THE **COMPLETE IDIOT'S GUIDE** TO

Tantric Sex

Second Edition

by Dr. Judy Kuriansky

ALPHA

A member of Penguin Group (USA) Inc.

To all those who are working toward more love ... and peace ... thank you.

ALPHA BOOKS

Published by the Penguin Group

Penguin Group (USA) Inc., 375 Hudson Street, New York, New York 10014, USA

Penguin Group (Canada), 90 Eglinton Avenue East, Suite 700, Toronto, Ontario M4P 2Y3, Canada (a division of Pearson Penguin Canada Inc.)

Penguin Books Ltd., 80 Strand, London WC2R 0RL, England

Penguin Ireland, 25 St. Stephen's Green, Dublin 2, Ireland (a division of Penguin Books Ltd.)

Penguin Group (Australia), 250 Camberwell Road, Camberwell, Victoria 3124, Australia (a division of Pearson Australia Group Pty. Ltd.)

Penguin Books India Pvt. Ltd., 11 Community Centre, Panchsheel Park, New Delhi—110 017, India

Penguin Group (NZ), 67 Apollo Drive, Rosedale, North Shore, Auckland 1311, New Zealand (a division of Pearson New Zealand Ltd.)

Penguin Books (South Africa) (Pty.) Ltd., 24 Sturdee Avenue, Rosebank, Johannesburg 2196, South Africa

Penguin Books Ltd., Registered Offices: 80 Strand, London WC2R 0RL, England

Copyright © 2004 by Dr. Judy Kuriansky

International Standard Book Number: 978-1-59257-296-0
Library of Congress Catalog Card Number: 2004111453

17   16   15   20   19   18   17   16   15   14   13

Interpretation of the printing code: The rightmost number of the first series of numbers is the year of the book's printing; the rightmost number of the second series of numbers is the number of the book's printing. For example, a printing code of 04-1 shows that the first printing occurred in 2004.

Printed in the United States of America

Note: This publication contains the opinions and ideas of its author. It is intended to provide helpful and informative material on the subject matter covered. It is sold with the understanding that the author and publisher are not engaged in rendering professional services in the book. If the reader requires personal assistance or advice, a competent professional should be consulted.

The author and publisher specifically disclaim any responsibility for any liability, loss, or risk, personal or otherwise, which is incurred as a consequence, directly or indirectly, of the use and application of any of the contents of this book.

Most Alpha books are available at special quantity discounts for bulk purchases for sales promotions, premiums, fundraising, or educational use. Special books, or book excerpts, can also be created to fit specific needs.

For details, write: Special Markets, Alpha Books, 375 Hudson Street, New York, NY 10014.

Publisher: *Marie Butler-Knight*
Product Manager: *Phil Kitchel*
Senior Managing Editor: *Jennifer Chisholm*
Senior Acquisitions Editor: *Mike Sanders*
Development Editor: *Ginny Bess Munroe*
Senior Production Editor: *Billy Fields*

Copy Editor: *Molly Schaller*
Illustrator: *Jody Schaeffer*
Cover/Book Designer: *Trina Wurst*
Indexer: *Angie Bess*
Layout: *Angela Calvert*
Proofreading: *Donna Martin*

Contents at a Glance

Contents

Appendixes

Foreword 1

It's exciting for me to see the tantric perspective coming more and more into mainstream thought. People might be drawn to tantric practices hoping to enhance their sexual satisfaction. It does an amazing job of improving what you already know and enjoy, but it also takes sexuality to another dimension entirely, an experience way beyond "normal."

Tantra is much more than a sexual teaching. Tantric practice can transform every aspect of your life, helping you to expand your physical health and vitality, emotional healing and expression, psychic sensitivity, satisfying relationships, creativity, productivity, and abundance. It is not unusual for someone to tell me after a few months of tantric involvement that he or she feels like a different person, much less stressed, much more comfortable, and more joyful.

Dr. Judy is uniquely qualified to be a major tantric communicator, to be the means through which this message goes forward to a broad population. Through her studies and research, her writings, her years on radio and in the media, she knows her subject and knows how to capture people's interest. She speaks directly of sexual matters, but she also appreciates the deeper potential of tantra.

In this book, Dr. Judy has presented a broad overview as well as specific things you can do to begin your personal exploration. Tantra is really a spiritual path, leading to self-discovery, to realizing you are much more magnificent than you ever guessed. If you have the courage to try something new, this book will guide you through your first steps, getting you started on a great adventure.

Bodhi Avinasha

Founder of Tantrika International and author of *Jewel in the Lotus* (bavinasha@ipsalutantra.com)

Foreword 2

Foreword 1

Tantra is a way of life that is needed now more than ever before in our times. In the face of intense intolerance, fear, and pain, what is essential is tolerance, love, and healing. Dr. Judy delivers this message in an intelligent and sensitive way—an impressive combination evident in her all of her work. She is the perfect professional to communicate these principles to help millions of people—and the world.

Besides overcoming fear, this is a time to finally get past sexual repression. The "sexual revolution" that began in the early 1960s is now an accepted part of sociological history. Although many feel that this revolution is dead, having tried all there is to try sexually and growing bored with it, I believe that the sexual revolution was the initial phase of a "sexual evolution." The 1960s seeds of a woman's right to pleasure and power in the world flowered in the 1980s. As we move forward into the twenty-first century, we are beginning to understand that feminine energy is awakening our consciousness and healing the planet. Tantric wisdom states that as a woman awakens her sexual center (second chakra) she naturally awakens her feminine and spiritual powers. It is time to embrace this wisdom.

At the foundation of our sexual structure is the typical early conditioning which filled us with guilt, fear, insecurity, and shame. This conditioning still drastically affects our ability to receive and transmit love and energy sexually, both to our partner and to ourselves. Even if we have a beautiful sex life much of the time, the foundation is still shaky and results in periodic relationship problems, sexual insecurities, and a lessened ability to enjoy sexual sharing. It is time to reverse this conditioning, to allow us to journey into the ecstatic spiritual potential of sexual love.

Tantra is one of the missing links for these puzzles. It is truly time for men and women to join together in their quest for sexual harmony. It is time for the dark age of sexuality to end; each of us must take the light and consciousness we've all awakened and put it into our sexuality, thus transforming its very nature.

Dr. Judy is a gifted therapist and writer, doing valuable work in the world. In this important book, Dr. Judy provides us with clear, easy-to-understand concepts and techniques of tantra, both ancient and modern. Learn to practice them well, and you will become a master in the art of love. You will watch your sexual love life become infused with more consciousness, energy, intimacy, pleasure, and the connection where the two become one.

Charles Muir

Director, Source School of Tantra, Maui, Hawaii
www.sourcetantra.com

Introduction

Tantra is a way of life whose time has come. It's been showing up in popular culture on TV shows, radio, and even in movies. Sting told Oprah on her TV show that he practices tantra with his wife, Trudie Styler. Tantra has been in scenes of the movie, *American Pie 2* and *Go!*, in the TV show *Sex and the City*, and even the subject of feature films like *Bliss* and the newly released *The Best Ever*. It's no surprise that tantra is catching on, given a few factors. Our world has accelerated, and new ideas are fast in coming in all arenas. Digital advances in our technological age are replacing person-to-person contact, leaving people isolated. And war in our new century has threatened our sense of safety and security. In the face of this, tantric practice offers hope.

Tantra originated thousands of years ago, but it is applicable to our life and needs today. It's a way of life that brings back true, deep, and intense connection. It's a spiritual way of being, consistent with today's increasing interest in spirituality. Most of all, it's a practice that emphasizes love—something we all want and need. And it's a practice that brings inner peace, which makes outer peace possible. I know; I've seen it happen for so many people!

What exactly is tantric sex? That's what *The Complete Idiot's Guide to Tantric Sex, Second Edition,* is all about: explaining the way of life the ancients knew and that we are rediscovering. In these pages, I will guide you through the basic things you need to know to practice this exciting and profound way of loving—and some advanced techniques, too! I'll tell you about specific tools that you can put into practice right away that will work for you, no matter what other path you are on in your life. You'll see—these practices will immediately infuse you with new peace, insight, and joy.

One of the most important things you'll discover in these pages is that tantric sex is about far more than sex. It is about using sexual energy to create more love, and having sacred sex as a means to *sacred love*. I had this special message printed for me by a street artist during one of my recent trips to China. It is a custom-made wording and depiction, and I am delighted to share it with you here. The beauty of the lettering shows how the art of truly loving also promises to make our lives more beautiful.

A message of "sacred love" printed in Chinese lettering.

Many of the exercises described in this book can be done either alone or with a partner. That partner can be anyone of your choice—even from a different background or sexual orientation. While the ancient practice of tantra is based on the opposite characteristics of yin and yang—male and female energies—the tantric practices in this book are equally applicable and fulfilling for any individual or partners regardless of sexual orientation or gender—GLBTOQ, as I like to list them: gay, lesbian, bisexual, transgender, "omnisexual" (meaning open to all possibilities), and those who are questioning.

Because tantric sex stimulates and encourages creativity, I encourage you to be creative in adapting the exercises for your own spiritual practice and then to integrate them into your practices with your partner.

In addition, be aware that there are many disciplines within the field of tantra and tantric sex. These might differ only in slight ways, such as instructing you in different ways to breathe (imagining a different pathway up and down your spine or through your body); or they might vary in more significant ways such as having a different emphasis (either on the more physical realm or on the more spiritual realm). I'll describe different approaches for you and give you some guidelines on how to make your choice.

The journey through this book promises to be an enlightening one, expanding your knowledge and your ability to love in new and exciting ways. You need not change anything drastic about your life; you can maintain your religion, beliefs, or any aspect of your lifestyle and just blend simple practices into the fabric of your life; or you can become immersed in a more major way. All is your choice, as you are the master of your destiny. Just by reading these pages, I promise you, you will embrace more bliss in your life. Get ready for an amazing and wonderful journey.

How to Use This Book

The chapters in this book are divided into six parts that take you through the practices of tantric sex and how you can integrate them into your life.

Part 1, "An Introduction to Tantric Sex: The Spiritual Path to Sacred Love," gives you the basics you need to know about tantric sex and how these ancient practices from the East can really work now, in the West. These five chapters teach you how to breathe, where your energy centers are, how to truly honor yourself and your partner, compassionate communication skills, and how to prepare for a union of male and female divinity.

Part 2, "Getting Started in Sacred Sex," tells you exactly what to do to turn your home, your inner self, and your body into a sacred temple and a clear channel for experiencing bliss. These five chapters give you specific things to do to set the stage for your tantra dates, and practices for beloveds to reach bliss.

Part 3, "Making Major Progress on the Tantric Path," takes you deeper into your practices for spiritual growth and healing. These five chapters reveal a new view of sex and orgasm, how to truly make lovemaking last, what to do to get fit together, and all the steps to having the most exciting and fulfilling nights together.

Part 4, "Going Deeper: Tantric Aids and Techniques for More Love and Better Sex," frees you to have the most playful and magical lovemaking and loving. These four chapters give you specific fun things to do together, games to play, tips on how to make magic, and more routines to tune up your love muscles and your whole body, to move to higher states of consciousness.

Part 5, "Dating and Mating Tantra Style," presents the issues in relationships that you'll face on the tantric path. These three chapters help you find the mate you're looking for if you're single; and if you're in relationship, you'll learn how to handle differences in your desires, and how to create the most memorable and sacred celebrations you can ever imagine.

Part 6, "The Tantric Path to Wellness and Peace for All," addresses ways to integrate tantra into your life. In these four chapters, you'll learn how tantra can enrich your life no matter what your age, lifestyle, or relationships status; how to harness this new loving energy; and how to create a strong healing force for you, your beloveds, and the planet.

In addition, you'll find three helpful appendixes: a glossary of tantric terms, resources, and tantric tools.

It's always good to ground yourself in some clear points when you're learning something new that could change your life, so I've included boxes that offer you information and advice to help you make this blissful transformation really stick:

 Ecstasy Essentials

Of course you want to experience ecstasy. But how? These boxes tell you what you need to know to make it easier for you to embrace the higher states of consciousness and bliss that tantric sex makes possible.

 Tantra Tales

It's always interesting to learn about other people's stories. These boxes tell you about the experiences of men and women who have decided to try out this new way of tantric relating, and how they—and you—can be successful.

Tantra Tutorial

With a new approach to life, love, and sex come new terms and concepts. These boxes clarify new words and ideas that you need to know and answer some questions you might have about the practices as you embark on your new journey in consciousness.

Dr. Judy's TantrAdvice

Every page of this book is filled with advice, but in these boxes, I add a few extra pointers. These include things you can do to enrich your life and loving. It's as if I were answering one of your questions and giving you some helpful suggestions in person.

Blocks to Bliss

Because the practice of tantra is transformative, there could be some cautions and controversial issues that arise along the way. These boxes prepare you for those dilemmas so you can avoid them and clear your path.

A Personal Note About My Own Journey

I am deeply grateful to everyone who has been part of my evolution at all stages of my life that has led to my latest reawakening into the more spiritual world. I'm amazed to reflect on some events that happened decades ago and are manifesting lately, consistent with the path of tantra. These include my dear childhood friend Rhea Ross insisting more than 30 years ago that I go with her to study yoga with Swami Muktananda and Swami Satchidananda (whom broadcaster Larry King also credits for teaching him gratitude), when doing so was avant-garde among people I knew. I've since visited the samadhis (graves) of these masters in India. Years ago, spiritualist Judy Hevenly insisted I come with her to receive shaktipat from Gurumayi. And it was ages ago that I went to classes with Mantak Chia, Chinese master of the Taoism of sex (now living and teaching in Thailand), which proved to be my introduction into this tantric path that I have so intensely studied in more recent years. Also many years ago, my friend Laurie Sue Brockway (a true goddess and now a minister who also works with the Red Cross, as I do, during emergency disasters) kept telling me how "we just have to go to

California to take one of Charles Muir's workshops in this terrific new thing called 'tantric sex.'" I've since been to many of Charles's seminars and his teacher trainings and become a good friend of this gifted teacher.

For years in between those early tastes of tantra and now, I followed a traditional professional path as a senior research scientist at the New York State Psychiatric Institute at Columbia Medical School. I did work on schizophrenia, depression, and cross-cultural psychotic disorders with a brilliant South African psychiatrist, Dr. Barry Gurland. In the late 1960s and early 1970s I became the protégé of the first professionals working in what was then the new field of sex therapy, who were collaborating with the "grandfather" and "grandmother" of sex therapy, Masters and Johnson. This led to many professional activities in the field of sex: becoming one of the founders of the first medical-centered based organization of sex therapists (the Society of Sex Therapists and Researchers); working on the sub-committee on the diagnosis of sexual dysfunctions for the American Psychiatric Association's Diagnostic and Statistical Manual; evaluating women's groups to teach women to have orgasm in 10 sessions with pioneer sexologist, Dagmar O'Connor; and writing some of the first professional papers about diagnosis, evaluation, and outcome of sex therapy. Along the way, I got my Ph.D. in clinical psychology at NYU and was fortunate to study "The Psychology of Love" with my supervisor Professor Irving Sarnoff and his wife and co-author, Suzanne, with whom he has written many wonderful books about sex and love.

The next phase of my work in the field of sex became more public as the host of radio call-in advice shows. This started more than 20 years ago on WABC Radio, but some of you are most familiar with my national radio call-in advice show *LovePhones*. What a special joy that was! Everyone has their favorites of the *LovePhones* radio calls, and so many of them come alive in the stories in my book *Generation Sex*. I am forever grateful to everyone who shared their touching stories—crying and laughing together—with my "radio family," co-host Chris Jagger, Badger, Jimmy, Sam, and Steve Kingston, who started it all.

We started talking about tantra on the radio so many years ago—and now it's become so much more well known! How glad I am to have been able to do that—to have everyone using terms like *goddess* and *honoring*, and to have broken radio ground by having the first sacred spot massage and female ejaculation to happen on radio airwaves, when tantra experts and friends Carla Tara and Sasha Lessin made love liquid flow right in our studio!

With tantra comes magic—if you want it to. It was at an advanced tantra training with the talented Bodhi of Tantrika International that this book was first born! And at another training, I set an intention to make more people aware of this amazing path, and to bring the messages around the world. I feel blessed to have done this—

especially in war-torn places that need a sense of peace and love. Since then, I have integrated tantra principles into my therapy with such amazing results, and so many patients tell me how much they have benefited. I have given so many speeches and workshops about tantra and presented the principles of Tantra with such enthusiasm because there is so much for others to gain from it. The spirit of love and healing has infused everything I do, making every moment of life so much more alive! In tantra, you set intentions. I made an intention at another advanced training to bring the messages of tantra back to the ancient world it originated in, that has "lost" the teachings; when I look back at how I have done this—in presentations, plenary addresses, workshops, and speeches from Hong Kong University to the Eastern Federation of Psychotherapy in Sagar India, to the China Sexology Association, and audiences all over China—I am amazed and ever so grateful.

I am more convinced than ever that tantra is a tool for peace. What a contrast it was, to be with a group of young teens who were enjoying the effects of increased self-esteem and inner peace as we practiced meditation and energy movement, while just blocks away there was a drive-by shooting. And what satisfaction there was, witnessing the changes in groups of people in the war-torn Middle East who were participating in my tantra groups for healing based on tantric principles of tolerance.

Acknowledgments

Tantra is about gratitude. I am ever so deeply grateful to my lifelong beloveds who have supported me from the core and taught me true unconditional love, including my mother, Sylvia, an angel epitomizing lovingness; my deeply soul-connected husband, Edward; my cherished siblings, brother Robert and sister Barbara; and my "daughter" Alissa Pollack, whose beautiful energy infuses this book and everything I do and who enriches my life every day with the best example of loving and support that I am blessed to have. Her light and devotion is a shining example of the love that is possible in this world.

Tantra is also about seeing the god and goddess in the people around you. I cherish all my true friends, who are such divine beings and who have taught and shared much love and growth with me in sisterhood and brotherhood on this tantric path. They include goddesses Carla Tara, Laurie Handlers, Marci Javril, Jaiia Earthschild (thanks for the magical music and Maui mud initiations), Voltage, Margot Anand, Sasha and Janet, Matt Feinberg, Brian Courtney, and many more, including those tantra teachers who so enthusiastically contributed their work to this book, such as Carla, Laurie, Richard and Antoinette, Francesca and John, Lexi and Kip, Lori Starr, Robert Frey, and Steve and Lokita. Profound blessings to Linda "Lexi" Hron for reviewing all my work with such love, brilliance, and soul. I am especially grateful to the dear ones there for me at the beginning of this book, like dear friends and "sisters" Carla and Nancy Froio, who offered brilliant inspiration the very first day this book was started during our third-level teacher training with Bodhi Avinasha; and to the dear ones who were there at the end, especially those tantrikas and dakas who read this manuscript and offered their love, support, suggestions, and gracious encouragement and enthusiasm for its contributions that went deep into my heart: Antoinette, Laurie, and Brian.

I offer the most profound of blessings and gratitude, too, to master tantra teachers and dear friends Charles Muir and Bodhi Avinasha, who have profoundly influenced my transformation. I have also been greatly affected on my path by "communicating" with Osho (who "left his body"); my training in Tibetan Tamang shamanism with Larry Peters and his shaman Amma; and my many trips to India, Japan, China, and Nepal, lands infused with astounding temples and god/goddess energy. Those trips led to quite an awakening about Hinduism and Buddhism, my friendship with His Holiness Guru Rinpoche and his family, and my "taking refuge" with a Buddhist lama Thrangu Rinpoche, who gave me the Buddhist name that translates into "Lake of Love."

This book is a labor of love, and I have felt the hand of spirits, divine beings, and angels guiding me in such a spiritually enlivening zone while doing this writing, that days passed with no need for sleep as the life force coursed through me. My sincerest gratitude to all of them, including wise ones who offered support, such as Norah Beraja and Spiritual Counselor Carole Maracle (my most profound love goes out to her now on the other side).

I greatly appreciate all my friends who support me through the excitement of being a pioneer. Sometimes it is scary to go into the unknown. Blessings to dear Richard Asimus, who sent me an encouraging e-mail, "Dear Judy, I love you. I honor your wild creativity. You truly are 'Shakti' creating new forms & essence from the emptiness of the void ... in awe, in joy, in spire with you." Some people ask me how I do it; the joy of creating and connecting with people and sharing joy and making people happy—that makes me happy.

My gratitude extends to all my friends and colleagues in China who have honored me by being so receptive to my presentations about their ancient culture as we practice it here now in the West. These friends greatly enrich my life these days and offer me an amazing view of how love can transcend all language and culture. These include Susan Lee and all my friends at Liaoning Education Press who published my other books, *The Complete Idiot's Guide to Dating* and *The Complete Idiot's Guide to a Healthy Relationship* in Chinese; dear "brother" Chuanliang Tong and all my extended family at the Shanghai Center for Reproductive Health Instruction (with whom I wrote the first book on sex advice in China based on questions to a unique hotline); and my other cherished Chinese colleagues who are dear friends, such as Zhang Zhigang and

Dr. Peicheng Hu, of the China Sexology Association, who has invited me so many times to teach about sexuality in China, and with whom I have collaborated on so many valuable projects, including doing the first pioneer training of Chinese professionals about Western sex therapy, which was featured on CBS-TV's respected *Sunday Morning* TV show and CBS-TV *Evening News*, produced by my friend Alec Sirken.

The physical world also matters in getting a book together, hence my gratitude to the talented artists who contributed their brilliant work to this manuscript. I had been waiting for years to work with Hrana Janto, having first seen her goddess drawings so many years ago. How amazing that not only is she connected to goddess, but also knew so much about tantra (and was as much a night owl as me!). And to Meadow and Al, who also contributed inspired art with a generous spirit and devotion to this volume. I shall always cherish Meadow's three couples on their journeys to tantric love!

Deepest gratitude to all at Alpha Books involved in this project and who have seen the value of doing this updated new edition: from my senior acquisitions editor Mike Sanders, who was kind, supportive, and helpful at every moment and with whom I love working through so many years; to senior production editor Billy Fields; to product manager Phil Kitchel; copy editor Molly Schaller, who surprised me with all her knowledge about tantra; to my "old" friends (because I've written several in this series): publisher Marie Butler-Knight, publicists Vicki Skelton and Gardi Wilks who have been so supportive, and development editors Lynn Northrup the first time around and then Ginny Bess, who contributed great ideas, loving support, and hard work at all hours (a combination I love!).

My deepest gratitude, too, to all my patients to whom I have taught tantra techniques for the betterment of the lives, and the men and women who have participated in the innumerable workshops and classes I have led, who have extended trust, shared innermost feelings, and shown courage in their transformation; and to everyone on this journey bringing love and light into their own and others' lives. A note of appreciation and praise, too, to my students at Columbia University Teachers College: Laura DeNoble who assisted me on my first tantra workshop with teens; Cathy Sullivan, Kristyn Simon, and Jessica Costosa, who worked on the report about the first research on this work; and Kiyoko Sasaki, who gave so generously of her kind and capable soul and helped me up to the last minute the first go-around and then my sweet and smart intern Lisa McIntire whom I found in my former dorm room at Smith College during my reunion, who wanted to be "me," so I took her on as my intern—what a joy! This edition is infused with so much excitement over tantra events I have led since the first edition, including an amazing teen tantra workshop, in a team of magical beings: my teaching assistant Michele Montecalvo (mystical Michele), and Teachers College students Heather Betts (Hopeful Heather) and Winnie Chen (Witty Winnie), with the awesome duo of Planned Parenthood of Nassau County's Heather Samel (Happy Heather) and Danielle Varney (Dynamic Danielle). I have so much love for the "tantra team" and their dedication and enthusiasm, as well as the teens who opened to moving energy for more love and AIDS prevention. I was blessed to meet Heather and Danielle at the American Association of Sex Educators, Counselors and Therapists conference, and hear of Heather reading the first edition of this very book and being inspired to teach tantra. And so, out cooperation and friendship was born! I'm proud of them as shining examples of the new generation of healers!

This book was first finished in momentous times, when terrorism struck New York and shook the world. Thousands sacrificed their lives in the terrorist attacks so the world could pay attention to the need for love and peace. The energy of that message infuses these pages. It made this effort timely then, as it is now when stress in people's individual lives as well as terrorism in the world, still plagues us. As people reach out now for safety and security, the message of tantra—of trust and love—offers hope needed more than ever to heal our individual lives, our relationships, and our planet.

Illustrators

Hrana Janto is an illustrator and painter who specializes in sacred art, on subjects about mythic, folk, and fairy tales, and in styles from fantasy to ancient history. Hrana created paintings of goddesses for the deck of cards in *The Goddess Oracle: A Way to Wholeness Through the Goddess and Ritual* (Element Books/Harper Collins, 1997) and also teaches dance. The creator of the Dr. Judy icon and the majority of goddesslike drawings throughout the book, her work has also appeared on calendars, logos, and in children's books and magazines.

Other artists who contributed the anatomical and some other drawings: Meadow is an illustrator, painter, and sculptor whose work is in the collection of the Smithsonian Institute in Washington, D.C. She has been shown in dozens of solo and group exhibitions in museums and galleries nationwide, from the New York Academy of Art to the American Crafts Museum. Her erotic artwork and poetry appeared in a book about women. A practicing reverend, Meadow is fulfilling her life's dream: establishing the first women's sculpture park, also a healing center and wildlife sanctuary called "Woodrock Sanctuary," the first park of its kind in this country. Meadow collaborated with Al Hughes, a New York fashion illustrator who branched out to write and illustrate children's stories and to draw humorous space beings and celebrity caricatures that have been featured on *ABC News*.

Testimonials

Here's what people are saying about Dr. Judy's speeches, workshops, seminars, and keynote speeches, as well as *The Complete Idiot's Guide to Tantric Sex*:

"*The Complete Idiot's Guide to Tantric Sex* is an empowering, satisfying, beautifully written book on sexuality today. I invite all of you who really want authentic pleasure in your life to read this empowering worldview on sexuality."
—B. Courtney, contractor, California

"Dr. Judy's new book on tantric sex is a wonderful act of service for the world and presents an impressive unified view of tantra as it is practiced and taught today, offering a wealth of techniques and opportunities to individuals and couples to integrate sex and consciousness."—Antoinette Asimus, executive director, Tantrika International

"This is the definitive book on tantra. Dr. Judy is so complete in her writing that one no longer has to sort through bits and pieces from competing schools of thought. She has included it all. What a great work and what a pleasure to read it."—Laurie Handlers, co-founder, Butterfly Workshops

"I learned more from Dr. Judy's lectures than any other experience. I am forever transformed. She taught with brilliance, sensitivity—and made it so much fun. We cried and laughed!"—Student in New York tantra seminar

"The audience was riveted to Dr. Judy's keynote address at our event. It was full of fascinating information and really good humor and got us all out of our chairs! Everyone wants her back!"—Texas executive, program chair

"Dr. Judy gave us rich information and we loved how she teaches, very unique. It changed my way of work and my way in my marriage."—Medical doctor in training class in China

"Dr. Judy changed my life in such a short time. She gets right to the core of the problem and really cares."—"Janine," radio listener

I feel particularly honored to have been an influence in Heather's path, and have taken her "under my wing" now. She describes: "After 4 months of dating, Dave's birthday was coming around. He had spoken about wanting to learn about Tantra and I really didn't know much about it. So I bought him *The Complete Idiot's Guide to Tantric Sex* that was perfect because all the other books seem philosophical and in depth, and this book with great illustrations and helpful tips just spoke to the common person. I was living in Georgia and Dave in New York so I got my own copy and we would read to each other over the phone about honoring your beloved, the chakras, and using your breath to create a stronger connection. When we finally got together and put what we had learned into practice, it was mind blowing. Not only did our physical experience exceed anything that we had ever thought possible, but our emotional connection with each other strengthened to a point we had never imagined. After a while, tantra was more than something we played with in the bedroom, it became a way of life. We have learned to surround ourselves with positive energy, to cope with challenges in a different way, and to interact with people with more patience and kindness. Dr. Judy's book has completely changed our lives and helped Dave and I realize that the answers truly lie within ourselves, our connections with people and with the world as a whole."—Heather Samel, sex educator

Trademarks

All terms mentioned in this book that are known to be or are suspected of being trademarks or service marks have been appropriately capitalized. Alpha Books and Penguin Group (USA) Inc. cannot attest to the accuracy of this information. Use of a term in this book should not be regarded as affecting the validity of any trademark or service mark.

Part 1

An Introduction to Tantric Sex: The Spiritual Path to Sacred Love

You're about to embark on a wonderful journey! Would you like to feel more intense excitement than ever before? Experience more love for yourself and others than you ever imagined possible? Have the best sex ever—truly, because it's not just sex; it's much more?

If you answered "yes," get ready to be transformed, to feel freer, and to be more enthusiastic about yourself and your life. I can make these promises to you because I know it's possible and because I have seen inspiring transformations happen to men and women of all ages when embarking on the exciting journey you can take in this book.

In this part, I'll introduce you to the ancient arts of lovemaking that started in the Eastern parts of the world thousands of years ago but that have been lost over the centuries until now—when we in America are reviving them. You'll learn powerful breathing techniques, ways to generate powerful surges of sexual energy through your body, how to honor yourself and your partner, how to communicate in a new way, and all the basics to get started on the tantric path to deeper intimacy and higher states of ecstatic consciousness!

What Is Tantric Sex?

In This Chapter

- What is tantra and tantric sex?
- How tantra frees your mind, body, and soul
- How tantra is compatible with the modern Western way of life
- Correcting myths about tantric sex
- The benefits of tantric sex
- Quiz: Are you ready for tantra?

Are you ready to experience more love and deeper intimacy than you've ever felt before? Imagine exploding with pleasure at even the slightest touch. Imagine being in such an embrace of joy and peacefulness that you "melt" into one another.

If you would like to have those experiences, you're reading the perfect book! This chapter helps get you started by answering the question of what tantric sex is and how it is much more than sex. You'll learn the benefits of following this path, as well as what's required, and why *now* is the perfect time for setting out on this journey.

What Is Tantra?

To understand *tantric sex*, first you must understand what *tantra* is. The word *tantra* comes from ancient Sanskrit language meaning "expansion through awareness." Tantra is a spiritual path that involves very specific practices that use breath, sounds, movements, and symbols to quiet the mind and activate sexual energy, directing it throughout the body to achieve states of consciousness and bliss. Tantra traditions come from ancient practices in India, Nepal, and China. Whereas at one time they were reserved for royalty, now they are for all of us.

The practices also help heal past hurts, which are often stored in sexual centers of the body, so that you can be more fully present in the moment and open to love. When practiced together, the techniques bring about a powerful flow of energy between you and your partner, which energizes your being and expands your love for each other and the universe.

Tantra Tutorial

Tantra is a Sanskrit word meaning the teachings and practices that use energy to lead to a high state of bliss and enlightenment. **Tantric sex** applies the teachings of tantra to the sexual union to reach these high states.

Sacred Sex the Tantric Way

Feel your sexual area now and sense any energy flowing there. Press yourself against the chair if you are sitting, or squeeze the muscles of your buttocks if you are standing. Therein lies a powerful energy generator, according to the tantric sex tradition—but the path does not end at just physical pleasure. Imagine feeling volts of electricity surging in your sexual area, which you could direct to your heart to feel more love—or to your mind for mind-blowing orgasms that last endlessly and put you in a state of complete joy and bliss.

Blocks to Bliss

The term *tantric sex* is often misinterpreted. It is used to refer to different paths; as a buzzword for wanton sexuality; or as an excuse for sexual affairs, sex addictions, and sex for sale.

Tantric sex involves the practice of various meditations and exercises (including yoga) to arouse and channel tremendous energy within the body, cycle that energy with a partner, and send it out into the world. It is intended for personal fulfillment, interpersonal intimacy, and connection to the entire world of beings. The energy generated by tantric sex can be used for either pleasure intended for blissful enlightenment or for healing. In Parts 1 and 2 of this book, I discuss tantric sex for pleasure. In Part 3, you learn how to harness that pleasure for healing.

The practices of tantra are the route to achieving high states of joy and intimacy.

So what is tantric sex? It can be any and all of the following:

◆ A way to experience deeper connection, more love, and intimacy.

◆ Techniques to create ecstasy by directing energy toward free expression and breaking barriers internally and interpersonally. Sex acts become elevated into divine practice that unites beloveds so that every sensation is alive and every touch and movement considered a divine gift.

◆ Achieving a balance between male and female energies within the self and with a partner.

◆ Aligning with another being and with the world through divine sexual experience.

◆ Celebrating sexual union as an honoring of all beings and creation.

◆ Practices that liberate the soul to experience the highest levels of inner peace and bliss.

How Tantric Sex Frees Your Mind, Body, and Soul

As in any meditative practice, a crucial key to achieving the wonderful benefits of tantric sex is to quiet the mind; you will learn many methods of doing this in this book. Tantric sex is *mindful* in that you pay attention to what you're doing in the exchange between you and your partner. Being mindful induces a sense of respect and reverence for the experience, which lends itself to honoring each other as god and goddess, as you will learn in Chapter 5. Consistent with mindfulness—but not at all contradictory—is the goal of tantric sex to free your mind and release your body. Through this kind of release you can freely express yourself and feel deep states of love outside of sexual pleasure that touch your soul.

Tantric Sex as the Path to Healing

An advanced use of tantric sex is for healing the body, mind, and spirit. Men as well as women suffer various hurts, rejections, and abuses—either real or perceived—from previous relationships. Through exercises and rituals explained in this book, tantric sex can heal these hurts and free the body, mind, and spirit to feel peaceful, empowered, and open to love without fear, guilt, embarrassment, shame, or anger.

Dr. Judy's TantrAdvice

You might enjoy renting the popular movie *Bliss*, which is about the healing and personal growth that is possible through tantric practice. However, be aware that the true spiritual aspects are barely touched upon, and the story is obviously skewed to conform to the needs of a marketable Hollywood drama.

As you will see, specifically in Chapters 10 and 18, sexual healing involves three steps:

1. Identifying past hurts (either real or imagined) through sexual stimulation and meditation.

2. Releasing powerful emotions attached to these hurts.

3. Replacing hurts with positive experience and emotions.

Tantric Sex as Magic

Throughout this book, and specifically in Chapter 16, I guide you through rituals and creative new techniques that will heal your hurts, make you feel young, and expand your ability to love and experience joy.

A Powerful Chemical Cocktail to Bliss

Tantric sex practices affect you in many dimensions—your senses, spirit, mind, body, and soul. Real changes occur in the body consistent with ecstatic states, including the flow of chemicals that lead to euphoria. These include *endorphins* (called "the pleasure chemical"), *oxytocin* (called the "cuddle chemical"), *phenylethlyamanime* (another pleasure chemical), and *adrenaline* (an activating chemical). Different practices stimulate the nervous system to create either excitation or relaxation. In fact, you'll find the most unique mixture of *both* of these states!

Although tantric sex practices have not been studied in any laboratory, research has shown how related activities that alter the brain and body are routes to bliss. Meditation, key to certain tantric practices, has been extensively researched and shown to have positive effects on brain wave activity, specifically causing relaxation responses. In preliminary research, a California sexologist measured women's brain wave activity during relaxation, imagery, and tantric-related masturbatory activity and showed that women who practice tantric activities can induce brain waves during self-pleasuring that are associated with pleasurable altered states of consciousness.

Ecstasy Essentials

After you discover personal sexual pleasure through tantric practices, apply them for grand goals, like the attainment of wisdom and the benefit of all mankind.

Find and Follow the Pathways of Energy

In tantric sex you discover energy pathways in the body and concentrate on controlling the movement of that energy within those pathways. You interweave those energies with your partner to dissolve feelings of separation and to become united. As you will discover in Chapter 3, tantric sex brings together key glands in the brain (the pineal and pituitary glands) that correspond to energy centers, or chakras. When this happens, you will see how grand it is!

How the West Is Reviving Eastern Tantric Sex Practices

Ancient Eastern cultures have been practicing some of these sacred sex traditions for centuries. Unfortunately, through political upheavals, religious objections, and cultural changes in those societies, the practices were suppressed or forgotten. It's amazing that these practices are being revived now in America and being returned to their origins by key figures in the field—as well as by me in my current extensive work in Asia. I call this the "Enlightenment Road" for new thinkers, bringing precious new ways of life from one country to another, much like traders brought their wares along the famous "Silk Road" through China centuries ago.

Although meditation from Eastern gurus, such as Swamis Muktananda and Sachidananda, became popular in the United States more than 30 years ago (I was among those who studied with them), and tantric sex practices were similarly introduced by Easterners such as Mantak Chia, the practices became mainstream only about a decade ago. Tantric sex practices were revived mainly by students of related arts of yoga and meditation in the West, who came upon teachings of tantra and integrated them into their own practices.

Dr. Judy teaching tantra to Westerners (a group of Americans in New York).

Though developed in the Eastern part of the world, the tantric sex practices are particularly applicable and appealing to the Western world today. Here are 10 ways tantric sex has modern-day appeal to the West:

1. Tantric sex promises simple steps and instant results, which appeal to Westerners who are conditioned to "instant" lifestyles (instant coffee, fast food, instant gratification) and quick fixes.

2. The practices are based on channeling and using desire, rather than denying desire. Most Westerners don't like the idea of abandoning desire, but adapting it to reach higher states is acceptable and even appealing.

3. The practices don't require the traditional retreat from society. Mainstream Westerners are not willing to find ecstasy and enlightenment by joining an ashram for years of quiet meditation, shaving their heads, wearing orange robes, or giving up worldly goods.

Tantra Tales

Perhaps one of the most notable bridges between Eastern and Western thought in our time is the Indian mystic Osho, who knew he had to adapt the most austere Eastern meditation practices to make them more appealing to Westerners. He set up a retreat center in America in the 1970s. His lectures were peppered with jokes and included freeform dancing to live bands and celebration, and his courses taught subjects like psychic massage, aromatherapy, and astrology.

4. Tantric sex is based on the principle of transformation of energy; Westerners are familiar with this concept in physics, electronics, and modern technology.

5. Westerners like to control (things, themselves, others); tantric practices harness control by channeling energy into different body parts and for specific purposes.

6. Tantric sex practices encourage experience and self-determination, practical day-to-day rituals, and a step-by-step approach to achieving higher states of peacefulness, bliss, and consciousness rather than blind faith, which is not as appealing to Westerners accustomed to questioning belief systems.

7. Tantric sex starts with individual practice that can be applied to practice with a partner, which can then benefit the whole society. This is consistent with the individualism that is the basis of Western society.

8. Tantric sex hails self-discovery, a practice consistent with the Western focus on self-improvement and self-mastery.

9. Tantric sex honors the human body, consistent with Western appreciation and focus on the body. Far from being a hindrance to enlightenment, the body is considered a vehicle for bliss.

10. Tantric sex practices encourage heightening the senses through beautiful clothing, attractive surroundings, and stimulation of all the senses, which is consistent with Western appreciation of worldly pleasures.

Sacred Sex

Sacred sex refers to the connection between two *higher selves* for the intention of a divine union—not for physical thrill, lust, or intent to use another person for personal sexual or emotional satisfaction. The coming together of two beings is considered an act of godliness, to be taken seriously and done with great reverence, serving as a bridge between the physical world and the spiritual world and reached via the vehicle of the body and breath.

Several different types of tantra are practiced and taught in modern times. Some of these preserve the ancient traditions; others have adapted

Ecstasy Essentials

To release the ego, you can call upon your **higher self**, or the wise part of you that is above judgments, worldly fears, and fear of the unknown. In quiet moments, some people find it easier to visualize this self as actually above the head, looking down on the problem or situation and witnessing it.

some practices to suit more Western or modern ways. However, most of the ideas are based on similar principles, such as …

◆ Sexuality is sacred.

◆ All beings are connected and equal.

◆ Sexual energy can be directed and channeled for the benefit of the individual, the couple, and all beings.

◆ Sexual union is the road to higher consciousness and ecstasy.

◆ The breath is key to releasing this powerful energy.

Even if you know nothing of tantra yet, you might know about, have heard a friend talk about, or had a taste yourself of an experience in which you were making love and "melted into" your partner, or "felt at one with the universe." Tantric lovemaking leads to this merging of the self with the beloved and the universe. This can be a challenge, because it requires suspending the rational mind—the thinking, worrying, critical part that defines who we think we are and our daily interests, needs, and problems. Oh, the mind struggles against giving up its worrying—after all, as tantric teacher Bodhi Avinasha says, "If it gave up worry, might the mind then be out of a job?" The mind constantly tells you, "I need this"; "I should do that"; "I don't like this." Tantric sex gives you a chance to stop the ego and the mind from this longing and worrying.

Myths About Tantra and Tantric Sex

Because tantra celebrates sexuality, it has become ripe for criticism and misunderstanding. Here are some myths and truths about tantric sex:

Myth: Tantric sex is all about sex.

Truth: Tantric sex practices sometimes do not even include genital contact—they are really about energetic and spiritual contact between partners. Intercourse or the connection of genitals only serves to heighten the energetic connection when a couple is ready for that intimate stage.

Myth: Practicing tantra means you give up pleasure.

Truth: This myth is the opposite of the mistaken belief that tantra is all about sex; neither extreme is true. Tantra does not require a renunciation of pleasure, even though some yogic practices do; rather, tantra is an enhancement of joy and pleasure. Desire is not something to be denied, as if you have to mimic a Buddha silently meditating cross-legged, alone, not thinking of anything—and giving up sex. Instead, tantra recognizes the powerful force that sex plays in our lives and harnesses it to achieve states of bliss beyond just physical pleasure.

Dr. Judy's TantrAdvice

To understand the difference between *allowing* pleasure rather than grasping for it, imagine a person you desire in front of you. First, picture yourself stepping forward and grabbing for that person, who stays out of your reach, and feel your frustration and pounding heart. In contrast, picture staying still and watching that physical being dissolving into a ray of light that either comes to you or not, and experience a more peaceful and expansive feeling within yourself.

Myth: Tantric sex encourages indulgences of the appetites, which leads to affairs or orgies.

Truth: Tantric sex does not advocate indulging uncontrolled sexual or other appetites, promiscuity, or wallowing in pleasure. In fact, it trains us to control desire to channel it to higher purposes. What's more, connection between two people is considered very seriously, and commitment highly regarded. Although some people use tantric sex as a way to rationalize having sex with many partners or several partners at once, this is not the spirit of true tantra. Sexuality is not meant to be flitted away thoughtlessly, but honored, and intended for the purpose of higher states of consciousness, rather than simply physical stimulation or satisfaction. A true tantric practitioner can even resist sexual contact with others because of being trained to connect with others emotionally and spiritually, without having to engage bodies in sex.

Myth: Tantric sex turns you into a sex maniac.

Truth: Tantric sex does release sexual energy and give you permission to express yourself— but acting out sexually misuses the practices. If you learn the practices responsibly, you will overcome any tendencies to have random, meaningless sex.

Myth: Tantric sex is for Easterners and is not consistent with how we experience sex in the West.

Dr. Judy's TantrAdvice

If a married woman feels attracted to another man, instead of having an affair, in tantric practice she would watch her feelings, meditate on them, and follow the force of that fantasy to bring new energy into her sex life with her husband.

Truth: As mentioned earlier in this chapter, tantric sex practices are actually quite consistent with the Western way of life, with focus on the individual, acceptance of pleasure, and clearly defined steps toward enlightenment.

Myth: Tantra is a religion and a cult that will trap or brainwash you.

Truth: Tantra is neither a religion nor a cult. The genuine ethical tantra teachers do not want to control you; they merely guide you in a series of practices that you choose for yourself and adapt to your life.

> **Blocks to Bliss**
>
> Beware of anyone, tantra teacher or otherwise, who demands that you follow him or her rigidly; give up your life, friends, or family; or sign over your finances.

Myth: It takes too long to learn how to do tantric sex.

Truth: One of the beautiful aspects of the tantric path is that the practices can be put into effect immediately and results noticed. In just one weekend workshop, you can learn enough basic ideas and practical exercises to immediately improve your sex life and general feelings about yourself, which will generate to every part of your life.

Why Tantric Sex Now?

Several factors have led to the popularity of tantric sex in modern times:

◆ Couples and singles still suffer great distress and frustration over relationships and are searching for solutions from an increasing number of self-help books, courses, and Internet sites, and a plethora of healing approaches and centers once considered "alternative" and now more mainstream.

> **Tantra Tutorial**
>
> Methods for personal growth and health, from bodywork or massage techniques to past-life regression (imagining eras in which you might have lived previously that helps explain your relationships, problems, or goals in the present), that were once considered "alternative" are now mainstream.

◆ Codependency and addictions of all kinds, which stem from lack of love and true intimate connection, have escalated. Sufferers and health experts are seeking, and willing to try, many new solutions to these problems.

◆ We are moving away from the view of relationships as "dysfunctional"—which emphasizes only negative patterns of behavior—toward a more positive view, which focuses on the potential for healthy interactions.

◆ People are looking for more than medications to relieve stress, depression, and anxiety, which have reached epidemic proportions.

◆ Pressures of corporate downsizing, increased consumerism, and technological advances have put increasing strain on relationships, causing loneliness and isolation and turning people toward Eastern philosophies, which shun materialism.

◆ The growing interest in improving relationships and attaining a deeper connection between lovers has led gradually to the resurgence of the Age of Aquarius, with its interest in what's come to be called *spirituality*. This spirituality focuses attention on the deeper parts of one's soul, instead of just rational reasons for coupling or particular ways that couples can stay together.

◆ World tensions, terrorism, and war have increased people's distrust and distress and therefore a desire for peace both internally and in their daily lives. Tantra stands for that trust and peace, in the internal and external worlds.

Twelve Benefits of Tantric Sex Practices

Devoting yourself to any practice has to pay off. There are many dividends from investing time and energy into tantric sex practices, such as the following:

◆ **Expand your possibilities for love.** Tantric sex shows you how to nurture and love yourself and then deepen the physical and spiritual connection with your partner.

◆ **Rejuvenate your health.** Practicing tantric sex has physiological and psychological effects that help you maintain—and regain—health. For example, breathing techniques bring more air into the body, nourishing the tissues and muscles. Research has shown a link between the effects of relaxation, meditation, and spirituality, and better physical and emotional health. People who are spiritual have lower blood pressure, lower levels of anxiety and depression, more stable hormone levels, and better functioning immune systems.

◆ **Tap into the fountain of youth.** For all the health benefits mentioned previously, practicing tantra can make you feel and look young again.

◆ **Empower women.** Many women suffer from low self-esteem. They might have a poor body image, not tell their partner what they want, or give in to sex when they really want to say "no." In tantric sex, women are treated with the respect and honor they desire and deserve.

◆ **Empower men.** So many men worry about the size of their penis and how long they last during sex. Many also don't know how to commit or really please a woman. When men feel more empowered in sex, they become more confident and open to being more caring in their relationship.

◆ **Achieve true satisfaction from sex.** When the sex act is over, are you ever left with the feeling that you're not really finished? This is often because the sexual act does not go beyond the genitals—it does not touch the heart. In tantric sex, you can reach the state in which every cell in your body feels nurtured from the soul connection you feel with your partner. When sex happens with this kind of heart connection, both body and mind are fed.

◆ **Alleviate anxieties and depression.** Statistics show millions of men and women suffer from anxiety and depression, including symptoms of fatigue and sleeping and eating disturbances. Tantric sex provides enormous energy to the body and peacefulness to the mind that overcomes these problems.

◆ **Elevate sex.** When you elevate sex to a level of sacredness, it takes on a richer dimension than a mere physical act.

◆ **Prolong pleasure.** Tantric sex techniques make lovemaking—including the afterglow—last a long time. This occurs through ejaculatory control and by directing sexual energy anywhere in the body or into spiritual manifestations.

◆ **Heal past emotional wounds.** Tantric sex helps you heal past hurts from all kinds of painful or traumatic experiences in which you felt betrayed or abused, and it creates healthy experiences of being honored and respected in sex and in life in general.

◆ **Deepen your connection to others.** Tantric sex gives more meaning to life and enriches your relationships.

◆ **Affect the world positively.** Your personal gains cause you to generate more positive and loving energy outward, extending to everyone you come into contact with, even altering the energy of the planet (because all things on a metaphysical or spiritual level are interrelated).

Tantra Tales

I've had so many success stories teaching tantra techniques to my patients. For example, Steve and Lori were happily married for two years, but since the birth of their little girl and Steve's company's downsizing, they stopped having sex. Worse yet, Lori suspected Steve of having an affair. In just a few therapy sessions with me, they learned preliminary steps in tantric connection, breathing together, and simple rituals to please each other (as in Chapters 2, 9, 11, and 12), and discovered renewed trust and love that was exhilarating.

Are You Ready for Tantra?

How do you know whether you're ready for tantric sex practices? Take this quiz to see. Share this quiz with your partner to see if he or she is also ready to begin these practices.

The "Are You Ready for Tantra?" Quiz

Check *Yes* or *No* for each of the following questions:

1. Are you willing to change the way you have sex now to have a deeper, more meaningful experience? Yes ☑ No ☐

2. Do you believe that how you breathe affects your sexual experience? Yes ☐ No ☑

3. Do you think that women can have multiple orgasms but men cannot? Yes ☐ No ☑

4. Do you think a man should be a "man" and a woman should be a "woman," with no crossover in those roles? Yes ☐ No ☑

5. Does a man have to ejaculate to achieve pleasure? Yes ☐ No ☑

6. Do you want lovemaking to last longer? Yes ☑ No ☐

7. Must a woman have an orgasm to be satisfied in sex? Yes ☐ No ☑

8. Do you need a certain type of lover to be happy? Yes ☐ No ☑

9. Would you like to have sex on a high, spiritual level? Yes ☑ No ☐

10. Do you think that your loving can influence more peace on Earth? Yes ☑ No ☐

Scoring: Count the total number of *Yes* and *No* answers you have to the preceding questions, according to the following:

Number of *Yes* answers to questions 1, 2, 6, 9, 10: 3 _____

Number of *No* answers to questions 3, 4, 5, 7, 8: 5 _____

My total score = 8 _____

My partner's total score = _____

If your total score is more than five, you are really ready for tantric practice. You believe in channeling pleasure for higher purpose and want to use lovemaking to achieve an energetic exchange with a partner. You are willing to enthusiastically participate in tantric training and are ready to learn the skills that will enable you to use sexuality in a sacred way.

If your total is between three and five, you have potential to start tantric practice and would benefit greatly from taking a tantric course. Read on to learn more about tantric sex and spark your interest and commitment to harnessing the potential you already have.

If your total is less than three, you have skepticism about how to harness sexuality, but you still should read on and consider how to integrate these new, exciting practices into your life. Trust that you are capable of new pleasure.

The Five Pledges of the Tantric Sex Path

After you are open to this new exciting path of tantric sex, see how the following pledges feel to you. Watch how a peaceful feeling washes over you—your breath becomes more even, your mind more restful—as you read these sentences:

1. I am open to achieving peace in my inner being and experiencing the extent of my ability to love and feel ecstasy and higher states of consciousness.

2. I am open to exploring new possibilities for love, intimacy, and bliss with my partner.

3. I am open to removing emotional obstacles from my own and my partner's past or present to free us to experience more joy.

4. I am open to honoring the divinity in myself and in all others.

5. I am open to using my energy wisely and judiciously for self-esteem, gentleness, empowerment, pleasure, harmony, freedom, and tolerance for the mutual good of myself, my beloveds, and all others in this world.

The Least You Need to Know

- ◆ The practices of tantric sex can lead to more satisfying, blissful sex; but more important, it can result in higher states of consciousness and better relationships.

- ◆ Although tantric sex practices originated in ancient Eastern cultures, they can be easily integrated into the Western way of life.

- ◆ Tantric sexual practices have many physical, emotional, interpersonal, and spiritual benefits.

- ◆ Anyone can follow tantric sex practices as long as they are willing to make changes in their attitudes and behaviors and make a commitment to an honorable and respectful way of life.

Chapter 2

Moving Energy and Breathing to Bliss

In This Chapter

- Powerful breathing techniques for better sex
- How to use the seven energy centers (chakras) in the body
- Seeing love more clearly through the third eye
- Sounds and symbols that evoke bliss
- The inner smile necessary for joy

You will explore many sacred practices in this book; I promise all will be fascinating and fun. They include using sights, sounds, and symbols in your journey to bliss. I'll tell you about these in this chapter.

First comes the most basic practice presented in this chapter. It's something that you are doing at this very minute: breathing. Breathing properly and directing the breath is essential to reach the deepest possible intimacy and highest possible states of ecstasy. After you have mastered these breathing techniques, you can integrate them into partner practices that I guide you through in Chapter 9.

The Importance of Your Breath

Proper breathing supplies necessary oxygen to your cells and frees emotions and sensuality. It can lead to euphoria and even orgasm. The breath is key to lasting longer in sex, having more intense orgasms, and feeling more intimate love. Sounds simple, doesn't it? Hold on! Here's the problem: we hold our breath too much! How are you breathing now? No doubt it's shallow and barely expanding your chest. Shallow breathing is not healthy!

Here are three simple practices that you can do now for better breathing:

- ◆ **The Source of Life Breath.** Take a breath now and notice the place in your body from which your breath is coming. Is it from your throat, chest, or stomach area? Put your hand there, and now inhale and make a deliberate effort to make the breath come from lower in your body. With each inhale, trace your breath and bring your hand to where it stops before you exhale. Lower your hand and make the breath come from as low down as your genitals—that is key to firing up your sex energy.

- ◆ **Egg to Eagle Breath.** This one is great to do if you're sitting. Exhale as you crunch down into a ball, bringing your elbows in close to your body and resting your hands gently on the back of your head. Feel the stretch across and down your back along your spine. Inhale, lifting up slowly, and stretch to bring your elbows as far back behind you as you can. Feel the stretch in your chest, throw your chest out, and arch your back. Feel all the air rushing into your lungs. Repeat.

- ◆ **The Bellows Breath.** The goal of this exercise is to take in as much air as possible by imagining that your lungs are a bellows. Keep your arms comfortably by your side. Blow all your air out forcefully, making a loud "whoosh," then suck in as much air as possible with as much noise as possible. Continue, taking longer breaths and making louder noises. Feel better already? (These are sounds you will eventually emit during sexual experiences—freer sounds allow more intense sexual responses.)

Dr. Judy's TantrAdvice

Don't worry (like I used to) if you yawn; that's a good sign that you are taking in more air!

Why We Don't Breathe Correctly

The more air you get, the better your body, brain, and organs are fueled; the more relaxed you are; and the clearer your thinking. Many factors inhibit your breathing.

Are your clothes too tight? Don't be vain—my whole life changed for the better when I started wearing looser-fitting clothes! Is your posture terrible? Do you slump, like I do, over the computer?

Some causes of poor breathing are more difficult to identify or change. Do you have a physical disorder? Side effects from medications? Undiagnosed food allergies? My life and breathing also changed for the better after I realized how creamy foods created phlegm in my throat and inhibited my breathing—not good for my work on the radio!

Another fault lies in fear. Shallow air protects us with shallow feelings. Emotions can come flooding out with intense breathing. For this result, many tantric workshops include emotional release exercises.

Tantra Tales

One patient of mine, Kate, protested that her boyfriend did not love her enough. When I asked her to take deep breaths and focus on her body sensations, she resisted. Whenever she complied, floods of tears would fall, revealing her pain. She was like a little girl desperately wanting love but being afraid that even if she received it, she would lose it. So she kept the breath—and the love—at a distance. With encouragement and understanding, she was able to take deep breaths, allow the emotions to surface, and feel more loved.

The Chakra Wheels

Energetics is the "in" word of the new millennium—and one of my favorites. It means focusing on energy. Physicists agree that everything in our world is energy. Think of how we talk about being drawn to someone "like a magnet," or feel "electricity" in his or her presence—all signs of energy.

According to tantric philosophy, energy centers known as *chakras* align along an imaginary axis through the core of our physical body from the bottom of our pelvis to top of our head. These are not physical entities but subtle energy fields associated with different qualities. If you could see them, they would look like energy forces spinning like seven wheels at different points in your body. Being familiar with these chakras is crucial to all the practices you will learn in this book.

Tantra Tutorial

Chakra is a Sanskrit word for "wheel, disc, or hub." Rather than being physical entities or points, the seven chakras are best considered as centers or energy forces.

The second chakra, located in your genital area, is the seat of the powerful force that I will refer to throughout this book. It is key to all the practices that you will learn—through breath and other movements—to bring you to deeper levels of intimacy and higher levels of enlightenment and bliss.

Energy centers, or chakras, and their aspects.

The following chart shows the colors, sounds, and issues associated with each chakra. The questions in the chart reveal whether you have strength or blocks in that area. The idea is to focus on a particular chakra (area of your body) and recite the sound associated with it, or think about the particular color, to connect with the energy in that center.

Another approach in using this chart is to read the issues and questions and see which ones are relevant to you (whether you feel good or bad about them). Then focus on the chakra, color, and sound to strengthen yourself regarding that issue. For example, if you're feeling stifled in expressing yourself (the fifth chakra), put your hand on your throat, visualize the color blue, and repeat the sound "ham" to give yourself more courage to speak up.

Chakra Chart Evaluation

Chakra	Color	Mantra	Issue	Question(s)
(1) Base	Red	Lam	Security	Do you feel insecure, needy, or helpless? Or safe, secure, grounded?
(2) Sex	Orange	Vam	Energy	Do you feel undesirable and inhibited? Or sexy and alive?
(3) Solar plexus	Yellow	Ram	Power	Do you feel weak, threatened, or powerless? Or confident and worthy?
(4) Heart	Green	Yam	Love	Do you feel unloved and abandoned? Or loving and compassionate?
(5) Throat	Blue	Ham	Expression	Do you feel unheard, misunderstood, or passive? Or expressive and truthful?
(6) Third eye	Purple	Ooo	Vision	Do you feel unclear, unauthentic, or confused? Or inspired and intuitive?
(7) Crown	Violet	Omm	Enlightenment	Do you feel spiritually void and disconnected? Or enlightened, ecstatic, and cosmically connected?

In another exercise, you can chant the sounds one by one (they are ancient Sanskrit words) as a way to connect with each chakra, experiencing the movement of energy through your body.

Breathe Through the Chakras

Your breathing practices help you create a clear channel in your body through which air can travel past these chakras, cleansing, feeding, and fueling you. Air going through a clear channel in your body is called an *inner flute* because of its sweet flute-like sound. You then can send your breath to your partner, who will cycle it through his or her chakras and return it, fueling and empowering you both.

As you breathe, picture the breath going through the chakras. Try the following two exercises:

♦ The *complete breath* relaxes you. Inhale deeply into your lower belly and chest (until it pouches out like a contented Buddha). You can do this on your own or with a partner, either face to face or back to back. Sadly, many people resist doing this breath, feeling unattractive with their belly popping out, but it is a good breath to do in the middle of sex. Say, "Let's do the Buddha breath," and press your bellies and chests against each other.

♦ In contrast, as its name suggests, the *fire breath* fires you up. Take continual rapid breaths in and out of the nose (like snorting), causing your stomach to pulsate quickly. You can accelerate the energy even more by raising and lowering your arms (a familiar motion if you exercise on a stationary bike).

After you get your individual breathing going better, you are ready to breathe with a partner for more powerful love connections. One word of caution, however: too much energy in the brain before you are prepared to handle it can cause you to literally "blow your fuse," like too many electrical appliances in an outlet. This results in headaches, confusion, passing out, or even a panic attack. For this reason, it's a good idea to take a workshop about tantric sex if you are going to practice the techniques intensely.

Three Breathing Practices to Create a Magical Connection

Breathing together gets you in tune and connected in a powerful, loving exchange. The following three breathing techniques are basic to the tantric practices in the rest of this book. It is best to learn them in order.

♦ **Step 1: The Synchronizing Breath.** In this exercise you breathe in and out at the same time as your partner to get on the same wavelength. Sit comfortably cross-legged, facing each other on pillows if necessary, as long as your spine is straight. Give each other a wink or touch, or make noises or hand movements to signal your pacing. After a while, close your eyes to sense each other's energy pattern.

Dr. Judy's TantrAdvice

I've counseled many people who start crying when they look really deeply in a loving partner's eyes and breathe. Don't be alarmed by this. The experience can trigger deep feelings about finally experiencing love you always wanted but never had.

♦ **Step 2: The Reciprocal Breath.** In this breath you send your loving energy into each other. Sit in the yab yum position (as shown in the following figure) and inhale while your partner exhales; then exhale while your partner inhales. Imagine that you are exchanging air, inhaling your partner's breath. Or imagine breathing for each other.

Reciprocal Breath: exchanging energy between beloveds.

◆ **Step 3: The Circulating Breath.** For this breath, inhale, imagining energy rising up from your sex center (second chakra) through your body (passing through all the chakras, as listed in the previous table), traveling to the top of your head, then back down to your genitals and the base of your spine on the exhale. Picture tracing a loop inside yourself and then out to a partner. This practice is called different names by different disciplines (the Hindu Circulating Breath is known to Chinese Taoists as the Microcosmic Orbit or the Golden Circle).

Circulating Breath: cycling energy through beloveds' bodies.

The following are some more advanced breathing techniques:

◆ **The Bliss Breath.** Inhale deeply through your mouth and exhale naturally and continuously, allowing any natural sounds. Smile.

◆ **Ecstatic Breathing.** To do this breath, lie on your back with your knees up and inhale long, slow breaths through the mouth; counting to five, expand the abdomen, and create an archway under the small of the back. Exhale to the count of five, bringing your back to the floor and tilting your pelvis slightly upward. Allow the air to rush into the chest, opening your throat. Repeat rhythmically to create a wavelike motion throughout the body. Release any tightness in the throat, neck, chest, shoulders, abdomen, buttocks, or pelvis by purposefully tightening and then releasing the muscles in those areas. Allow sounds and feelings (sadness, anger, joy) to emerge freely on the exhale. This technique was developed by Lori Star in her California "Celebrations of Love" courses (see Appendix B).

Ecstatic Breathing.

Tantra Tutorial _____

The cobra breath involves a particular pattern of breathing with moves and imagery (invoking the shape of a snake) that are powerful tools for mind expansion. To ensure that tantra students are prepared for its powerful effects, some traditions, such as Tantrika International, insist that this breath be taught orally and only by those given permission to do so by experienced tantra teachers.

◆ **The High Consciousness Breath.** Eventually you can cycle your breaths through each other's body in all kinds of directions and then ultimately to a higher place, beyond the mind. This is shown in the Tao of Sex illustration on the following page.

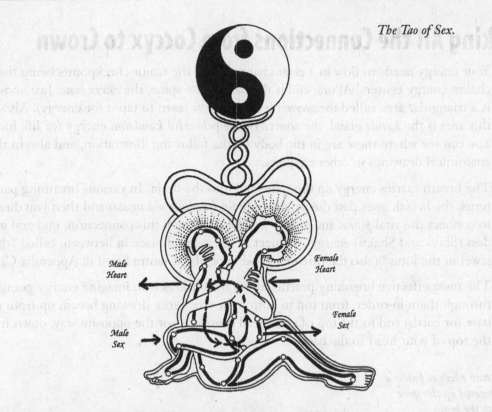

The Tao of Sex.

Male Heart

Female Heart

Male Sex

Female Sex

The Third Eye as Window to the Soul

No doubt you have heard the phrase, "The eyes are the window to the soul." In tantra, the most effective door to your soul is not your real eyes, but that symbolic eye called the *third eye* (actually, it's behind your eyes, in the middle of your brain). Opening your third eye helps you delve deeper into your own being and connect on a higher level with your loved one. Fortunately, more men these days want the intimacy that women have always craved; that kind of connection is possible only when both people really want it to happen. To do this, put your finger on that spot on your forehead to connect with the third eye deeper within, and imagining breathing into that spot when you want to tap into deep relaxation and inner knowing.

Dr. Judy's TantrAdvice

To help you with different breathing patterns, play a CD to pace yourself. Excellent choices are any of Gabrielle Roth's CDs, the CD called *Tantric Sexuality,* and Osho's *Dynamic Meditation* CD (see Appendix C for more information).

Making All the Connections from Coccyx to Crown

Your energy needs to flow in a clear channel, with the major checkpoints being the chakra energy centers. At one end is the base of the spine, the *coccyx bone*. Just above it is a triangular area called the *sacrum* (you will later learn to tap it for energy). Also in this area is the *kunda* gland, the source of the powerful *kundalini* energy (or life force). You can see where these are in the body on the following illustration, and also in the anatomical drawings in other chapters.

The breath carries energy up the spine and into the brain. In various breathing patterns, the breath goes past the primitive brain (*medulla oblongata*) and then you direct it to connect the vital *pineal* and *pituitary glands*. Through this connection, god and goddess (Shiva and Shakti) energy can meet in the magical place in between, called "the jewel in the lotus" (also the title of a good book about tantra listed in Appendix C).

The most effective breathing practice using the chakras is to imagine energy going through them in order, from top to bottom or vice versa; drawing breath up from the base (or earth) and to the top of your head (the sky)—or the opposite way, down from the top of your head to the base.

The breath needs to follow a clear channel up the spine and into the brain.

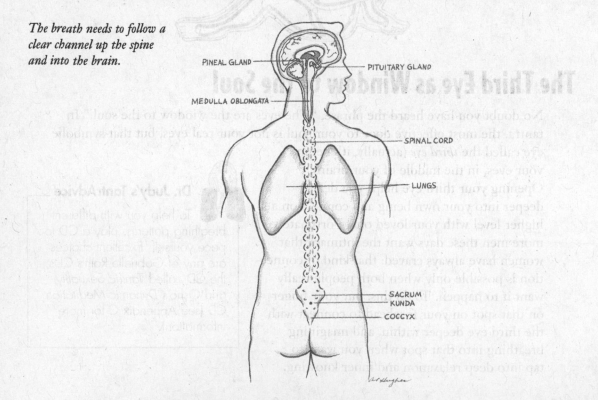

PINEAL GLAND

PITUITARY GLAND

MEDULLA OBLONGATA

SPINAL CORD

LUNGS

SACRUM
KUNDA
COCCYX

Your Inner Smile

Smiling is a powerful tool for happiness and bliss. It boosts your confidence and makes you and everyone around you happier. Research has even proven that smiling triggers the *limbic system* in the brain, which is the center for pleasure.

You know about the smile that is visible on your face, but tantric practice teaches about another smile. It's called the *inner smile*. Imagine it happening in the back of your brain, at the nape of your neck, in the primitive brain. Picturing it creates not only a positive attitude, but also helps you reach the desired state of bliss that tantra is all about. Put your best smile on your face and imagine an equally broad inner smile when you look at your partner and at yourself in the mirror. This will boost your self-esteem and create good energy in your inner and outer world.

Try this exercise. Allow yourself to have any facial expression, even a scowl. Now purposefully put on an outer and inner smile and notice how your energy shifts. Make this inner smile while doing the exercises described throughout this book.

Be Both Participant and Observer

Key to stilling the mind for tantric sex (as well as many other meditative practices) is being in a mental state in which you are simultaneously participant and observer. This means that while you are "doing," another part of you is also observing what is going on. This part is called the *witness*. It might sound distracting, but actually, the witness acts as a referee, keeping you on track, being present and authentic, processing feelings, and alerting you about what you need to do or share. For example, so many men and women complain about distracting thoughts that cause sexual performance anxiety, like "How long can I last?" "Will I please her?" "Does he think I'm attractive?" To solve this problem, in tantra, you notice (witness) yourself having these thoughts (instead of fighting them as many people do, which only makes them more persistent!) and then refocus your attention on your breath and the sensations in your body.

Tantra Tutorial _____

The commonly used Sanskrit chant, *Om Mane Padme Hum*, is the oldest and most famous Buddhist mantra, written on prayer flags and chanted thousands of times by Tibetan and Nepali people as well as tantra practitioners. It expresses the idea of enlightenment through union of male and female. Chant it for five minutes alone or with your partner to create a peaceful and joyful space.

Mantras

Mantras are spoken or silent sounds, or a series of sounds that trigger specific reactions in the body and mind because their vibrations correspond to specific chakras. Repeat any sound, and notice its hypnotic effect. Try drawing out the sound "om" and feel the vibration move from your body up into your head. The sound helps you focus your mind and move energy where you want it in your body. You probably already know how sound can affect you (and send you into other realms) when you listen to your favorite music and feel sensations in your body, or feel like you are carried into another world. Using sound in mantras allows you to control what you feel and where your mind goes.

Mantra sounds are usually short and repetitive (to help quiet the mind) and range from a single word ("om") or a verse (such as the Lord's Prayer). You can recite a known mantra or make up your own. Any word or phrase that you enjoy saying will work fine.

Yantras

A *yantra* is a geometric figure that you concentrate on to still your mind and be stimulated by the particular state that the symbols are meant to evoke in you. The idea is to focus on the figure and then close your eyes, letting the symbol be projected on your inner mental screen. There are symbols related to each of the seven different chakras. These yantras are used like mantras, to focus your energy on a particular issue related to that energy center.

The six-point Star of David is a popular yantra that I will talk more about in Chapter 10.

Mandalas

Mandalas, a kind of yantra, are patterns with concentric rings that come out from the center and contain symbols, figures, or forces of nature (like deities, waterfalls, or dolphins) that reveal mysteries of the universe. Psychoanalyst Carl Jung is credited with introducing mandalas into the West, using them as a therapy technique and map of the psyche to "uncover the mystery of the unconscious and the soul."

California artist Paul Heussenstamm, a master of painting mandalas (see the following illustration), often depicts patterns that evoke tantric sex imagery in the union of god and goddess surrounded in exquisite nature. Heussenstamm makes custom mandalas and teaches classes on how to make this art in California and on journeys to countries like India and Nepal. "You don't have to think of yourself as an artist," he says. "Just close your eyes and notice the lights and colors that appear in the visual field. People draw what their mind has conjured up, and it gives you clues as to what's really in your soul." (See Appendix B for contact information.)

An original mandala by artist Paul Heussenstamm.

The Least You Need to Know

- ◆ Breathing practices are key to directing sexual energy to other parts of the body to connect with the beloved, maintain health, achieve ecstatic states, and melt into unity.

- ◆ There are seven energy centers called chakras throughout the body, each associated with colors, sounds, and issues. Tantric practices help you connect and use the energy in these centers to achieve desired feelings and connections in yourself and in a relationship.

- ◆ Practicing breathing exercises with a partner can greatly intensify your love connection and achievement of mutual sexual satisfaction.

- ◆ Quieting the mind and directing energy is key to reaching high states of consciousness in tantric sex and can be accomplished through meditation on sounds and designs.

Chapter 3

More Basics: Yes, Yin Yang, and Yab Yum

In This Chapter

♦ Achieving balance and uniting male and female, yin and yang, Shiva and Shakti

♦ A test of opposites

♦ The lovemaking position of yab yum

♦ A new view of desire

♦ Setting boundaries of "yes" and "no"

Now that you know the basic breathing practices and are embarking on the study of tantric sex, you'll find yourself changing how you view certain aspects of yourself, your relationships, and the world—likely a paradigm shift from what is familiar to you. Through this new exploration, you will learn to look beyond the physical to see the divinity in every being. You'll view sex as sacred and spiritual rather than simply as a physical act. What's more, you'll learn a new language of love as you progress to higher states of consciousness and bliss.

As you embark on this journey, suspend limiting beliefs of how you have to be, what you think you need from a lover, and what has to happen in sex for you to be fulfilled. As you read this chapter, allow yourself to embrace new ideas about who you are, what a really happy partnership entails, and how to have truly great sex.

In this chapter, I'll introduce you to those basic concepts and practices of tantric sex that are important to your understanding of this exciting new way of life and loving. Get ready to grow—I promise it will be worth it!

Sex as Energy—Not Activity

The most basic principle is that sex is energy! Sex in the Western world has all too often been a matter of performance (how much the woman moans, how long the man lasts) or behaviors (such as oral sex or intercourse). Tantric sex redefines what sex is—not as an action, but as movement of energy within you individually, and between you and your partner. The practices guide you to generate sexual energy, transform it into love energy, and transmit it to your partner and even to the universe. (I'll discuss this further and give you specific techniques on how to do this in Part 3.)

Dr. Judy's TantrAdvice

A man's energy "enters" the woman (and vice versa) through penetration or the exchange of body fluids—an important reason to be selective about with whom you have a sexual embrace or physical encounter.

Ecstasy Essentials

Tantra asserts that all problems, fears, and unhappiness in relationships derive from feeling that we are not whole and are searching to complete unfulfilled parts of ourselves. Yet each of us has the capacity to embrace our male and female energies, to become whole, and to come together in a healthy union.

Yin and Yang: What Is Male and What Is Female?

I'm sure you're familiar with traditional stereotypes of men as assertive and powerful and women as soft and nurturing. We also know too well the criticisms that men don't express feelings (thinking that's a "female" thing to do) and that women don't speak up or take credit for what they do (characteristics considered more "male"). Fortunately, an increasing number of men and women are allowing themselves a broader range of behaviors.

Tantric sex might seem to affirm these opposite characteristics, because a fundamental principle of tantra is that male and female are considered polar opposites. According to Eastern theory, yin represents feminine characteristics, and yang represents masculine traits. However, that's not to say that a woman can't be "yang" or a male "yin." Rather than taking this principle literally, try to imagine male and female as energies. The path to bliss in tantra is the union of these two powerful forces.

> ### Dr. Judy's TantrAdvice
>
> Consistent with the principles of tantra, gays, lesbians, transgendered persons, and omnisexuals should read everything in this book as applying as equally to them as to heterosexuals. Rather than getting hung up on "male" and "female" as if they refer to men and women, think of masculine and feminine energies—within yourself or between partners.

The Circle of Coupled Consciousness

You've undoubtedly seen the circular yin yang symbol before, with one white side and one black side. It's the classic Chinese symbol of the male and female energies uniting into a whole. According to Eastern theory, the circle represents the union of yin as the feminine or female energy and yang as the masculine or male energy. Yang is the force of father, heaven, sky, and all that is logical and penetrating. Yin is the feminine force of the earth and mother, representing aspects of being that are nurturing and receptive.

Yang is quick to fire, whereas yin is slow to heat. Think of how similar this is to the typical sexual response cycle of men and women—he's always so ready for sex while she needs more romance to get in the mood. In fact, men need only 3 minutes to get excited, whereas it takes women 15 minutes to reach equivalent arousal.

Yang corresponds to the upper part of the body, including the throat, brain, and power center; yin is linked to the heart and lower body (the womb and sexual organs). I'll discuss more about these energy centers in the next chapter. Again, these ideas are consistent with stereotypes that men are more "in their heads" and into power and women are more in touch with their body and emotions. Tantric sex practices give you specific tools, disciplined practices, and fun games that bring these two parts and characteristics into balance, assisting your journey to cosmic bliss.

The Chinese symbol of the union of yin and yang, male and female energies.

Shiva and Shakti

Another common image in tantric tradition is the Hindu couple in the form of Lord Shiva and his female consort, the Goddess Shakti. He is considered the mighty creator, and she the essence of energy. Their symbolic union inspires us to expect to be treated like a god or goddess and to surrender to the god or goddess in our partner. I'll discuss more about how honoring in this way leads to sacred love and magical sex in Chapter 5 and in Part 3. There you'll learn exactly how to treat each other to have awesome and enlivening loving experiences.

Lord Shiva and Goddess Shakti as the union of male and female energy.

Shiva's male energy also represents bliss, and Shakti's female energy represents wisdom—another magical combination of two essential elements necessary to reach enlightenment. The perfect pair is often depicted in statues and paintings in many entwined positions—embracing, sitting, standing, balancing on one leg, or dancing, with Shakti wrapped around Shiva's body or hiked on his hips. (Dancing, as I'll tell you later in this book, is a sacred ritual to free the spirit and facilitate enlightenment.) The pair also might be sitting inside a *lotus* (a plant in the water lily family, considered in Hinduism to be the source of life).

Tantra Tutorial

The left side of the body is considered the receiving side (yin); therefore many tantric sex practices in this book are meant to be done while gazing mainly into your partner's left eye, or by visualizing energy entering through your left hand and flowing out toward your partner from your right hand.

Getting in Touch with Opposites

To reach the balance of opposite energies, first you must recognize any divisions you have made. Consider the following pairs of stereotypic opposite characteristics. Think of ones that you identify with or that best describe you; then read the opposite quality and see if you can imagine being like that as well. Add other qualities you can think of:

Giving	Receiving
Active	Passive
Light	Heavy
Being a day person	Being a night person
Happy	Sad.

Imagine going from one extreme to the other and then what it would be like to embrace both characteristics.

Achieving Balance and Union of Opposites

An ultimate goal of tantric sex is to balance polarities, which you explored in the previous exercise. Different cultures might use different terms, but all similarly search for balance of opposites and use rituals to achieve sacred union of male and female energies. Some of these practices seem esoteric to us; others are familiar. For example, prayers invoke both energies, as in "God's will be done on earth as it is in heaven." In tantric practice, energy from heaven (also considered male—yang or "father" energy) must unite with energy from earth (also considered female—yin and "mother" energy) in a cosmic circle to reach the desired higher states of bliss.

People often ask me whether opposites really attract. Think of your past relationships. Have you and your partner been opposites in any way? Perhaps one of you was the pursuer and the other the pursued. Perhaps one was more emotional and the other more rational; one more extravagant and the other more prudent. These couplings are common and represent the self seeking balance. These relationships can certainly work, and being different can create excitement, but it's unhealthy to seek

Tantra Tutorial _____

In ancient times among certain groups, **androgyny** (exhibiting both masculine and feminine qualities) was honored, and **hermaphrodites** (people born with genitalia of both sexes) represented perfection.

Dr. Judy's TantrAdvice _____

When assuming the yab yum position, choose a place to sit that is comfortable for you. Experiment (try sitting in a chair). Using a pillow to be more comfortable and aligned is helpful, especially if one partner is much shorter than the other.

an opposite to fulfill a part of you that is lacking (as in the case of a woman choosing a man who is extremely logical because she feels too emotional).

Position Yourselves for Love in Yab Yum

The Hindu term *yab yum* refers to the position you might have seen in tantric art: The man sits with legs crossed and the female straddles in his lap; their legs are wrapped around each other and, if possible, meet behind the back (the same position is called *Cranes with Necks Intertwined* in Chinese). The words *yab yum* represent the union of opposites, like the male and female forces of yin and yang. This position accomplishes several goals, as it …

Tantra Tutorial

Tantric sex is commonly associated with the **Kama Sutra**, the ancient Hindu texts of love that contain advice on love and many positions for lovemaking. Some of these are presented in Part 3, where I'll tell you about many specific practices for pleasing your partner.

- Enables lovers to look directly in each other's eyes.
- Aligns your energy centers (something I'll discuss in the next chapter).
- Gives easy access to each other's bodies.

Couple sitting in yab yum position.

A New View of Desire

You feel desire every time you feel the urge to have something you think will make you feel better. "That chick is hot," you might say about how a woman looks, or "I want that guy," you might exclaim about a man you think will make your dreams come true. These desires can come from feeling incomplete, expressing the feeling that "If only I had (him or her, this or that), I would be happy," reflecting a neediness and driving you to possess someone or something. Ironically, after you have what you desire, you often become disillusioned; for example, you might search for someone prettier, richer, or more interesting. Tantric sex practices teach you to be no longer desperate or attached to superficial needs, allowing you to create healthier relationships.

Empowered to Say "Yes" or "No"

When people are empowered to set their boundaries, both in sex and in general, they gain valued self-esteem. In tantric sex, you are in charge of your body and soul. A lover should always ask your permission to enter your sacred space, and you have the right to say "yes" or "no." Are you ready to say "no" to being disrespected, pressured into sex, or touched in a way that makes you uncomfortable? When you speak your truth in this way, your partner is empowered as well, by knowing your limits and how to please you. Are you also ready to say "yes" to longer lovemaking, ecstasy in multiple orgasms, deeper satisfaction and intimacy, and spiritual love connected to blissful sex? If so, you're reading the right book!

Dr. Judy's TantrAdvice

One of my favorite homework assignments to give patients is the "yes/no" exercise; to say "yes" to three things you would ordinarily deny yourself, and "no" to three things you would ordinarily agree to but wish you had turned down. This builds assertiveness and self-esteem.

Taking Care of Your Body Temple

According to tantra, your body is your temple. To reach enlightenment through tantric sex, you have to take care of that temple. Any fitness routine you prefer is helpful, although many tantric practitioners mix their sexual practices with some form of yoga (a gentle choice). Yogic poses have roots in tantric lovemaking positions from ancient texts (although they also became the route to asceticism and abstinence). Read more about useful, interesting, and fun routines you can use individually or with a partner in Chapters 7 and 15.

Tantric sex practices also balance what seem like opposites: relaxation (through meditation) and activation. This is done through breathing practices that send breath through your body, as I described in the previous chapter.

The Least You Need to Know

♦ Tantric sex involves the union and balance of opposites, female and male energies referred to as yin and yang that symbolize dark and light, moon and sun, receiving and giving, heaven and earth.

♦ Yab yum, the position for lovemaking described in ancient Hindu texts in which the woman sits in the man's lap, helps align energies necessary for a powerful tantric love connection.

♦ Tantric sex is not simply an act but the buildup, movement, and transmission of energy through your own body and between you and a partner.

♦ Setting boundaries by saying "yes" or "no" to what you want builds self-esteem and empowerment that is essential for a healthy interaction with a partner in tantric sex.

♦ Honoring and respecting your partner is essential in tantric sex. It is accomplished by asking permission for any sexual act and in using terms like "beloved" to refer to your partner and "sacred space," "yoni," and "lingam" to refer to sexual organs.

The Goals of Tantric Communication

Chapter 4

Communicating the Tantric Way

In This Chapter

- ◆ What is special about tantric communication?
- ◆ How partners should address each other
- ◆ Words to use in tantric love talk
- ◆ Body language for tantric love

What you say and how you say it can make a big difference in how connected and intimate you feel. In this chapter, I describe some new ways to communicate that heighten your inner awareness and intensify your love connection with your partner. These techniques are meant to facilitate the tantric practices that will bring you to higher states of individual consciousness and inter-personal intimacy and bliss.

What Is Tantric Communication?

Tantric communication is the language of the heart, whereby you are not just sending messages consisting of intellectual thoughts, but rather intending to express love. When speaking from the heart with love, the sender and receiver connect through their spirits at a level that goes beyond superficial conversation. Loving tantric communication is meant to be directed toward oneself, the beloved, and any others in your world.

There are three sources of tantric communication:

- ◆ Nonverbal connection, as happens, for example, in looking deeply into one another's eyes.

- ◆ New words for concepts, body parts, and feelings. These new words are often derived from the Sanskrit language, and using them creates a different feeling, that is, a sense of more love within oneself and for the other.

- ◆ Body language consisting of unique body movements that also create a higher state of awareness and connection to the partner.

The Goals of Tantric Communication

The language of the heart used when practicing tantra is meant to enhance the tantric experience of ecstasy and higher consciousness. As such, it is intended to diminish motivations or negative emotions (such as blame, shame, manipulation, guilt, fear, and threat of punishment) that incite distance, distress, and defensiveness between people. Thus, the language is meant to …

- ◆ Convey respect for oneself and others, valuing each person.

- ◆ Honor the other person as a sacred being by seeing beyond physical attributes and looking into his or her soul and seeing good.

- ◆ Bless the other person by wishing them the best.

- ◆ Show compassion by acknowledging what is going on with another person and being sensitive of his or her fears and needs.

- ◆ Show empathy by understanding, as well as feeling, what the other person experiences.

- ◆ Demonstrate honesty and trustworthiness.

- ◆ Bring about nonjudgmental relationships and engender openness rather than defensiveness.

Body Language Tantra Style

I'm sure you know that actions can speak louder than words. Motions in tantra are also meant to express love.

Greeting

The tantric greeting involves holding the palms of the hands together with fingers outstretched, and bowing the head, while stating the word "*namaste*," which means "the divinity (high spirit, god/goddess) in me honors the divinity (high spirit, god/goddess) in you."

Dr. Judy's TantrAdvice

In an advanced greeting, the edges of the thumbs (with palms pressed together) are pressed into the sternum, to activate the heart, or in the area between the eyebrows, to activate the third eye.

Holding Hands

The left hand is always held palm up, because it is the receiving hand, and the right hand is placed on top of it, palm down, as it is the giving hand.

Shaking Hands

Tantra revives the ancient Celtic tradition of shaking both hands; while over time, the left hand shake dropped out, leaving only one hand from each person connecting.

Eye Gazing

The eyes are the window to the soul, nowhere as keenly as in tantra practice. In looking into someone's eyes, gaze primarily into the left eye, which is the receiving eye.

In the eye lock (described in Chapter 9), beloveds look deeply into each other's eyes. Try not to notice the eye color, hair color, or facial features of the person; look deeper, gazing behind the eyes into your beloved's soul.

Heart Tap

Also described in more detail in Chapter 9, the heart tap involves placing a hand on the heart to activate love energy, the source of tantric bliss.

Verbal Tantric Communication

Certain rituals in speaking, as well as particular words, are consistent with the spirit of honoring in tantra. Their use assists in reaching higher states of consciousness and deeper states of intimacy.

Greeting

The Sanskrit word *namaste* is the time-honored greeting to honor each other's divinity. It is used in meeting (in place of *hello*) and in parting (in place of *good-bye*).

Addressing the Partner as the Beloved

Tantra is about sacred love; so, the partner is considered a *beloved* to be honored, cherished, and loved unconditionally. This term can be used for a boyfriend or girlfriend, or for a spouse, and is meant to imply that this person is of primary importance and someone with whom you share deep love and intimacy. Use the term "beloved" when you speak to your partner—say, "John, my beloved, I would like to …"—and see how the word alone arouses loving feelings, both in you when you say it, and for your beloved who hears it. Using this term might seem strange at first, but with practice it will come more naturally.

Dr. Judy's TantrAdvice

Refer to your partner as your "beloved" when speaking to someone else. You will send out loving energy to the person with whom you are speaking, who will share in that love and feel more loving.

New Terms for the Sex Organs: Yoni and Lingam

Tantric sex gives you a new vocabulary for genitals to honor the sacredness of those parts of your body and their roles in sex. Labels help communicate how you feel.

Look over these lists of names for the female and male genitalia and add ones you can think of. See if you can identify the ones that are tantric, that connote a ring of honoring. Circle ones that you feel sound positive and make you feel good about yourself and your body, or your partner's body. Put an "X" through the ones that you feel are negative and pejorative.

What Do You Call the Female Sex Organs?

Vagina	Clitoris	Pussy
Lips	"Down there"	Pleasure pot
Mystic rose chalice	Sacred cave	Cunt
Heavenly gate	Pleasure cave	Doorway of life (Chinese)
Kohe (Hawaiian)	Other: _____	Jewel gate (Japanese)

What Do You Call the Male Sex Organs?

Penis	Phallus (Greek)	Prick
Pecker	Whonker	Johnson
Whacker	Peter	Family jewels
Arrow of love	Sacred arrow	Wand of light
Jade flute (Chinese)	Other: _____	Other: _____

Consider using these words for genitalia (which are used throughout this book) from the tantric sex traditions:

♦ *Yoni* is a Sanskrit word meaning "womb" and "source." It refers to the vagina, a woman's sacred temple.

♦ *Sacred Space* refers to the divine insides of the female, meant to be treated with great reverence, as it is the source of Shakti, female power and feminine divine energy.

♦ *Pearl* is a word for the clitoris.

♦ *Lingam, vajra, wand of light,* or *thunderbolt* refers with respect to the male phallus and evokes the male energy of the Hindu Lord Shiva.

> **Dr. Judy's TantrAdvice**
>
> Using these tantric terms for genitalia might feel stilted to you or your partner at first, but with practice, it will become more comfortable and infuse you with positive energy. Honoring words convey more respect. Practice saying, "I adore your lingam" or "What a beautiful yoni."

Stating Intentions

When coming together for tantric sex, the couple states intentions about what they want to happen in the lovemaking. This ritual commonly starts with sitting in yab yum position, looking into one another's eyes, palms pressed together, and then declaring desire, for example, "I intend for this to be a beautiful exchange of our love for one another, feeling peaceful in our hearts, and sharing a deeper level of closeness than ever before," or simply, "I want us to have the best time," or "I want to laugh a lot!"

Making Dedications

Because tantra is intended for the expression of love for one another and for a greater good of all, the couple would dedicate the lovemaking to some higher purpose. One couple made me laugh by telling me, "We dedicated our last tantric lovemaking to getting the BMW that Paul always wanted!" A common dedication that one partner would say to the other is, "I dedicate this time of our being together for your achieving your dreams, for peace in the war-torn areas, and for the enrichment of the lives of peoples not feeling as graced as we in this moment."

Asking "May I?"

Tantra requires respecting one another's boundaries. As such, tantric partners always request permission when making advances, to test the partner's comfort with sexual approaches and to obtain the partner's agreement and consent. Asking permission from your partner for any sexual act (or anything else) you would like honors the other person. I'll discuss this in more detail in Chapters 11 and 12, which cover pleasing your partner.

Asking permission is especially important when it comes to intercourse, when the man should always ask, "May I enter your sacred cave?"

Giving Thanks

The way of tantra involves expressing gratitude to others for their contribution to your life. A beloved in particular enriches your life in untold ways and should be acknowledged for doing so. Saying "thank you" not only makes others feel good and helps them know how to please you further, but makes you feel good about yourself as well as the giver. Say, "When you touch me in that way (specify how), I feel happy because it meets my needs to be adored." Allow yourself to receive, and resist fears of what you might owe someone for their gift.

The Least You Need to Know

- Communicating consistent with tantric principles involves using words and gestures that express respect and honoring and avoid judgment and negativity.

- Use of new words in tantric communication helps achieve desired intimacy and heart connection for higher states of love.

- Body language also enhances tantric connection by movements, positions, and interactions that allow a deeper opening of the heart.

- Stating your intentions helps you be clear about what you want and helps a partner understand how to please you.

5

Honoring the God and Goddess in You

In This Chapter

♦ The role of god and goddess energies in tantric sex

♦ Significant deities from varying traditions, cultures, and eras

♦ How to connect with divine forces within you

♦ How to use deity meditations

♦ Uniting your god and goddess as beloveds

♦ Festivals and temples that honor god and goddess energies

This chapter helps you connect with the essence of the god and goddess in yourself and in your partner because it is so important to your practice of sacred sex. I introduce you to different gods and goddesses related to tantric practice and techniques of using their divine energies on your journey.

What Is God/Goddess?

In tantra, the terms *god* and *goddess* refer to treating yourself and others with the respect and honor you would extend to revered beings. Through this honoring in tantric sex practices, your divine consciousness will embody the power of the universe.

Deities in tantric practice are essentially archetypes of spirits, guides, angels, and light beings that are symbols of various energies, qualities, or relationships. Other terms for male and female deities are deva and devi, daka and dakini, and priest and priestess. Although deities are portrayed as external beings, they can be considered projections of qualities within our own nature.

The word *goddess* is widely used in the tantra community but has become more mainstream and is often used to refer to a woman who is proud of and in touch with her power as a feminine force. The goddess embodies a range of qualities of a woman, from being soft and nurturing to being strong and fierce. The term *god* is not used as popularly, possibly partly due to the reverence in Judeo-Christian tradition for God as a superior being.

Ecstasy Essentials

Even if you are skeptical, deities and spirits might be helping, supporting, and guiding you. Suspend disbelief for the moment; notice how these energies might help heighten your experience of love and blissful sex.

Some traditions promise that you can be gods or goddesses in another life or by changing in some way to become more divine. Tantra proposes that being a divine being is your birthright. You are divine now, without change.

Being a god or goddess refers to your energy, creative force, and cosmic power. Every woman is a goddess. That means she is the embodiment of all that is feminine to be honored and worshipped. She is a lover, seductress, healer, and nurturing mother, as well as a hunter and wild woman. She must reveal and embrace all these parts of herself and be similarly honored. Similarly, every man is a god, the embodiment of many roles, including being a provider, protector, and a symbol of power, as well as being nurturing, healing, and surrendering. He must embrace and be honored for all these parts. These qualities are present in all people, regardless of age, race, culture, or status. We either display these qualities, or they are potentially available to us.

Integrate All Your Roles

As a start on your path to embracing the god or goddess within you, think of all the roles you play in your life and how you feel about yourself. Are you a parent? An entrepreneur? Are you feeling nurturing? Sexy? Powerful? Introspective? Review your qualities in your mind and write them down. I often have participants in my workshops make a collage of their roles (as shown in the following illustration), with a picture of themselves in the middle surrounded by symbols, photos, and written words for their feelings.

Integrating the goddess self.

After you read about the gods and goddesses later in this chapter, go back over your list and write in the names of deities you most relate to. For example, if you feel sexy, write in Ishtar; if you feel powerful, write in Shiva.

Seeing Beyond the Superficial

You likely know the unpleasant experience of judging others or being judged by looks, job, or stock portfolio. You might also know the pain of statements such as "She's too fat" or "I need a guy who has more money," where your body or bank account becomes your eligibility quotient in the wide world of dating and mating. But in the tantra world, there are no such criteria; you are encouraged to see beyond superficial characteristics into the divinity of each being.

Three essential steps in worshipping the divine in the tantra tradition are ...

1. Embrace the divinity within yourself.

2. Acknowledge divinity in your partner. Tantric sex emphasizes the equality of both male and female deities to achieve the necessary balance of energies.

3. Unite god and goddess in the union of you and your beloved. This achieves the perfect balance of male and female energy necessary to achieve bliss and higher consciousness.

The Importance of Worshipping Each Other

Through my years of work as a therapist, I know how happy people become when they are acknowledged. Do you know what it feels like to be truly appreciated? To really be noticed? To be deeply known, like when someone "gets" who you are? Tantric sex takes acknowledgment one step further—to being *worshipped!* Worship doesn't mean blind obsession; it means loving unconditionally and limitlessly. Nor does it mean having power over someone who is your slave; it means serving each other equally from the highest state of personal power and mutual respect.

Think of all the compliments you would like to hear about yourself and wonderful things you could say about your beloved. That's what it means in tantra to be worshipped like a god or goddess.

Clearing Up Confusion About Gods and Goddesses

All deities are involved with life and death. However, understanding their roles can be confusing because some are claimed by several cultures and have multiple incarnations or *manifestations*, which represent different aspects and therefore have different names. I remember being very confused by the most dramatic example of these: the Hindu Lord Shiva, who is also called Brahma and Vishnu, and who has more than a thousand different manifestations ranging from his Protector form to his more evil form called Bairab. Similarly, the power of the goddess Kali can be seen in her "light" form as powerful but also in her "shadow" aspect as manipulative and controlling. The goal is to accept and merge these aspects within yourself.

You might like or dislike or want to emulate or discard these qualities. As you read about them in this chapter, see which resonate with you. Do the exercises later in this chapter to understand their role in yourself and your relationships.

Getting to Know the Ancient Goddesses

Male and female divine figures come from ancient cultures such as the Sumerian, Teutonic, Egyptian, Greek, and Roman, as well as from modern times. Let's take a closer look at some of the deities from around the world, starting with goddesses.

Major and Well-Known Goddesses

Most goddesses represent fertility. Goddesses are loving and nurturing in their light manifestations; however, some are also portrayed as seductresses engaging in ritual prostitution. As you read through this list of goddesses from various cultures, circle names you find yourself drawn to:

◆ **Lilith.** A Near Eastern goddess portrayed in many legends as an independent woman refusing to be dominated by men (a music festival a few years ago that celebrated female artists was given the name Lilith Fair). In one myth, she is the first woman in paradise, but unlike Eve, she did not submit to Adam. In ancient Sumerian lore, she gained a reputation as a seductress and harlot, using her secrets of sexual techniques to lure men to the temples of Inanna, Ishtar, and Astarte to worship her, hail infidelity, and participate in tantric sexual rites.

◆ **Ishtar.** The Exalted Light of Heaven, with her sweet lips and beautiful body, is known for her eroticism and sexuality but is also depicted as the goddess of battle, carrying a bow and sword and riding on a lioness. Deriving from ancient Sumeria as Inanna, she later appears in the Babylonian era as well as in Egypt, and even is claimed as Aphrodite born on Cyprus, giving the island its name as the "Island of Love." She is symbolized by the evening star and revered for her prophecy, leadership, and healing of the sick. In annual rites, this high priestess unites with the king in sacred marriage.

Ishtar, the great goddess of eroticism.

◆ **Guan-Yin.** This is the great Chinese goddess of compassion, whose statue is sold everywhere in China. I've been moved after seeing one of her tallest statues on Puduo Mountain, the site of three of her most revered temples; another statue of her stands in the water at China's most expansive Buddhist gardens, the Nanshan Buddhist Monastery, on the island of Hainan (the Hawaii of China), meant to evoke the impressive welcome of our own Statue of Liberty.

Guan-Yin, the Chinese goddess of compassion (statue at Nanshan Buddhist Monastery on the island of Hainan, China).

◆ **The Virgin Mary.** She is the ultimate Christian symbol of purity and motherhood.

◆ **Greek goddesses.** The Greek goddesses are centuries old, and many temples were built in their honor. Later they were adapted by the Romans, who changed their names.

 ◆ **Aphrodite.** This popular goddess from Greek tradition is associated with love, desire, ultimate sexuality, and ecstasy, and she is often symbolized by a dove, dolphin, rose, apple, or even an opium poppy. She is also popularly known as Venus, famous Roman goddess of love, known for purity and supposedly invented by the Romans to turn the citizens toward chastity.

 ◆ **Athena.** The warrior goddess whose statue once stood in the center of the Parthenon is a symbol of wisdom, protection, and virginity (she sprung full grown from the father God Zeus). Her temple, Athena Nike, is testimony to victory.

 ◆ **Demeter.** The Greek goddess of motherhood and nurturance.

 ◆ **Artemis.** In Greek mythology, she is the virgin goddess of the hunt and the moon. She is the female counterpart to Ares, the god of war.

Statues of goddesses from different cultures in the collection of real-life goddess author and interfaith minister Laurie Sue Brockway.

◆ **Hindu goddesses.** Various goddesses are of great importance in India and Nepal. I have witnessed ceremonies, seen temples to many of them, and also have many small statues that I keep in my home and even carry in my briefcase.

   ◆ **Durga,** the mother of goddesses.

   ◆ **Tara,** a goddess representing kindness and wisdom.

   ◆ **Lakshmi,** the goddess of abundance, wealth, happiness, and prosperity.

   ◆ **Saraswati,** goddess of the arts.

   ◆ **Kali,** the goddess of power and strength. I have witnessed many sacrifices at her shrine outside Kathmandu, Nepal, where goats and chickens are slaughtered and their blood offered to her statues as a request for her protection.

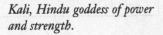

Kali, Hindu goddess of power and strength.

Other Goddesses Around the World

Almost every culture has goddesses who might be equivalent to deities from other cultures and eras. Even if your own background differs, you might identify with these entities (especially if you believe in past lives; you might have lived in those times and places). Here are several countries and some of the goddesses associated with them:

◆ **Africa.** Mboze is the goddess of the Woyo people; she represents fertility through rainfall. Odude is a Northwest African goddess, whose name means "the black one" and who is often imaged as a serpent, evoking the tantric kundalini energy rising.

◆ **Egypt.** Qadesh is the goddess of love and sex from the Akkadian and Babylonian empires often depicted as a ruler of fertility in the animal world; her worshippers also practiced prostitution.

◆ **Haiti.** The Voodoo goddess Erzuli, also called Empusae, is known as a sexual vampire, sucking out men's strength by seducing them while they sleep and inducing erotic dreams or ejaculation. She is worshipped in modern times with champagne and perfume.

◆ **Ireland.** Maeve is considered a magical goddess of Ireland. On one hand she is associated with wanton sexuality, but on the other she is a warrior who uses her sexuality to win battles.

◆ **Israel.** The Hebrew goddess Shekinah, whose name means "creative force," is equivalent to the Hindu Shakti and is meant to establish balance. Ruth is a real woman revered to have saved her people in ancient times, and thus can be considered a goddess.

◆ **Japan.** The goddess Benzai Tennyo is associated with sexuality and fertility, but also with granting good fortune and with the art of music (similar to the Hindu goddess Saraswati).

◆ **Mexico.** Tlazolteotl is the Aztec goddess of love and sexuality whose worship included prostitution. Her dark side is associated with death and human sacrifice.

Tantra Tales

Some women today rename themselves with Sanskrit names of goddesses, such as Lakshmi, Kamala, and Usha. Or they might refer to a goddess to describe their own behavior. For example, one tantra friend of mine talks about her expressions of anger or confrontations with other people by saying, "My Kali came out!"

Tantra Tutorial

Greek goddess prototypes, such as Demeter as mother and Artemis as the warrior, are described in Agapi Stassinopolous's book, *Conversations with the Goddess: Revealing the Divine Power Within You* (Stewart, Tabori & Chang, 1999).

◆ **Middle East.** The Islamic goddess Al'Lat (also called Hecate) is the feminine form of Allah and is similar to the Hindu Lord Shiva in that calling her is like saying "the Lord" or simply "God." She symbolizes three aspects of the moon: the virgin, the mother, and the aging wise woman. Her reign ended when her shrine was taken over by the prophet Mohammed, signaling the change from matriarchy to patriarchy.

◆ **Near East.** Cybele is reputed to perform both fertility and castration rites. Archaeological finds, usually in the form of a black stone, dating back to 6000 B.C. prove her early worship.

◆ **Scotland.** Riannon is a Welsh goddess often depicted mounted on a white horse or who transforms into a white mare for a marriage ceremony. In mythology, she was chased by a prince who could not catch her until he asked her permission—a story evoking the importance of a man's surrender to the goddess (a key tantric sex principle).

◆ **Thailand.** Tap-tun is celebrated in Thailand (and as Chao Mae Tuptim in China) with offerings of hundreds of symbols of lingams (male sexual organs).

◆ **United States.** Mother Maui is the goddess of the New Age movement; Gaia is the goddess of the earth; and Pele is the goddess of fire, often depicted as arising from a volcano. (Having spent much time on the island of Maui in Hawaii, I know firsthand the powerful goddess energy there and recommend you visit to experience it, too.)

Go back over this list and circle the goddesses whose energies you connect with. For example, I connect with all the goddesses in Nepal because that is such a scared place; Guan Yin because I spend so much time in China; the Greek goddess of the hunt, Artemis, which was the name of the women's rock band I played in; and the Welsh goddess Riannon, the subject of a Fleetwood Mac song I sang when I played in a band of six women.

Blocks to Bliss

Some beings are considered to have given tantric sex a bad reputation. Aghora is a rebellious manifestation of the Hindu god Shiva, famous for orgies and cruelties, such that his devotees have sex in cemeteries. Bhogi supposedly volunteered as a human sacrifice to achieve sacred status; his dying wish was to have sex with many women.

Gods from Different Cultures

Like goddesses, gods come from every culture, tradition, and era. Despite their association to a particular religion, many gods similarly represent a higher power, such as Jesus in Christianity, Allah in Islam, Buddha in Buddhism, or the Hindu Lord Shiva. See which ones you relate to:

- **Hindu gods.** These include the most important, Lord Shiva; also known as Vishnu, god of all gods, with more than a thousand manifestations, including his dark side as Bairab. He is worshipped in the form of the Shiva lingam (a phallus) in temples throughout India and Nepal. As I mentioned in Chapter 3, Shiva's consort is Shakti (the female force); together they are a union of energy and enlightenment. The oft-beloved Ganesh, known for his kindness and removal of obstacles, is well recognized as a boyish-looking figure with a human body and an elephant head.

- **Christian God.** Jesus is considered the Son of God and savior of the Christian people who performed the ultimate self-sacrifice to deliver others from their sins.

- **Greek gods.** As in the case of goddesses, there are many Greek gods, all of whom have equivalents in Roman culture. The highest god among all other Greek deities, Zeus is symbolic of power and domination. He is the archetype for the macho, alpha male. Other Greek gods include the following:

  - **Eros.** Called the god of love in Greek times and Cupid in Roman days, Eros evokes a familiar image as a cherub who mischievously aims arrows at people's hearts to make them fall in love. He also has been depicted as androgynous (not clearly male or female).

  - **Dionysus.** Called the god of lust in Greek times and Bacchus in Roman days, Dionysus symbolizes overindulgence of wine, women, and song and is known for wanton feasts and drunken orgies.

  - **Priapus.** A Greek phallic god and son of Aphrodite and Dionysus, Priapus is known for his unusually huge erection, symbolizing men's sexual potency (his name now refers to an erection that lasts too long!). Virgins would also deflower themselves on his erect lingam.

  - **Satyr.** Related to Pan and Eros, Satyr is well recognized as the half-man, half-goat mythical creature who symbolizes unrestrained male passion and the pursuit of erotic adventures.

  - **Hercules.** Endowed with great strength and cunning, this Greek hero of classical myth is most often portrayed as a slayer of monsters and beasts.

◆ **Apollo.** One of the greatest and best-known Greek deities, Apollo is called Mars by the Romans and is pictured as a handsome young man. He is god of the sun, music, poetry, medicine, and fine arts. We know his name well from the series of manned spacecrafts, one of which landed on the Moon, marking one of the greatest achievements of our time.

◆ **Ares.** The Greek god of war, he is equivalent to the energy of the female warrior, Artemis.

◆ **Egyptian gods.** Ra is the god of the Sun, and another god, Osiris, is infamous in stories of dismemberment, incest, and adultery.

◆ **Japanese gods.** These include Musuri-Kami, a Shinto deity honored at annual fertility festivals where hundreds of people march through the streets toting huge phalluses made of stone or wood.

The Essence of the God/Goddesses Within You

As I've mentioned, certain gods and goddess and their essences will resonate with you, giving you insight into how you are or how you want to be. Review the previous list of deities, and consider whether you are like them or want to be like them.

Notice when you read their names whether you feel drawn to that deity in a positive way (excited, energized, happy). Or do you feel something negative in your body (tightness, pain, pressure)? You might have a negative charge on the qualities he or she embodies.

Ask yourself, "What am I trying to avoid?" For example, because Kali is the goddess of power, some women might feel attracted to her to express more assertiveness in their life; others might be frightened by that energy. Don't judge what you feel, just notice it. Don't worry whether the deity's sex matches yours. Remember that according to tantra, you have both male and female essence within you and must embody both.

Have your partner do this exercise, too. Discuss the energies stimulated in each of you as a way to learn more about yourselves, each other, and your relationship.

Modern-Day God/Goddess Icons

Modern-day figures (alive or dead) also serve as cultural icons of gods or goddesses, usually because of their media exposure. Some believers think that the spirits of ancient figures are channeled through these people. Modern goddesses might include Marilyn Monroe and Madonna (the rock star) as sex goddesses, Mother Teresa as the Chinese goddess of compassion Guan-Yin, or even Barbara Bush as the strong mother energy of the Hindu goddess Durga. Modern-day sex gods might include *People Magazine*'s picks for most handsome men, such as Sean Connery, Brad Pitt, or the late John F. Kennedy Jr.

In the following exercise, write down some modern-day figures who embody energies you either like or want.

Your Modern-Day Deity Exercise

Name of Person	Qualities This Person Has That I Like
_____	_____
_____	_____
_____	_____

God and Goddess Counterparts

Tantra is a partnered as well as a personal practice, as evidenced by tantric gods and goddesses depicted with partners, called *consorts*. Entwined in embrace, they project the male/female balance that is central to tantric practice. Think of some famous people—deities, heroes and heroines, or historical figures—who are linked together. What feelings do they evoke in you? How are those reactions related to the relationships in your life? Make your list, adding to some of the examples I give you here. Have your partner do this exercise, too, and then discuss your choices.

God and goddess pairs.

Couples Qualities	
Name of Couple	**Qualities This Couple Evokes in You**
Shiva and Shakti	Ultimate ecstasy, perfect balance
Samson and Delilah	Displays power and strength
Romeo and Juliet	Tragic love thwarted by disapproval
Lancelot and Guenevere	Passion tainted by infidelity
Edward of England and Wallis Simpson	Love so compelling that he would give up the throne
Elizabeth Taylor and Richard Burton	Passionate love that causes turmoil
Other (fill in): _____	_____

Using Deities in Your Sex Practice

The gods and goddesses can add great power to your tantric practices. In Chapter 17, I'll discuss more advanced ways to draw from their energy.

You can buy a form of the deity as a statue, photograph, mandala, or thangka. Ask at local yoga centers or check local Yellow Pages for stores specializing in Eastern artifacts, or check out the websites listed in Appendix B.

Reclaiming Goddess Juiciness

Tibetan nuns preserved ancient practices that cultivate healing energy in the body and send it to the earth and the world. With many monasteries having been destroyed, many of these *Vajrayogini* practices were in danger of being lost, but they are now being made available to women in the Western world to continue the tradition. California Tantra teacher Lexi Fisher teaches the practices to groups of women, accompanied by another healer playing

 Tantra Tutorial

Vajrayogini was/is a female Buddha who taught erotic practices that recognize that within the body lies the powerful wellspring of sexual energy that can be cultivated and applied to personal restoration, replenishment, and rejuvenation.

the crystal and Tibetan bowls. The Vajrayogini practice is a series of gentle, flowing movements that marry yoga and T'ai Chi with the added excitement triggered by doing locks (holds) of the root chakra (Mula-banda). The locks lift up the pelvic floor with each inhalation and release and relax the pelvic floor with exhalation.

Dr. Judy's TantrAdvice

Visualization using pure light, described here to identify with qualities of a deity, has also proven effective in other situations. For example, some cancer patients who have been taught to imagine healing light through their bodies have been shown to produce fewer cancer cells.

In a Vajrayogini practice CD designed to help women who have experienced the practice at least once incorporate it into their lives, Lexi leads listeners through each of the movements with the music of Sharon Stevens's crystal and Tibetan bowls, wind chimes, rain stick, and other wonderful sounds. Says Lexi, "These practices are an elegant way for women to reconnect to their juicy, sensual creativity."

Festivals and Other God/Goddess Gatherings

All kinds of celebrations honoring deities have existed in every age. The following are some that relate to tantric principles.

Fertility Festivals in Japan

Each spring hundreds of worshippers parade through the streets of small towns, carrying effigies of the phallus and chanting testimonies to its power and potency. Legend has it that every time a princess lay down with a mate, he woke up the next morning with his penis bitten off. A suitor who was a smithy proved his worth and finally cured the princess by forging a steel phallus that was inserted into her vagina, whereupon the steel teeth lodged inside her vagina gripped the rod and were extracted. His prize was her hand in marriage. Local worshippers and hundreds of tourist onlookers (like myself!) attend the charming circuslike parade that has more recently been turned into a street fair (selling phallus-shaped candy) and distributing educational materials about AIDS prevention.

At the annual fertility festival in Kawasaki, Japan, worshippers carry effigies of the phallus through the streets.

Clean Monday in Greece

Every year on the first day of Lent, people in a town in central Greece host a no-holds-barred celebration of the phallus. Similar to the fertility festival in Japan, paraders follow floats featuring the male reproductive organ, vendors sell phallic-shaped Popsicles, men sport ceramic penises on their head, women dance clasping clay phallus replicas, children drink from penis-shaped straws, and lines form to take pictures with the towering phallic-shaped monolith. The carnival, complete with raunchy songfest, is a remnant from ancient rituals of phallus worship during Dionysian festivals, practiced in the mythological home of Greeks' ancient gods, but also in ancient Rome, Egypt, India, and, of course, Japan. After the first day of Lent, all returns to normal, as if the carousing never existed.

Burning Man Festival in Nevada

Although it's dusty and 107 degrees, thousands of free spirits journey to the annual Burning Man festival at the end of summer for the weeklong experiment in temporary community dedicated to radical self-expression. Participants set up villages and theme camps (such as Fertility, Outer Space, and The Seven Ages) in a psychedelic maze of art installations (such as the "Boom Boom Womb" or "Impotence Compensation Project") and rest stops. The scene is unique, and some participants recall their days at Woodstock, sharing food, art, music, and love.

Many tantric devotees come to Burning Man each year because of its kindred spirit to tantric energy, creativity, lovingness, and sense of community. A favorite attraction in past years had been the Temple of Ishtar (www.ishtartemple.org), a magical community dedicated to raising awareness; educating; and expanding and healing sacred sexuality, sensuality, and relationships.

Goddess Gatherings

During the women's movement of the 1970s, women formed "consciousness-raising groups," meeting in homes and talking about men, sex, and how to have orgasms. Similar gatherings today often are called goddess groups, in which women come together to share their stories, support each other in careers or relationships, and connect with their priestess energies. Often they perform ritualistic ceremonies, lighting candles, invoking feminine spirits, forming drum circles, declaring intentions, and celebrating femininity.

These can be held on a private, small scale with selected invited friends, or they can be large gatherings, workshops, or retreats for women to connect with their feminine spirit.

Temples

A tantric temple is a place where tantric rituals take place. There are several varieties of such temples. In ancient cultures, women were considered priestesses and goddesses because they were the holy creators of life, thought to be sent to earth from heaven with secret powers as healers. Girls were brought to buildings, called temples, before puberty and taught all the secrets of using sexual energy to heal by older women; they learned the sacred arts of sex, including love, lust, rituals, magic, and spiritual practice. These temple goddesses also taught younger men how to reach realms of bliss through the pleasures of the female body, rejuvenated older men by practicing their skills of lovemaking with them, and healed warriors with sacred waters. Some tantrikas today form collectives for similar purposes.

The town of Khajuraho, south of New Delhi in India, was the heart of medieval tantrism. The ancient temples here are renowned for their erotic sculptures. Figures in a seemingly infinite variety of combinations and positions adorn the edifices from the base to the top. The relief sculptures at ascending levels become more refined, as a symbol of the ascension to higher states of consciousness. Many were destroyed in wars, but a large number remain. I can assure you—because I've done it—that visiting them is an awesome and educational experience.

An erotic scene from a temple at Khajuraho.

Museums

Many museums of sex exist around the world, such as in Prague and Barcelona. I have visited many of these, and some have tantric treasures in their collections.

The Shanghai Sex Museum in China has innumerable items from the tantric tradition, including phallic statues and Shiva and Shakti figures. They are worth a visit!

The Least You Need to Know

- Every man and woman is a god or goddess. Consider yourself as having the qualities of divine beings, to embrace the highest level of self-esteem and to confront powerful characteristics you consider positive or negative.

- Gods and goddesses whom you might relate to come from every era and culture.

- Think of lovemaking as a divine act that expresses the sacred union of you and your partner as enlightened beings (god and goddess).

- Visiting sacred temples and festivals can inspire you to embrace the divinity within you.

Part 2

Getting Started in Sacred Sex

Now that you're breathing right, communicating in an honoring way, and sending powerful surges of sexual energy through your body and out to your partner, you're ready to start using that energy. When you can turn up the heat or calm it down at will, you're more in control and therefore more ready to lose control—into bliss.

In this part, you'll learn specific practices to amp up your sexual energy—or to bring it down a few notches—at will to prepare you for long-lasting lovemaking. You'll discover how to look at love through totally new eyes and learn techniques that will take you further into sensuality than you ever thought possible. Discover the secrets of the sacrum tap, Shakti shake, eye lock, heart hold, and muscle locks that unlock your door to sexual pleasure. You'll learn how to break through any blocks you have to embracing bliss, opening the door to a whole new world by setting your stage for love—preparing your room, your mind, and your body as a temple of love.

Chapter 6

Preparing Your Body Temple for Bliss

In This Chapter

◆ Getting to know and learning to love your body

◆ Simple movements that boost your tantric sex life

◆ Inner muscle holds for better control in sex

◆ How to keep your spine healthy and straight

◆ Eating right the tantric way

Tantric practice asserts that your body is your temple. You must keep it healthy and fit for your journey to bliss. In this chapter, I introduce you to some principles and routines that help you honor this temple. I'll also share with you some ways to tone your body to facilitate the important practices that you are undertaking to heighten, channel, and control your sexual energy to reach a higher consciousness.

Your Body as the Bridge to Bliss

When studying tantra, be prepared to experience a thrilling ride: energy soaring up and down your spine, electrifying every cell in your body from your toes to the top of your head. Your entire body becomes the bridge between the earthly and the spiritual on your road to bliss.

All too often we are not even aware of the body temple we live in. We take it for granted—usually until we have some breakdown (pain), or look in the mirror and get distressed about what we see. Worse, we abuse our body temple with toxic food, lack of sleep (I'm guilty of this one!), overeating, drugs, alcohol, and even sex that we've regretted afterward. Another abuse is self-criticism—but to be ready for tantric love you must turn body hate into body love.

Building Body Love: Through the Looking Glass

A fundamental part of every sex therapy seminar or workshop (I have taught a vast variety of them over the years!) involves looking at your body and changing any negative attitudes. Often called "homework," I prefer to refer to such exercises as "homeplay," because everything you do to increase pleasure should be play and fun, rather than work. Do this exercise for your whole body and private parts:

1. Stand naked in front of a full-length mirror (a good time to do this is after a bath). Look at every part of you, starting from your feet and moving slowly up to the top of your head (as in Chapter 2, when you moved your energy through the energy centers). If you catch yourself criticizing, stop and say something kind instead; for example, "My breasts are too small" becomes "My breasts are nice and firm"; "My thighs are too bulky" becomes "My legs are so strong." Don't obsess that you are not telling the truth; you are simply shifting your focus and being gentler with yourself.

2. Examine your genitals. Women can sit on the bed and use a hand mirror (and flashlight) because the female genitals are less obvious than men's. Open the lips and notice colors, moistness, and shapes.

3. Examine your first chakra (your base center located around your anal area, the symbol of security). An easier position to do this for both is to squat. As in the genital exam for women, men can use a mirror and flashlight to see more clearly. Notice colors and skin texture.

Dr. Judy's TantrAdvice

Women have rarely seen inside their vagina at the view their gynecologist sees. You can get a plastic speculum (the instrument the doctor uses for your examination) from a reputable outlet such as Eve's Garden (see Appendix C). Carefully insert it inside your vagina, creating an opening. Position a mirror and flashlight so you can see.

Examining, and loving, your body temple.

Describe Your Sexual Parts Inside and Out

Most men have looked at their genitals, because they're so accessible every time they go to the bathroom. In contrast, women have been taught not to look—and even today most females are shy or unsure of what's "down there."

I am always surprised at how little even sophisticated men and women know about their sexual parts. I remember not knowing much when I was young—my mother just gave me books to read, and my confusion lasted until I was well into my 20s. Compare your descriptions of your body to the following figures, which show the major parts of the male and female genitalia.

Both men and women should note the following:

♦ There are actually sets of muscles in the pelvic area—including those around the genitals anal openings—that play an important role in sexual toning and excitement. These are affectionately called the "love muscles"; I'll tell you more about them a little later in this chapter.

♦ The sacrum is a triangular area above the tailbone which, when tapped, awakens energy, as I'll describe in Chapter 9.

♦ The kundalini gland is the seat of blissful energy that lies dormant within the spine until activated by tantric practices. It is often depicted artistically like a coiled serpent.

A closer look at the female anatomy shows …

◆ The clitoris is more than the bump, knob, or tip that you can feel. It actually has a shaft that extends into the body, which is also pleasurable to stimulate.

◆ The urethral opening is in front of, and separate from, the vaginal opening.

◆ There is a spongelike tissue surrounding the urethra (called the "urethral sponge," consisting of glands, ducts, and blood vessels) that produces fluids emitted through the urethra during high states of arousal. These "love juices," also called female ejaculate, can be triggered from stimulation inside the vagina in the goddess space (commonly called the G spot). This process will be described in Chapters 11 and 18.

A closer look at the male anatomy shows that you can reach (and stimulate) the prostate gland from the outside along the perineum and from the inside through the anal opening, as will be described in Chapter 18.

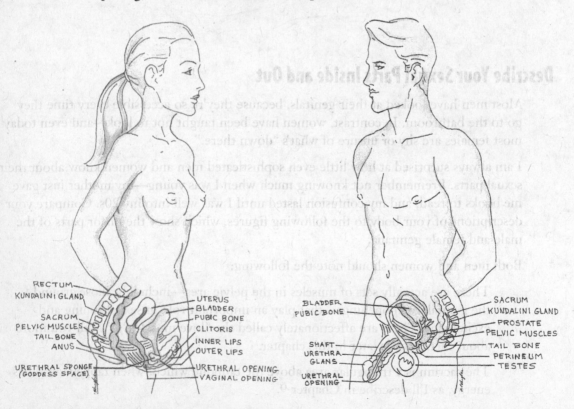

RECTUM
KUNDALINI GLAND
SACRUM
PELVIC MUSCLES
TAIL BONE
ANUS
URETHRAL SPONGE
(GODDESS SPACE)

UTERUS
BLADDER
PUBIC BONE
CLITORIS
INNER LIPS
OUTER LIPS
URETHRAL OPENING
VAGINAL OPENING

BLADDER
PUBIC BONE

SHAFT
URETHRA
GLANS
URETHRAL
OPENING

SACRUM
KUNDALINI GLAND
PROSTATE
PELVIC MUSCLES
TAIL BONE
PERINEUM
TESTES

A closer look at the female and male internal sexual area.

If Your Penis or Yoni Could Talk

Fans who listen to me on the radio tease about hearing me ask callers, "If your penis could talk, what would it say?" The truth is, our bodies do talk to us—and we talk back. Try this exercise, and say aloud what your genitals might say to you (such as "Why do you criticize my size?" or "Can't I have a rest?" or "I'd like to be adored").

Go On a Genital Exploration

Take some deep breaths. Center yourself. Now that you've looked at your genitals, touch them with the primary intention to explore. Notice the colors, shapes, and textures. After your exploration with a more objective view, get emotionally involved. Allow yourself to touch your genitals with pleasure in mind. Watch what happens in the mirror, or just lie back and enjoy the sensations. Focus on the smallest sensations, without any expectations.

> **Blocks to Bliss**
>
> Tantric homeplay often includes a genital display for your partner, where the partners "play doctor" for each other, showing each other what they have learned about their bodies. This is not only educational, it also helps overcome embarrassment and increases intimacy.

> **Dr. Judy's TantrAdvice**
>
> Touching yourself to turn yourself on (masturbation) might bring up old feelings, particularly from early childhood when you might have learned it is "wrong" or "bad." Tell yourself the opposite: self-pleasuring is healthy and will benefit your sex life.

The Yoga Connection

Yoga is an integral part of the tantra path. Many tantric masters are also yoga masters who have studied and practiced poses for many years. Yoga helps you focus on your body, still your mind, strengthen and stretch your body, and control your movements. All that can help you achieve ejaculatory control and multiple orgasms and also benefit your overall health as well as the physical experience of the transcendent energy you share with your beloved.

Take a course at a local yoga center or contact resources listed in Appendix B about whether they offer yoga classes. Most tantra workshops include simple yoga routines in their teachings.

Some Simple Yoga Movements

Here are some simple yoga movements in many individual routines. See Chapter 15 for interesting yoga poses you can do with your beloved as part of tantric practice.

- **The head lift.** Stand up as straight as possible. Reach your head up to the sky as if a string were pulling it upward from the middle of your crown. Inhale through your nose, pulling your shoulder blades back toward each other. Exhale and press your feet solidly into the ground, as if rooting yourself like a tree. Relax and repeat.

- **The cobra pose.** Lie fully extended on the floor on your stomach. Place your hands under your shoulders, arms close to your body with elbows back, and slowly lift your upper body and head in a curve, looking upward.

- **The cat pose.** From cobra pose, bring your head down slowly and rise up on your knees, rounding your back to stretch your spine in the opposite direction from cobra pose.

- **The resting pose.** From cat pose, lower your chest to your knees and your forehead to the ground, keeping your arms outstretched. Breathe naturally.

> **Blocks to Bliss**
>
> Always move slowly, and always have a teacher instruct you on proper breathing, form, and progression of yoga poses for maximum benefits and to protect your spine.

Hold It: These Are Called Bandhas

In certain yoga poses or breathing practices in tantra, you hold a body part a certain way or create muscular contractions to control your energy; these are called *bandhas*. They act like waterway locks in that energy is pooled in a certain area by tightening muscles there, then the energy is released in a stronger force and sent wherever you want it (up or down the spine, or up to the sky).

The three most common holds are …

- **Throat hold.** To do this, inhale and turn your chin down toward your throat, drawing the back of your neck straight; then lift your chin and exhale slowly.

- **Belly hold.** Exhale, suck your navel back toward your spine, and pull your belly up toward your throat.

- **Pelvis hold.** Tighten your PC (pubococcygeal) and anal sphincter muscles. (I'll discuss more about how to exercise those PC muscles in the next section.)

The bandhas greatly benefit your sex life. Here's how:

♦ The three-step lock, as I call it, incorporates the three most common holds and helps men control their ejaculation without losing their erection. Inhale and do the throat hold. Exhale and do the belly hold. Squeeze the PC (or "love") muscles for the pelvis hold. Repeat.

♦ Pelvis holds help both women and men to strengthen their pelvic muscles, which results in more powerful orgasms.

♦ Muscle holds help men and women condition the entire body, strengthen lower back muscles, and intensify the effects of love muscle exercises to create more intense sensations in self-pleasuring or intercourse.

Tantra Tutorial _____

Bandhas increase the energy you can cycle within your own body or out to your partner. As you breathe in, do the pelvis hold and imagine drawing energy up from the earth, through your body, out to your partner, and cycle it back again.

You can do these holds any time—while you're waiting in a movie line or stuck in traffic—for an energy rush. (Once while teaching a class I was saying that no one would notice, but when demonstrating how you can practice in secret, the students laughed at how my skirt was lifting!)

When doing yoga, keep the following important tips in mind:

♦ Always check with a doctor before starting a yoga program or any physical routine.

♦ Warm up before each routine.

♦ Never force your body beyond its limits.

♦ Rest when you feel tired.

♦ Always balance movements; for example, bend forward after you bend backward.

Love Muscle Exercises for Men and Women

There are sets of muscles all along the pelvic floor in both men and women. Exercising, or "pumping" them (also referred to as "deer exercises") have many benefits besides sexual toning, readiness, and stimulation: stimulating the nervous system, invigorating the endocrine system, tightening sagging skin, flushing out toxins, and releasing tension.

Women's pubococcygeal (PC) muscles run along the sides of the entrance to the vagina. Strengthening and toning them creates more pleasure during sex for the woman and her partner (and tightens the muscles, especially after childbirth). Locate them by squeezing, as if to hold back urine, and then release as if forcing the urine out. Now purposefully contract them in faster and faster progression for about 30 seconds. Do this several times a day. You can even insert a finger to help you better focus on gripping with these muscles.

Ecstasy Essentials

The secret to using the PC muscles to send powerful energy through the body and brain is to coordinate your breath. Inhale through your nose as you pull up your muscles, hold your breath as you contract as many times as you can, and then exhale through your nose.

Men's PC muscles run through the perineum and connect to both the anus and the scrotum. Locate them by squeezing as if holding back the flow of urine, then release as if forcing the urine out. Contract and release 10 times, at an increasingly faster pace, several times a day. This also provides powerful training for men to control the timing of their ejaculation.

Contracting and releasing the anal sphincter muscles for the man and woman also increases sexual pleasure. Locate these muscles by squeezing as if to prevent defecating, then bearing down as if forcing yourself to eliminate.

Follow a Conscious Workout

There are many workouts that will tone your body and build your strength. These can complement your tantric sex practices as long as you stay aware while you do them, which means focusing on how the particular exercise is moving your energy and how you are moving your breath. These workouts can include …

- Western-style workouts such as weight lifting, aerobics, or specialized routines from your own gym or trainer.

- Eastern-style practices such as T'ai Chi or the increasingly popular QiGong (pronounced *chee-gong*) are systems of Chinese yoga movements that open the body to allow the flow of life-force energy. Some exotic-sounding movements include T'ai Chi Bo Balancing to build a strong and supple back and Bagua Xun Dao Gong, which stretches and strengthens the legs.

The Spinal Tap

Having a healthy spine is crucial to the practices of tantric sexuality. The spine is the pathway of the breath through the body, from the base (first) chakra through the inner flute to the top of the head (the crown chakra). It brings the sexual energy from the genitals through the body and into the head for transformation and awakening.

Pay attention to your spine! At this very moment, how is it positioned? How is it when you walk, sit, or stand? Your spine is, of course, directly related to your posture. Take the following quiz to see what kind of shape your spine is in.

Your Spinal Condition

Check *Yes* or *No* to each of the following questions:

1. Are you slumped over when you stand? ❑ Yes ❑ No

2. Do you slump over when you sit? ❑ Yes ❑ No

3. Do you stand in a crooked position (leaning to one side)? ❑ Yes ❑ No

4. Is your neck protruding forward (instead of sitting on top of your spine)? ❑ Yes ❑ No

5. Are your hips thrust decidedly forward when you walk? ❑ Yes ❑ No

6. Do your feet turn inward or outward when you walk? ❑ Yes ❑ No

If you answered *Yes* to any of these questions, you need to pay more attention to your precious spine and your posture.

Everyone worries about getting that slumped-over look as they age. Not only is this unpleasant aesthetically, it's also not good for your breathing, which is necessary to send that crucial breath carrying life energy (called prana) through your body. Pay attention to keeping your spine as clear a channel as possible. For help getting your spine in correct alignment, see a doctor or a chiropractor.

Many variations of chiropractic practices help realign the spine for more freely flowing energy; one new trend is called *network spinal analysis* (*NSA*). California NSA practitioner Lexi Fisher explains that this gentle form of chiropractic adjustments (developed in 1979 by Dr. Donald

> **Tantra Tutorial**
>
> Life experiences or traumas (physical, emotional, or biochemical) that are left incomplete get stuck and stored up in the spine just as they do in your unconscious, preventing the body from healing or responding freely.

Epstein) consists of a series of very light contacts (pressure similar to that you might place on closed eyelids) to areas of the spine along the vertebral column. These contacts re-awaken the body to unresolved experiences and traumatic tension patterns to release them and free up the channel for more energy.

Fisher explains how it works: "Gentle rocking of the vertebrae frees what was stuck there, allowing it to be integrated back into us. As the nervous system becomes more flexible, chronic holding patterns let go as a wave of muscular contractions and pulsation moves through, discharging tension stored there and reorganizing the nervous system. Once the spinal cord becomes more flexible we experience increased ease and more energy flow through the body, as we give up old ways of resisting life."

Food for Thought: You Are What You Eat

Just as important as how you move your body to achieve total good health crucial for tantric practice is what you put into it. That means, pay attention to nutrition. Food is the body's fuel, so it is crucial to pay attention to what you eat. Of course, you know that fatty foods are bad for your health, and that eating heavy meals is not conducive to good sex. However, healthy eating practices go beyond this; they must be part of your entire tantric life routine.

Blocks to Bliss

Never go on a fast or other radical dietary routine without proper consultation and supervision about what's right for you.

A clogged or unclean digestive tract can seriously interrupt the flow of energy. Some tantric devotees do an occasional "cleanse" to purify their body of toxins. Cleanses range from eating raw foods to juice fasts. Not all approaches are right for everyone. To find the right one for you, get a medical evaluation, consult a nutrition expert, read books on nutrition, and ask friends and tantric teachers for recommendations.

The Least You Need to Know

- ◆ Your body is a temple of love; pay attention to how you treat it as a sign of how you treat yourself.

- ◆ Exercise routines such as yoga draw your attention to your body, promote health, increase your sexual energy, and prepare you for tantric sex.

- ◆ Pay particular attention to the position of your spine, because it is the channel of life energy through your body.

- ◆ A healthy eating plan contributes to your general health, which in turn contributes to a healthier relationship.

Chapter 7

Amping Up or Damping Down Your Sexual Energy

In This Chapter

- ◆ You are in control of your energy
- ◆ Exercises to calm down your energy
- ◆ Reducing stress with air yoga
- ◆ Exercises to amp up your energy
- ◆ The sacrum tap, chakra thump, and pelvic thrusts to shake up your Shakti energy
- ◆ How a partner can help

Now that your body is in good shape, you can progress to the next step: controlling your energy by relaxing or intensifying it as part of your tantric practice. It's important that I discuss these two states together because they are consistent with the tantric principles of opposites. That is, energy can be still or active, dynamic or in motion. You need to know how to move your energy in both of these directions.

In this chapter, you'll learn some exercises to put you in a mellow mood, with your sex energy at a calm, flowing pace, or to amp you up so you're fully energized and hot to trot. Remember that you are in control of your body temple; as long as you have been properly prepared, it will respond to what you ask it to do.

Ways to Calm Down

Life is stressful, so it's understandable that it might be difficult to do some of your tantric practices if you aren't in the right frame of mind. Worrying about work, a health problem, or a relationship can prevent you from directing your energy as you would like.

Here are some ways to calm down and relax your energy:

♦ Control your breath. Take a deep breath in to the count of seven and exhale to a longer count (see how high you can go). Exhaling longer than you inhale relaxes you and decreases your heart rate. Refer to Chapter 2 for more details about using your breath to direct your energy.

♦ Sit still and empty your mind. Let thoughts come and go without focusing on them. Or try meditating on a single word, such as "om," to calm your mind.

♦ Adjust your environment to eliminate distractions such as ringing phones, irritating street noise, or glaring bright lights.

♦ Light candles and soak in a warm bubble bath.

Dr. Judy's TantrAdvice

Notice the level of your energy at any particular time by rating it on a scale from 0 to 10, with 0 being the least energetic and 10 being the most. Watch how the rating changes by activities you purposefully do to raise or lower your energy.

♦ Take a long walk, play with the dog, or toss a ball around with your kids. Just about any physical activity reduces stress.

♦ Close your eyes and picture a soothing scene, such as the ocean. Imagine the smell of the salt air and the feel of the sand between your toes.

♦ Soothe yourself with massage. Use long, smooth strokes to calm you while you breathe slowly and deeply. Use cream to glide your hands over your skin.

Air Yoga as a Stress Reducer

You likely have a basic idea about yoga, even if you don't already practice it—but *air yoga?* What's that? It's a variation on more traditional yoga that incorporates tantric principles. Developed by London-based tantric teacher Joshua Smith, it involves moving your body into traditional yoga poses, then letting your body settle comfortably into positions it feels it wants to move into.

Start by assuming a simple yoga pose. Stand with your feet shoulder-width apart, knees slightly bent, looking down. Exhale fully through your mouth, focusing on a spot on the ground, falling deeper and deeper into your body with each exhale. Close your eyes, inhale through your nose, raise your head, and allow your hands to drift upward as if holding a balloon in each hand (until they are level with your head). As you exhale through your mouth, allow your arms to arch forward, letting your head and body be guided gently toward the ground. Relax your head, arms, jaw, and shoulders, feeling like a rag doll.

Now move in whatever way your spine and body want to move. This is different from other yoga, Smith explains, because you are not following poses that are defined in a book or established practice, but moving completely in the unknown. "With each exhale," Smith instructs, "allow your body to move in a different way. Stay tantrically aware of your breath and you will be carried into a state of transcendent stillness."

Amping Up for Good Loving

Sometimes you really feel too tired for sex or not interested enough, even if part of you really want to make love or satisfy your partner's desire. The good news is there are many ways tantric sex practices can help you energize your body for lovemaking.

Control Your Breathing

Take a deep breath in to the count of seven and exhale to a shorter count. Inhaling longer than you exhale increases your heart rate. (This is the opposite of the technique that I described earlier to calm down your energy.)

Another breathing technique that can recharge you is the fire breath, described in Chapter 2. Inhale and exhale rapidly through your nose. Let your belly fill up and then deflate with the air.

Practice the Sacrum Tap

Tap on your sacral area (the triangle above the end of your tailbone and below your waist).

Blocks to Bliss

Consider your physical condition in any activity that alters your energy, especially because accelerated breathing can make you lightheaded or dizzy. For example, people with heart conditions should be especially careful; consult your doctor.

This is the home of powerful energy (called "kundalini" energy because it is released from the kunda gland located at the base of the spine). Tantra workshops, such as those taught by a highly respected organization called Tantrika International (see Appendix B), often include more elaborate variations of this practice. For example, one partner lies down and the other adds motions (running thumbs up the spine, breathing warm air up the spine) to move the energy up the spine after tapping the sacrum.

Taps to awaken energy.

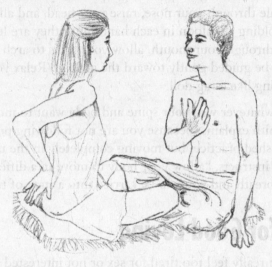

Do the Chakra Thump

Tap on any of your chakras to awaken the energy there. This doesn't mean tap dancing with your feet! Rather, it means making rapid, repetitive, up-and-down tapping motions on the body with the pads of your fingers. You can also make a fist and use the softer edges of your hands. Review the locations of the chakras in Chapter 2.

Practice Streaming

Streaming is a variation of the previous exercises. The giver taps forcefully on either side of the receiver's spine with the fingertips, starting from the sacrum and progressing up to the neck. As a nice addition, when you get to the shoulders, give the receiver a massage!

Dance Up an Energy Storm

The benefits of dance as movement, body conditioning, and just having fun are endless! I'll discuss this more in Chapter 16, when I share some playful things to do with your partner. Put on some music at home and let yourself sway, bob, shimmy, and shake. Improvise. When I do this, I go from imagining being a ballet dancer to thinking of myself as a Chinese god wielding a sword. Don't worry if you don't have a partner to dance with. Consider taking a dance class, whether modern, jazz, ballroom, swing, or tango (which is quite popular now).

Get That Pelvis Moving!

Pelvic thrusts are essential to generating sexual energy and pleasure in sex. Doing them is like downing a power bar for your sexual energy. This is the movement men naturally make when they have sex—but usually don't prolong long enough to get the true benefits.

Pelvic thrusts are one of the favored and fun exercises in tantra workshops. It's quite a sight to see a room full of men and women standing or lying on the floor, each arching their back and thrusting their pelvis forward. When everyone adds sound to the movement, the energy in the room is nearly enough to lift off!

Pelvic thrusts can be done from a standing position, progressing to the floor through various levels of squatting; or in the opposite direction (starting from a lying down position and getting up). Doing them basically involves thrusting the pelvis forward and backward. It's important to coordinate your breath (exhale through the mouth as you thrust forward and inhale through the nose as you arch backward). After you get the hang of it, you can move your arms to help move your energy. When you do these exercises alone, you can picture yourself thrusting against a partner, having intercourse to help allow yourself to get really sexy and seductive. Or you can do these exercises facing a partner—and feel as if you are already in the sex act!

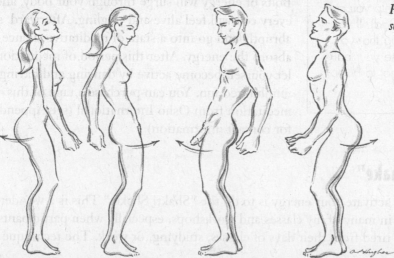

Pelvic thrusts to build sexual energy.

Fantasize

It's normal and even healthy to have sexual fantasies—fleeting thoughts or extended stories in your mind about past experiences or imagined situations that are arousing. Give yourself permission to have these thoughts without worrying about whether they are bad or wrong. However, keep in mind that tantric practice requires that you always bring your attention back into your body sensations and the present so you fully appreciate your real experience, your partner, and what is going on in the moment.

Let Yourself Go!

An important principle in building sexual energy is to free your thoughts and movements from inhibitions. One technique to do this is called "the dynamic meditation." This is a technique developed by the Indian mystic Osho, who originated many tantric practices to bring about enlightenment. The first time I did this practice, at the Osho retreat center in Pune, India, I was impressed with how brilliantly and artfully it can help move energy.

Tantra Tutorial

Spinning—twirling around in a joyful dance movement—is part of energizing ceremonies in Sufism, an Islamic mystical movement that some Westerners follow. Spinning is intended help you connect with the divine (God). If you try it, don't spin so long that you become dizzy and lose your balance, and take care not to bump into anything.

The dynamic meditation is done in several parts. In the first part, shake your body for up to 15 minutes while breathing in and out forcefully and quickly. Flap your arms (you'll look humorously like a chicken!) to get more energy flowing. Let your voice go and say gibberish. Free your mind and loosen your jaw, and let your limbs fly where they may. Bolts of energy will surge through your body, and every cell will feel alive and tingling. Afterward, stop abruptly and go into a state of meditative silence to absorb the energy. After this period of meditation, let yourself become active by dancing and having uninhibited fun. You can purchase a tape of this meditation from Osho International (see Appendix B for contact information).

Do the "Shakti Shake"

Another way to activate your energy is to do the "Shakti Shake." This is a wonderful technique I use in many of my classes and workshops, especially when participants come in feeling tired from their days of classes, studying, or work. The technique is very simple. Put on some music that you can't resist moving to. Start by shaking just your right leg, then your left leg. Keep up with the beat of the music. Get your hips, arms, and hands moving. Rock your shoulders. Let your head go (careful with your neck!). Get your whole body into the action. Notice how alive you feel.

Take Lama Breaths

Lama breathing is one of my favorite ways to amp up. When I give lectures I have the attendees do it to refresh themselves, sometimes even in the middle of my speech! It's quite an exhilarating experience—and quite a sight! The monks in Tibet use these movements and find them so effective in warming the body that they can go up in the mountains naked and stay warm. The movement consists of an extended series of moves in sequences. Here are two simple techniques that I have adapted for use in my groups with great effectiveness:

- Stand straight with your knees slightly bent and shoulder-width apart. Inhale and raise your arms straight out to your sides. Exhale, dropping your arms to your sides, blowing the air out and making a bellowslike sound until your arms come to rest at your sides. Notice how you feel. Repeat this three times.

- Stand firmly rooted to the ground, legs shoulder-width apart. Inhale and raise one arm, making a fist up above your head, and drop it while exhaling, blowing out the air forcefully and letting a sound come out. Alternate arms. (Twice might be enough to jazz you up.)

Lama breaths.

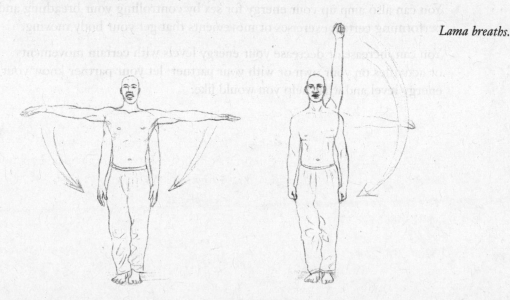

Ask Your Partner for Help

All the techniques in this chapter can be done alone or with a partner. Letting your partner know the level of your sexual energy and your willingness to adjust, or to match his or her interest, increases trust and intimacy between you.

For example, Andy knew that his partner Ali had planned a special evening for their anniversary and would want to be especially close and to make love. But he had had an unusually bad day at the office; an important deal fell through, leaving him feeling fatigued and discouraged. Not wanting to disappoint her, he explained the dilemma. She happily allowed him time alone to calm down by breathing, meditating, and taking a shower, and then helped him shift his mood by giving him a long, relaxing massage.

Moving your energy alone or with a partner prepares you for sharing nights of pleasure, as described in the following chapters.

The Least You Need to Know

- ♦ You control your energy and decide whether you want to be sexual; don't give up, feeling that you're just too tired and can't do anything about it.

- ♦ It is possible to calm your energy for tantric sex by controlling your breath, thoughts, and movements.

- ♦ You can also amp up your energy for sex by controlling your breathing and performing certain exercises or movements that get your body moving.

- ♦ You can increase or decrease your energy levels with certain movements or activities on your own or with your partner; let your partner know your energy level and what help you would like.

Setting the Stage for Your Tantric Pleasure Date

In This Chapter

- ◆ Making time for lovemaking
- ◆ Preparing for your tantric pleasure date
- ◆ Bathing rituals to boost bliss
- ◆ God and goddess attire to spark your desire
- ◆ Arranging your temple of love and your love altar
- ◆ What to do and where to go on your tantra date

Consider lovemaking as your "tantric date," a special get-together in two steps: planning and preparing for your night of pleasure, and spending the actual time together. Having sex is not just an act; it is a ritual experience that requires thought and deliberate actions as part of the seduction.

Every action serves a multiple purpose: to quiet your mind, put you in the mood, build anticipation, and honor yourself and your partner. Dress up yourself and decorate the space where you will make love, paying attention to the smallest details. Attention to detail is a sign of honoring each other and your time together; it shows the value you place on each other, your relationship, and your environment. Your tantric night of pleasure starts with setting aside time to be together—something many couples neglect.

Making Time Enough for Love

We never have enough time for sex. This is one of the most common complaints I've heard from couples over the years! Of course you're busy with work, family, friends, and a full calendar, but what could be more important than making time for this special kind of loving?

Set aside time to do these practices. Start with an hour on two different occasions during the week. Agree on the specific time, and write it in your calendar. This will affirm that your relationship is of primary importance from which other aspects also flow, including your job, family relationships, hobbies, and life in general.

Ecstasy Essentials

Falling into a passionate embrace—spontaneously, anytime, anyplace—is exciting and certainly adds quick fire to a relationship, but preparing for that special encounter can build a steady burn. Putting time, energy, and care into preparing for your time together makes you both feel special!

"But where's the spontaneity?" complained Donald when I told him to set up such a tantric sex schedule. "Who wants sex to be so organized? That sounds like no fun." Donald's objections are common, especially for men. However, every new exercise or self-improvement effort requires allotting time and expending effort, whether it's yoga, weight lifting, or a weekend workshop. To keep your priorities in order in our busy world, you have to insist on scheduling, at least at first; later you can be more spontaneous. Use a calendar to check off when you will be together for your tantric sex practices. Start with one hour twice a week, and add more time as you advance in your practices.

Ensuring Privacy

Of course there are always distractions! Be sure you have private, uninterrupted time. That means turn off cell phones, beepers, computers, telephones, and anything else that will take away your attention from each other. This is particularly important for parents. Brainstorm how to occupy the kids, whatever age. Pack them off to some activity or someone else's care. Or put a sign on your door, or have a clock that shows when you will be available. Get them used to your taking private time.

The Conscious Cleanup

Surely you know the experience of dressing your best for a special date, or a quick cleanup if you anticipate taking your date back to your place (tossing newspapers in the garbage, hiding piles of magazines, throwing clothes in the closet). If you've been together a long time and take each other for granted, it's time to go back to those days of dating when you were making an effort to impress. Consider the following 10 tips for conscious cleanups, both alone and with your partner:

1. Always keep your fingernails clean and neatly clipped. Neatly trimmed, clean nails are not only attractive (dirty nails are mentioned as turnoffs by both men and women), they are important for hygiene, because you'll use your fingers to stimulate your partner's skin and pleasure his or her internal organs.

2. Brush your teeth regularly, especially before a romantic interlude with your partner. Like nails, unbrushed teeth are high on the list of turnoffs mentioned by both men and women. Use toothpaste with baking soda for a good cleansing, and swish with mouthwash for an extra feeling of freshness.

3. Wash each other's hair. This is particularly good for the man to do for the woman, as it is often the first time he has done such an act for her.

4. Shave each other (do his beard or her legs), paying careful attention to tender areas on the skin. Trusting your partner to do this will make him or her feel proud and pleased.

 Tantra Tutorial _____

In the Arm and Hammer First Impression Study of more than a thousand men and women, top turnoffs included body odor (89 percent), unpleasant personality (86 percent), bad breath (84 percent), discolored or yellow teeth (70 percent), too much perfume (62 percent), and dirty fingernails (60 percent). More than half of those surveyed said fresh breath becomes more important the longer they are in a romantic relationship. People with bad breath were described as unclean, unhealthy, lazy, unattractive, and unsuccessful.

5. Paint her toenails. Do his nails, too, for something new, as more men are letting themselves enjoy this primping without thinking that it is unmanly.

6. Adjust the lighting in the bathroom. Most bathrooms have harsh lighting, especially over the sink. Replace the bulbs with rosy colored ones for a special evening, or bring in a special lamp. Place candles on sink counters, bathtub ledges, and the floor to create a sensuous atmosphere.

7. Take turns preparing a bath for each other, or share a romantic bath together (more on that in the next section). Check the water temperature. Although a cool bath is stimulating, warm water usually is best for relaxation and to generate feelings of warmth.

8. Play music during your bath. One couple I know mounted stereo speakers in their bathroom! A simpler idea is to bring in a CD player or radio (be careful, of course, that electrical appliances don't fall in the water!).

9. Buy special scented soaps, bath oils, soft brushes, and even bath mitts. Most department stores have large sections for bath items, and stores such as Bed, Bath and Beyond and The Body Shop specialize in all kinds of accoutrements for the bath.

10. Prepare your exit with a mat (to avoid stepping on a cold floor), cozy bathrobe, and large, plush towels. Keep the latter two items separate from what you use every day, to make the experience special.

The Tantric Bathing Ritual

I'm sure you're familiar with taking a quick shower or dunk in a tub after a stressful day to get ready for sex. But when's the last time you languished in the bath with your lover? Languorous, deliberate showering and washing together is an essential part of tantric sex. Time in the tub is for far more than getting clean; it also is to …

◆ Enjoy the experience of being together in the water.

◆ Get in touch with your bodies.

◆ Arouse your sensations.

◆ Build your awareness of each other.

Tantra Tutorial

Bathing is an ancient tradition as a prelude to lovemaking. Ancient Roman and Greek lovers stepped down into large, open baths, and in Japanese tradition, lovers went from an extremely hot tub to an extremely cold tub to stimulate circulation, a practice continued at Oriental spas.

The most important aspect of tantric bathing is to make washing each other a ritualistic act, done with deliberate attention. Instead of swishing soap quickly over body parts, linger on certain spots. Be creative, as you would during a massage. Soapy hands offer a wonderful opportunity to slide over your partner's skin. Use different touches to delight the skin; from long, smooth strokes to circular tracings around areas such as the back and buttocks. Alternate your touch, using the soapy palms of your hand on especially sensitive places and light fingernail scratches on places such as arms and legs.

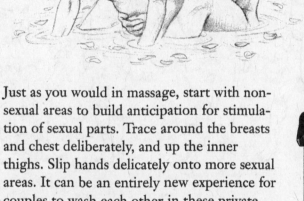

The beloveds' bathing ritual.

Just as you would in massage, start with non-sexual areas to build anticipation for stimulation of sexual parts. Trace around the breasts and chest deliberately, and up the inner thighs. Slip hands delicately onto more sexual areas. It can be an entirely new experience for couples to wash each other in these private parts. Clean with an air of innocence—still intending to stimulate your partner—to add an element of teasing and tantalizing.

Dr. Judy's TantrAdvice

Water striking the skin can be pleasurable. If you don't have the luxury of jets in a hot tub, buy an attachment that can be installed in your tub to circulate the water, or a showerhead that emits either diffuse or pelting flows.

God and Goddess Dress Up

On your tantra date, let yourself have fun dressing up; play with styles and fabrics, pick clothes you might never imagine wearing, or use that finery in your closet you've been saving for a special occasion.

Most men get quickly to the stage of being naked in lovemaking, and of course you can choose to be *au naturel*, but tantric sex involves dressing up before you undress. Dressing up to seduce your lover—and to feel good about yourself—is a meditative act to draw attention to your body, to put you in a seductive mood, and for just plain fun. Let yourself be creative, following these suggestions:

♦ Tantric clothes are usually loose fitting and diaphanous, to match the feeling of flowing energy. Sensuous fabrics such as cut velvets and silk encourage touch. Tantric men are not afraid to wear wrapped materials in colorful patterns (commonly worn on exotic islands such as Hawaii and Tahiti) called *pareos*, which look like skirts but are actually quite masculine and sexy-looking.

♦ Be sure these clothes are special and not the same things you wear every day, working around the house, or just hanging out.

God and goddess dress up.

♦ Be dramatic with jewelry; she can let a string of pearls dangle into her cleavage, and he can dare to wear a bracelet or necklace—as men did in ancient Roman or Egyptian times.

♦ Use color. The traditional tantric colors are red and purple. Refer to Chapter 2 to review the colors associated with different chakras, and choose colors of clothing to stimulate and accentuate certain energy centers. Wear orange underwear to awaken the sex center, a yellow scarf around your waist to boost your power, a necklace with a turquoise stone at your throat to help you express yourself, or a purple shirt to inspire you to achieve a more spiritual state of mind and union.

You can undress alluringly for your partner, even putting on a strip show. Or undress each other slowly and seductively, or even rip each other's clothes off in a fit of passion.

Your Ideal Romantic Setting

Lights! Camera! Action! Think of a movie set for the most romantic or exciting love scene you can imagine. What does the set look like? Fill in the following chart for yourself and with your partner. Do you have the same ideal lovemaking space? Talk about your different ideas of a perfect setting for lovemaking. Take turns describing your scenes fully and enjoy your partner's scene, allowing yourselves to imagine being there.

Describe how the most romantic scene would look if you were directing a love scene in a movie. For example, for Place, your ideal scene might be outdoors in a field of lilies, whereas your partner's choice might be indoors in a bedroom with a crackling fireplace. For Era, you might choose ancient Rome as being most exciting or romantic; your partner might choose seventeenth-century France.

Our Ideal Love Scene

	What I Like	What My Partner Likes
Place:	_____	_____
Lighting:	_____	_____
Furniture:	_____	_____
Clothing:	_____	_____
Era:	_____	_____
Other characteristics (specify):	_____	

Prepare Your Sacred Lovemaking Space

Think of the most elegant temples, cathedrals, and synagogues you have ever been in. Remember your awe at the stained-glass windows, elaborate ceiling paintings, marble floors, gilded wood carvings, gold satin, or red velvet drapery. Consider your lovemaking space with the same reverence and care as such temples.

Dressing up your lovemaking space follows the same principle as dressing yourself up before a special date. Think of going to a special event. Just as you'd put on your best finery, dress up your room. Be mindful of stimulating all the senses, following these tips:

- ◆ Light candles all around the room. Put dimmers on your lights, replace harsh lighting with softer fixtures, or put colored bulbs in lamps. If you have overhead lights, place lamps strategically. Drape scarves over lampshades with lights that are too bright (a favorite tantric trick). Think of yourself on TV or in a movie, where lighting creates flattering views of the people's faces and the environment.

Dr. Judy's TantrAdvice

Don't inhibit lovemaking by fearing that your fancy satin sheets will be ruined by oils or body fluids. Buy them for that purpose, replace them when necessary, or put down towels for protection. Use silk sheets for sensuality or put on flannel sheets because they are warm, absorbent, and feel comfortable on the skin.

Ecstasy Essentials

One tantra teacher I know recommends not always making love in your bed, saying it can trigger physical reactions and mental associations with sleep and the release of melatonin that induces drowsiness. In addition, a too-soft mattress or waterbed does not provide as much friction of body parts pressing against one another as a floor (padded, of course).

◆ Add scent. Put fresh flowers in the room, light incense, or spray aromatic room oils. (Don't overdo it, and, of course, be attentive to any allergies you or your partner have.)

◆ Dress up your bed. Put on a new coverlet, drape it with colored materials purchased specially for these occasions, and add soft pillows as decoration and to support body parts. Spread rose petals on the bed!

◆ Keep love toys handy, including massage oils, feather boas, and silk scarves to run over your partner's body to awaken sensations.

◆ Have sacraments nearby to stimulate your taste buds and toast your lovemaking. These can include anything from chocolate-covered strawberries to the traditional glasses of chilled champagne.

◆ Neaten up. Store messy piles of papers in a closet, stash exercise equipment under the bed, cover distracting items (such as stacks of videos or books) with scarves or attractive swatches of material.

◆ Put the children's toys away; this is your night together for romance, remembering how you are as lovers, not as parents.

Change Your Setting

Be creative in your lovemaking. Make love in different places inside your home, blessing each area with your love.

Consider having your tantric encounter outdoors. Flowers will bloom and trees will grow taller where you come together with blessed intention and spiritual union. Choose a private but beautiful setting.

*Choosing an inspiring setting
for your tantric date.*

However, making love in the same setting and keeping your love altar in the same place are also good ideas, as your lovemaking creates an energy vortex that builds and intensifies your union when you return to that space. Cellular memory and mental associations are triggers, so even if you are not in the mood, entering that space can get you there.

Music to Make Love By

Music stirs the soul. Research has proven that certain sounds and tempos directly affect our breathing and heart rate, which in turn affects our mood. For these reasons, music will play a very important role in your tantric date. Choose music you and your partner enjoy, whether it is classical, operatic, or even rock-and-roll. Most important, select music consciously to create the mood you desire. I'll go into more detail about this and give you suggestions about what kind of music to play in Chapter 19. Check out that chapter and Appendix C when it's time to stack your CD changer for your date.

Building an Altar

An altar is a space on a ledge, table, or on the floor where you place sacred objects symbolic of your prayers and respect for spirits. Just as in a religious institution, looking at these objects inspires you to a higher state of consciousness. Be on the lookout for sacred objects to decorate your house that trigger spiritual feelings when you look at them. Collect the objects and design this space together, as an experience that brings you close together and as a testimonial to your togetherness. Approach this altar before your lovemaking and say a prayer together—silently or aloud—to bless the items and your upcoming union.

Items on your altar might include ...

◆ Photos of yourselves that you cherish, or photos of revered religious leaders or tantric masters.

◆ Objects from your life together that are especially meaningful (shells from a trip to Fiji, promise rings you wore, figurines of lovers from that antique outing you took).

◆ Items representing the elements: earth (a special stone), fire (candles), water (a bowl), air (a feather), and spirit (crystal).

◆ Flowers, especially fresh flowers.

◆ Special gifts that you've given each other (his class ring he gave you, the crystal she bought for you in a small shop in the mountains).

◆ Sacred objects such as statues of Shiva and Shakti in embrace, or the bell and *dorje* (symbolic of the male and female spirits).

Ecstasy Essentials

As is done in ancient Native American traditions, light sticks of sage (available at health food stores) to purify the air with its pungent aroma. Move it around the room, into each corner, and around your body.

Honoring Rituals to Sanctify Your Space

Love rituals involving movements and dedications help create a safe space and a sanctified area in which to surrender to each other. Here you can achieve transformation and trancelike states that lead to ecstasy. The following are some ways to sanctify your special space:

◆ Walk around the space in each of the four corners, saying a prayer at each corner. Make up your own prayer, such as: "I dedicate this experience to you, my beloved. May it fulfill all your heart's desire." Or recite a prayer that comes from your ancient people. Maria Yraceburu, an American Indian descendant who writes about being in touch with her spiritual heritage in her book *Legends and Prophecies of the Quero Apache*, suggests this chant:

> *We come from the Earth Mother, We come from the Sky Father,*
> *We come here to be all that we can be,*
> *The legacy unfolds here in life,*
> *Moving like soft warm rain, Our love ascends*
> *Cascading to Earth. Spirit's saving grace.*
> *Daaiina, and so it is.*

♦ Walk around the space in each of the four corners, invoking and inviting the spirits of the four directions of the universe, and any other spirits you would like (good guides, holy spirits, or ancestors) to bless and protect you in your lovemaking. For example, walk to the north corner, ring a bell, and say, "We invite spirits of the north to send their blessing and protective energy to our lovemaking." Say something similar at the south, east, and west corners.

♦ Give each other a gift as an offering of your love and devotion, and to sanctify the space as holy and honoring. This can be a small gift that does not have to cost a great deal of money. Make it something thoughtful that you can use immediately in your lovemaking ceremony, such as a CD of his favorite music, a scarf, or scented oil.

Giving gifts of love.

Quiet the Mind

Settle down into your space after bathing and honoring the space rituals, and quiet your mind to allow your energies to mingle. Sit in the yab yum position, as described in Chapter 3. Do eye gazing and breathing techniques as described in Chapters 2 and 9. Chant to synchronize your energy and quiet your mind. Follow the repetitious mantras of a particular CD, do traditional ones (such as simply repeating "om" or "aum"), or make up your own.

Set Your Intention Together

All too often couples jump into bed—and sex—silently. But because tantric sex is a dedication and not a mindless act, face each other and set an intention for your lovemaking. Sexual and love energy is powerful energy; say what you would like to manifest in this lovemaking session, and it will be more likely to come true as you let your energy expand and merge. Take turns, speaking from your heart, allowing whatever needs to be said to come up. Ask for anything from your partner or from divinities, including personal happiness and world peace.

> **Tantra Tales**
>
> Barry's intention in making love with his girlfriend Beth was: "I intend for this time together to bring us to a better understanding of each other, to cleanse our hearts from the anger of last week, and to blend our bodies so that we feel higher states of pleasure than we ever have before." Beth said, "My intention is for us to go deeper in our love than we have ever gone before; for me to feel better about my body; and for the love energy that we generate to spread out to heal the children in other parts of the world who are suffering, and the men and women who are the victims of cruel unloving acts from others, and to inspire all those who do not yet know the joys of these practices." Alex had a similarly touching blessing for his beloved, adding a dedication to her health, but also a humorous request: "… and may you have that Mercedes Benz car that you drool over!"

Going Out on Your Tantra Date

The tantra date refers to your lovemaking ritual in a private space, whether at home or away, indoors or outdoors. However, the prelude to this date can certainly include activities you do on a regular date, in which you actually go somewhere to do something—before coming home for your special evening. Excitement can build when you are out somewhere together. What are the most exciting things you can do together that will increase your feelings of togetherness and build your anticipation for private time together?

Review the following list and check off activities you would most enjoy. Add to the list. Write down pleasurable activities you can think of, ask your partner to do the same, and compare your lists. Did you come up with similar activities? Read your lists to each other and discuss what you would most enjoy about each one. Go over them one at a time, slowly, enjoying the description of what you would do. Notice how you feel when you imagine the activity. Where is the pleasure in—or resistance to—these activities? What fears do each of you have about doing what each of you chose?

Activities List

Activity	I Like:	My Partner Likes:
Have a romantic dinner	❏	❏
Walk in the park	❏	❏
See a movie	❏	❏
Go dancing	❏	❏
Ride bicycles	❏	❏
Visit friends	❏	❏
Attend a concert	❏	❏
Work out together	❏	❏
Other: _____	❏	❏

The Least You Need to Know

◆ Even if you have a full calendar of work, family obligations, and other commitments, it's important for you and your partner to make time for love.

◆ Prepare for your tantric date to make your encounter special by pampering yourself and setting up your ideal love scene (your bedroom or wherever you choose to make love), paying attention to appeal to all the senses.

◆ Create a sensuous bathing ritual not just for cleaning but for adding to your sensual pleasure.

◆ Dress up for the special occasion, selecting apparel that flatters your shape and seduces and adornments that draw attention.

◆ Sanctify your body and your space with ritualistic purifying and prayers, and set your intentions that honor the special event you will make of your union.

Practices for Beloveds to Reach Bliss

In This Chapter

- How to reach the state of bliss
- Simple methods to synchronize your energy
- Spicing up your senses and stimulating your partner
- Finding your tantric love triggers
- Learning "sex in the flow lane"
- Rituals that make lovemaking special

Now that you've set the stage for your tantric connection, what are you to do? A natural answer would be to do what comes naturally. But because tantra is a ritualistic practice, there are some activities and ceremonies you can do together to facilitate your pleasure and help you reach higher realms of bliss. This chapter introduces you to some of those practices.

What Is Bliss?

Have you ever been so happy you almost couldn't believe it? Do you know what it feels like to be so attuned to everything around you and smiled so hard that your face hurt? Would you like to feel a bright white light enveloping you and maybe even transporting you to another dimension?

That's the state of bliss—deeper than delight, juicier than joyful. You're enraptured and have the feeling that all is perfect. "Bliss" is the highest happiness; in a word, *heaven*, says Bodhi Avinasha, master teacher of spiritual transformation and author of *Jewel in the Lotus.* "Bliss means feeling so good that every cell in your body feels alive," says tantra teacher Laurie Handlers, who leads workshops titled "Tantra in Bliss."

How do you get to that magical state of bliss? By being present in the moment, breathing, channeling your energy, feeling your love, and practicing the techniques I'm sharing with you in this book.

Synchronizing Your Energy

Because life is so stressful and you can't always expect that you and your beloved will be in the same mood, it is very important before beginning any tantric practice that you do as much as possible to be on the same wavelength. The magic of tantra is that you can start out in different spaces and places, figuratively speaking, and through certain practices, you can get into the same groove.

One way to synchronize your energy is by breathing together. Review the breathing practices I described in detail in Chapter 2. You'll recall that the breath guides your energy in various ways that you want it to go.

You can do these breaths in different positions to achieve interesting new sensations. For example, sit back to back while you do the breaths (instead of facing each other) and feel your partner's chest, sides, and back expanding through the contact with your back. You can feel this easily if you both have taken a full breath so that your chest and back expand. As you breathe, make up a sound to chant together (use "om" or any sound both of you like). Adding a sound to breathing together intensifies your connection to each other.

Look Into My Eyes: Eye Gazing

Eye gazing is a basic tantric sex practice, widely taught by tantra teachers of all schools of thought. It's a fundamental practice that leads to intense experiences when you do it right. It sounds so simple—looking at each other—but in fact, think about how difficult it can be to actually look into anyone's eyes for any amount of time. Fears of intimacy can make it even more uncomfortable to look into a lover's eyes deeply for an extended period of time. How do you feel when a lover looks deeply and directly in your eyes? You might be delighted, but you might also feel vulnerable, self-conscious, or embarrassed. These feelings are normal!

Eye gazing in tantric sex practice means looking deeply into your partner's eyes, to see behind the obvious (eye color, eyelashes, expression) into his or her soul. It can be challenging and take practice.

Eye gazing with deep breathing and energy connection.

Incorporate eye gazing into most of the exercises throughout this book because …

◆ It stills your mind and focuses your attention on what you are doing rather than on distracting thoughts, to keep you present and in the moment.

◆ It gives your partner a good feeling that you're totally paying attention and are present for him or her.

◆ It enables you to confront your fears of deep connection with your beloved.

◆ It transforms your relationship to each other by getting beyond mental distractions and physical judgments to enter each other's soul.

Ecstasy Essentials

Teachers Michaels and Johnson recommend starting with the classical practice of *Tratak*, in which you fix your gaze on a candle flame for several minutes, usually just before bed. This helps you develop the concentration necessary to exchange intense gazes with your partner.

Eye gazing is the favorite sexual practice of the husband and wife tantra teaching team of Mark Michaels and Patricia Johnson. "When people first fall in love, they often spend extended periods gazing into each other's eyes," says Michaels. "In perfecting eye gazing you are consciously re-creating the experience of falling in love."

To do eye gazing, stand facing your partner in a relaxed and open posture and gaze softly into each other's eyes for at least three minutes. (You can also do eye gazing while sitting in yab yum or any comfortable position as long as your energy centers are aligned.) Look predominantly into each other's left (receiving) eye. Remember it's not a staring contest; keep your eyes relaxed, and blink if you have to. Come back to gazing if you get distracted. Instead of focusing on the outward act of looking, be receptive so you can melt deeper and deeper into the union with your beloved. Notice whatever feelings come up (fear, embarrassment, attraction, love). Keep breathing. Notice your body's reactions (lips tightening, squinting, coughing, shifting). Eventually you will be able to keep more still.

The Heart Hold

This exercise sends love energy through your hands and into each other's heart. Place your right hand over your partner's heart. At the same time, your partner places his right hand over your heart. Imagine sending out your love energy through your heart down your arm and out your right hand into your partner. You have several options for where you can put your left hand to run the energy between you:

◆ Over your partner's right hand, pressing it over your heart.

◆ On your partner's middle back, directly in back of where his or her heart is.

◆ On your genitals or on each other's genitals.

Experiment with different places to experience heart energy cycling through your body in various ways. On each occasion, go slowly, breathe, and feel the energy actually passing between and through you.

The heart hold sends love energy through your hearts.

The Partner Passion Pod

Being encircled by your lover's arms feels secure, comforting, and even exciting. Tantric practice encourages connecting between partners in all types of positions and situations. In this exercise, approach each other slowly while eye gazing and let your bodies float into each other and embrace in any way that seems comfortable. As you embrace, do the synchronizing breath while slowly inhaling and exhaling. As you breathe, feel your bodies melting into one another. Stay in this position as long as you like. When you separate, move apart slowly, still maintaining eye contact; abrupt separations should never occur in tantric connections. Look at each other and notice how different you look. After such a connection, you might look as relaxed and happy as you do after a massage.

Stimulating the Senses

All the senses are honored in tantric lovemaking. That means all the organs involved with these senses are also centers of the body. Here are some examples of exercises you can do with your partner to create bliss between you that activates each of the senses:

◆ **Mouth and face.** Trace around your beloved's mouth with your fingertips and pull the lips apart gently. The lips are related to the genitals, according to Eastern tradition, and licking and sucking them can stimulate the sexual organs. Press your lips to your partner's and make motions. Extend your touch to the area around the mouth and to the cheeks and face. Blindfold your partner and feed him or her various tasty morsels with different textures (try strawberries, chocolate-covered cherries, a spoonful of ice cream, a slice of crunchy cucumber). Tantalize your partner as you do this. (See Chapter 16 to read how this feeding will get more playful.)

Sensuous touch.

◆ **Eyes.** The eyes truly are the window to the soul. At the beginning of this chapter, I mentioned the importance of eye gazing as fundamental to all tantric connecting. Go a step further by touching your partner's eyes gently around the eye sockets and across the lids, making circles at the corners and tracing out to the temples. Let your gaze roam from each other's eyes down to other parts with wonder and appreciation.

Ecstasy Essentials

Consider aromatherapy and the use of essential oils in your individual and partner practices. Research has shown that such scents actually have particular effects on the brain, facilitating certain mood states.

◆ **Nose.** The nose is cherished in tantric practice, because along with the mouth, it is the entrance for the vital breath that is the life force (*prana*). In addition, its function (smelling scents) plays a vital role in attraction! Stimulate your partner's sense of smell by blindfolding him or her and passing various scents (scented oils, oranges, wine) under his or her nose. Sniff various parts of each other's body in a natural, uninhibited way, as animals do, as if scouting each other out. Use your nose as you would your fingers to stimulate each other and see what new sensations you can create.

◆ **Hands.** Touch has been proven to have healing effects, and the role of massage is paramount in tantra. As I've mentioned, it is an excellent idea to take a massage class, read a book, or watch a video about tantric massage to hone your skills.

Here's an exercise I use in my workshops to teach participants how to enjoy sensations through touch. Taking turns as giver and receiver, close your eyes and hold your partner's hand. Feel the energy of the hand you're touching and that of your own hand, so you can identify the different sensations of touching and being touched. Breathe deeply, sending energy through your hand, and explore your partner's hand. Feel the different textures (bony parts, soft palm, sharp nails). Massage, using different strokes and pressures, with the intention of making your partner feel good. Give each other feedback about the different sensations of touching and being touched.

Dr. Judy's TantrAdvice

While you and your partner are both in the shower, soap up, turn your backs to each other, and rub your backs and backsides against each other. Bump up against each other's sacrum to stir up energy.

◆ **Ears.** Too often neglected, this part of the body can be very erotic. Press your thumbs into the openings of the ears, pressing around the inner skin. Stretch and tug at the earlobes (they can take pressure) and around the outer ear. Whisper sweet nothings into your partner's ear. Sing a song; it doesn't matter whether you can really sing, just let yourself improvise to express yourself into your partner's ear.

As I mentioned, music is so important in your tantric practice (music is discussed in more detail in Chapter 19), so improvise making music together. That means you don't have to play someone else's CD; instead, use anything around the house on which to keep a beat, or get some simple percussion instruments (drums, rattles, bells, chimes) from a music store. (As a musician, this is one practice I particularly enjoy!)

Making Time for Each Other to Connect

I often hear couples complain that they have no time for each other—much less for sex. Everyone is too busy, and other priorities can push quality tantric time together to the back burner. So it's important to find practices you can realistically do together to keep the energy flowing between you. Here are some simple practices you can do that don't require much time but that maintain an intimate connection in your relationship.

Couple's Morning Blessing

Tantra teacher Robert Frey suggests doing this daily morning practice with your partner before getting dressed for your day. Begin by sitting on your knees facing each other. Bow to each other with hands in prayer pose. Take 10 deep belly breaths in unison, the first 5 with eyes closed, and the second 5 making eye contact with your partner. Take turns saying the following blessing to each other, with a breath between sentences and three breaths with eye contact between turns (writing these words on a 3 by 5 index card can be helpful). Feel free to improvise and make up your own words for this blessing:

> I recognize you as an important ally for me, and I am grateful that you are in my life. I feel blessed to be co-creating with you. My life is enriched by knowing you. I want you to feel fulfilled, victorious, happy, and at peace today. I wish for you love, wisdom, creativity, and a flowing, meaningful experience today. I love you.

After you have both said the blessing, take three more breaths while maintaining eye contact and end with a bow, hug, and kiss. Further conversation is optional; usually the best choice is simply to get up and move on with other activities, with your beloved in your heart.

The Ten-Minute Connect

In his workshops and book on conscious loving, Charles Muir poses a solution to couples who don't connect due to lack of time or interest: a simple exercise called the "10-minute connect." I have often heard Charles emphasize how couples should do this connect even if they don't feel like it because it keeps the love flowing. He's right!

Here's how to do the 10-minute connect, along with two other simple exercises you can do to connect with your partner:

- **The 10-minute connect.** The couple takes 10 minutes at some point in the day, preferably at the beginning or end, to lie quietly together, just feeling each other's energy. This can be in a spoons position, with synchronized breathing.

- **The 10-minute sharing.** Take 10 minutes to talk about what happened in your day, how you feel, or anything that is on your mind.

- ◆ **The 10-minute acknowledgment.** Take 10 minutes to tell each other what you most appreciate about each other. Recognition makes us feel alive and loved.

The sharing and acknowledging connects can be done in addition to the silent 10-minute connect, or at another time in the day when you can both give each other your complete attention.

Connections can also be accomplished through body stances. In one example of this, tantra teacher Laurie Handlers trains couples to assume an Egyptian posture together, where the matching of their poses creates a union of souls, and of heaven and earth in the Egyptian tradition (Ra and Ma, where *Ra* means father and *Ma* means mother). The couple stands face to face, with their left feet stepping out toward the other and hands outstretched on top of one another but not touching. The left hand faces up and the right hand faces down, creating a matched hieroglyphic body position. They place their tongue up in the roof of the mouth and inhale hearing the internal mantra sound "Ra" and then exhale through the mouth hearing the internal mantra "Ma." The result is that the partners feel the energy of the integrated whole by balancing male and female energy in the Egyptian way.

Call It Sacred: Finding Your Tantric Love Triggers

Consider your relationship as sacred, meaning that you hold it in the highest esteem, reflect on it with awe, and treat it with the utmost respect. To infuse your love with this quality, preface any descriptions of your relationship with the word *sacred*. Infuse this sacredness with words or symbols that are special to the two of you and evoke your tantric union (I call these *tantric triggers*). One of my personal tantric triggers is the depiction of the dragon and the phoenix, two magical beings and auspicious symbols in China often paired together as statues, etched on sidewalks, or printed on wedding invitations.

The auspicious pairing of the phoenix and dragon.

Sex in the Flow Lane

Tantric sex requires an awareness of every sensation—but so often we're so busy *doing* that we don't really *feel* how we're moving. Personal coach Greg Ehmka developed a technique he calls *Sexyhan* (I call it "sex in the flow lane"), in which you don't move any body part until your body feels the motion from within. Ehmka describes this technique in his book *Money, Sex, Power and You: Transforming Your Ego*. Many tantra teachers, including myself, use a variation of the process in their workshops. It is quite wonderful to run a workshop where everyone starts moving in slow motion and gets the experience of this sensation of allowing experience to happen instead of forcing it!

Ehmka, who lives in a tantric community in Austria, recommends doing this exercise on your own for 20 minutes and then with a partner. Start by sitting or standing together with your eyes closed, making low sounds and being still until you get motivated to move (called *inner guidance*). As impulses come, you can touch each other gently, curl up together, or over time get more vigorous even to the point of screaming—as long as it's not a preconceived or automatic motion. "After this practice, measure on a scale of 0 to 10 how joyfully empowered you feel," says Emhka, "I guarantee the more you do it, the higher will be your rating."

Advanced Body Exploration

There are endless secrets hidden in your body temple, to be uncovered though your tantric practices, either alone or with your partner. Don't be afraid to show yourself. Even if you have been making love together for years, or doing tantric practices, your partner's genitals might still be a mystery. Here are some exercises that go a step further than the body explorations and physical sharing that I have mentioned in previous chapters.

Her "Yoni Show" for Him

This exercise is an ultimate act of trust and intimacy. It's also very exciting—physically and energetically—to allow your partner to truly see you inside. Most women are embarrassed about how their genitals look and how they look in their most sacred space: the vagina.

In this exercise, the woman is given tremendous encouragement to display her most private, sacred temple for her beloved. It must be preceded by many of the rituals described in Chapter 8, so that she is extremely relaxed and feels adored by his bathing and massaging her. She then either disrobes or he lovingly disrobes her. As I've emphasized, he must ask permission to see her. At her own pace, she reveals her most private parts, using her fingers to direct his attention and open her lips more.

Some couples worry that this exercise will be too clinical—like a medical examination—but actually, if you have prepared together using tantric breathing, it is inevitable that the mood and spirit will be one of loving rather than objectivity. If you feel objective, do not criticize yourself. Realize that this is a way of controlling any fears or self-consciousness. Breathe deeper, and let these feelings transmute into more calm, connected ones.

This exercise could evolve to another activity; for example, a demonstration of how she likes to be pleasured, or more free-flowing play leading to a tantric sexual interaction. However, there should never be a goal, as the purpose of the exercise is for her to be relaxed.

> **Tantra Tales**
>
> When Matt and Julie did this exercise, she was excited for him to truly see her but extremely frightened and embarrassed. With his reassurance, she could continue, slowly opening her thighs. "I needed to hear him say that he really wanted to see," she said. After he did, she was more reassured.

His "Love Arrow Show" for Her

In tantric sex, lovers always take turns at different activities, usually with the woman going first. After her show of her sacred gates to heaven to him, it's his turn to show her his lingam (or to use other tantric terms as described in Chapter 3, the "jade stalk" that can enter her "gates of heaven"). As with other exercises, remember not to have any expectations or make any demands, but to simply enjoy the experience with a spirit of curiosity and adoration. As mentioned for her yoni show, his love arrow show is best preceded by many of the rituals described in Chapter 8.

Making Sacred Water Magic

Water serves many purposes in tantric sex practices—it's cleansing, healing, playful, and a turn-on. I've already mentioned in other chapters many ways you can pleasure each other in the bath or shower. For example, you can do many of the breathing exercises, eye lock, and heart hold. Sit in the bathtub in yab yum position with your genitals close together. Breathe slowly, and rock your pelvises toward each other on your exhale. Do this for a few minutes.

Some tantric experts use these interesting techniques to awaken powerful energies in water. For example, California tantra teachers Steve and Lokita Carter are experts in a bodywork technique called *Watsu Water Shiatsu*, in which the receiver is cradled, stretched, and slowly moved in warm water, interspersed with intervals of stillness. The resulting experience can be a wonderful combination of feeling loved and peaceful. But powerful emotional releases can also happen (I know from experience!).

Although working with an expert is certainly helpful to work through any strong emotions that arise, couples can do a more elementary variation of this technique together. It's a wonderful opportunity to melt together in stillness, trust, and relaxation. It's also a sensual experience! Next time you have the chance to be in a pool of warm, still water (a moving sea or cold ocean won't work because you have to be relaxed) you can try this exercise that the Carters recommend. (As in every exercise throughout this book, always greet each other first with loving words and compliments.) Take turns in water about waist deep. For example, the man stands in the water and helps the woman lean backward in the water. He gently sways her from side to side, holding her by the rib cage or hips, keeping her nose out of the water and pressing her sex center (yoni) to his genitals or belly. (It's a nice addition to put a water pillow under her head, leaving his hands free to gently stroke her chest, belly, and sex center.) Change places. When you're done, thank each other for this special time.

Tantra Tutorial

AquaTantra is a term used by expert Rainbowheart who teaches couples and paired singles choreographed movements, holding and guiding each other while floating in a warm pool to dissolve stress and create bliss.

Watsu: connecting deeply in warm water.

Staying in Bliss: The Afterplay

What if neither of you wants to fall into that post-sex syndrome in which he falls asleep and she lies there unfulfilled? Tantra teacher Robert Frey has a favorite tantric solution for this dilemma, which he calls the *afterplay*, to keep you in bliss.

After ejaculating, says Frey, keep the lingam in the yoni and sit up in the yab yum position. Take a deep breath in, and picture drawing that powerful energy of the ejaculation up the spine, like heat rising. Then picture a golden light or mist coming down the spine as you exhale.

Frey suggests doing this for up to a half an hour—and promises that if you do, you could build into a profound full-body orgasmic state for both of you. "Both the man and the woman may have several additional orgasms, simply from being completely turned on by the power of the circulating energy," he explains. In this way, afterplay means there really isn't any "after," because bliss just keeps on coming.

Tantra Tales _____

Who wouldn't want love to last and last, much less build! By staying with the practices, this can happen for you! It did for Richard and Antoinette Asimus, a highly experienced Cincinnati-based Tantra teaching team who have been deliriously in love with each other for decades, but are also dedicated to practicing what they preach. "Our relationship has deepened and become more passionate because we devote time to our sacred loving," says Richard. For the last four years, they have not missed a day of doing their daily tantric connecting practice, which includes 60 to 90 minutes of making love! How can that be, you wonder? Explains Antoinette, "We do all kinds of creative variations of the five stages of the Ipsalu practice involving body movements (called rishis), breathing, generating sex energy through pelvis thrusts, and bringing it to our hearts. Then we play!" Play might be massage, laughing, or dancing together. Richard adds, "The benefits are enormous, not only to each other, but our morning hour gives amazingly strong and beautiful love energy to everything we do all day, from our teaching and coaching to daily life routines that have taken on more joy."

The Least You Need to Know

◆ Bliss is an ecstatic feeling of connection with a loving energy that expands inwardly and outwardly.

◆ Simple exercises can create intense pleasure and deep connection; for example, looking deeply into each other's eyes, sending energy through each other's hearts.

♦ Stimulate all your senses for a truly all-consuming experience; explore tastes, smells, sights, sounds, and touches.

♦ Each of us has particular thoughts, sounds, or symbols that can trigger sensuous feelings; know what these "love triggers" are for yourself and for your partner.

♦ The most blissful sexual experiences can happen when you do not force any actions, but rather when you are still and allow the urges to move to come from within (sex in the flow lane).

♦ Instead of abruptly ending your lovemaking, stay in bliss by taking deliberate actions to stay connected.

10

Breaking Through Blocks to Bliss

In This Chapter

◆ How issues from the past interfere with your practice of tantric sex—and with your life in general

◆ The power of releasing intense emotions

◆ Ways to connect and make time together

◆ Getting past anger, attachment, and anxieties

◆ Seven ways to balance your sexual energy

◆ Lifestyle practices that keep you clear and healthy

On any new path of self-discovery, self-improvement, or spirituality, you can make exciting discoveries about yourself and the world around you. However, as you make changes in yourself, your relationships, and your lifestyle, blocks can arise from resistance, conflicts, or anxieties. These blocks can come from unresolved problems in your past, your partnerships, or even your upbringing. You need to be free of these blocks so you can experience pleasure not only in love but also in all areas of your life.

Many therapeutic techniques offer help. I use a wide variety and combination of these in my workshops and with private patients as well as in my work giving advice on radio, TV, and the Internet. In this chapter, I'll address some tools and techniques that will be especially helpful in solving conflicts and clearing emotional blocks so that you'll be free to explore the tantric sex path.

When Big Emotions Burst Forth

Sexuality is a powerful force, and these tantric sex practices generate intense sexual arousal! As a result, it makes sense that you could confront some strong previously suppressed issues. It can be scary when upsetting feelings emerge unexpectedly, but it's important to allow them to come up and resolve them. Instead of repressing problems or traumas, welcome the opportunity to work through them. Trust that their appearance means that you are ready to deal with them. To ease your fears, seek the help of a trained person, ideally a tantric master schooled in psychotherapeutic and clinical techniques.

To release blocks caused by unresolved issues in your past, some tantra teachers include what's called *emotional release* in their workshops. Deep-seated emotions stored in the body can be freed through particular patterns of breathing and movement. A partner can also act as a witness and guide. It's amazing to be in a workshop, such as the ones held by those of us trained in the techniques of Tantrika International (see Appendix B), in which a roomful of people are lying on the floor, doing pelvic rocking, breathing, and making sounds, when suddenly a large number of people connect with intense past experiences. Some people might be joyful and laughing, while others express explosive or angry outbursts when remembering a past experience that made them feel that way.

Blocks to Bliss

Critics of emotional release, such as tantra teachers Mark Michaels and Patricia Johnson, maintain that emotional release exercises focus on potential pain, which they say can become a self-fulfilling prophecy. They assert that tantric practices themselves are healing, and deeper work is best left to professional therapists.

Not all emotional releases are loud or connect with pain; I've had many that are calm and blissful. One of my emotional releases was so powerful that I began to see colors radiating from my body, leading to a feeling of jubilance. Some lead to astounding, physically obvious transformations. When facilitating one woman in an emotional release, I witnessed her transform from looking sad and haggard to looking joyful and 20 years younger!

Transformation as a result of an emotional release process.

Overcoming Feelings of Separation

Tantra is about connecting; therefore, when you are in pain or feel a block impeding the progress of your practices, you are probably experiencing some degree of separation. You could be feeling separated from your own self, from your beloved, from your work, from your family, or from the world in general; indeed you might know that terrible feeling of being isolated or not belonging. Tantric practices heal this separation by opening your heart.

Think of the ways you create a feeling of being separate from others: judging yourself, judging others, or having unrealistic expectations. In my classes and workshops, I lead people through experiences of separateness and connectedness by facing each other and saying "I feel separate from you when I …"; then saying "I feel connected to you when I …." This gets you in touch with how you create those feelings and empowers you to choose which situation to create.

Dr. Judy's TantrAdvice

Anytime you protest that you don't have the love you want in a relationship, consider how you might be creating the blocks yourself. Perhaps you are not ready to receive the love you say you want.

Diffusing Your Anger

It's inevitable that at times you and a partner will get angry at each other, but instead of storing that anger or confronting it head on, tantra offers another option. The *lion's play* is an exercise that California tantra team Steve and Lokita Carter find highly effective for couples who have tension between them. Put your hands together and roar loudly like a lion, and push on each other's hands with equal strength. It might sound silly, but try it! After a few minutes, even the most skeptical of you will probably start laughing. Keep it up until you and your partner are both laughing, and watch your anger dissolve.

The lion's play exercise can help diffuse anger.

Tantra Tales

Beloveds Francesca Gentille and John Mariotti, who describe their work as "Passionate Living Coaching," include sexual and emotional healing work in their tantric lovemaking practices. As Francesca says, "We've found that blocks to love and intimacy come from our past. They often arise as feelings of disconnection, numbness, or irritation. We watch for these feelings both in and out of bed. When they come up we slow down, breathe deeply, gently ask questions, 'Where does it feel numb?' 'What feeling is present?' 'When have you felt that before?' 'Do you see an image?' Often, a disintegrated aspect comes to the surface; the little one rejected as a child, the teenager told she was unattractive, the vampire self who feeds off energy. Or the destroyer who enjoys inflicting pain. When we dialogue with these lost, hidden, or suppressed selves we heal. Even aspects that are considered dark or dangerous become allies. It's like returning lost pieces of our souls. It's very intimate work that brings us emotionally and sexually closer and gives us more energy."

Frustration Over Who's on Top

Many relationships are about control and battles of control. In tantric terms, the center for control is in the third chakra (the area below the belly). To help resolve control battles in your relationship, do exercises related to this center. Pick exercises in this book and hold your hand on your power center to empower you as you do the exercise. For example, you could do eye gazing with your partner and put your left hand on your power center to receive more strength. Breathe. Then bring your right hand onto your throat to feel your right to be heard and then have a discussion with your partner.

Ghost-Busting Relationships

As I've mentioned, resolving past relationships, particularly when they have been painful, is essential to free you up for pleasure. These include relationships with lovers as well as early childhood patterns with parents. Tantra offers invaluable opportunities to face and embrace shadows of inner feelings often labeled as "bad" (anger, hurt) and prior wounding to make way for joy.

Tantra instructor Rundy Duphiney runs tantra groups for men to help them open up to deeper intimacy by resolving issues with their fathers. "Many men had dominant and unavailable fathers and grow up being the same way; that prevents them from being vulnerable and opening to intimacy," says Rundy. "Men have trouble releasing control," he adds, and they have to free the wounded little boy inside. Tantric breathing, sharing their stories together, and lots of laughter and play helps. One game in Rundy's group is a race where men learn trust, cooperation, and sharing while having fun. Pairs of men stand side-to-side, shoulder-to-shoulder with their arms linked and one leg tied together (making a three-legged unit), with one man blindfolded and the other not allowed to talk. Then the teams race to get around an obstacle course.

Sexual Healings

Past pains about sex get locked in the body and particularly the pelvic region. Many tantric practices help release these pains, as described in more detail in Chapter 18.

Balancing Your Male and Female Energies

In Chapter 3, I explained that uniting male and female energies is key to tantric practice. Sometimes blocks come from the inability to balance these energies, which throws you off balance and causes tension or incompatibility between you and your partner.

The Sexual Relations Review

As a therapist for more than three decades, I certainly know how past relationships affect present ones. Painful pairings keep us panicked about their repetition. In my previous books, *The Complete Idiot's Guide to Dating* and *The Complete Idiot's Guide to a Healthy Relationship* (see Appendix C), I presented many exercises to free yourself from the ghosts of the past. Do those exercises to see how patterns in your past relationships affect your present ones.

The following Sex Relations Review exercise is based on the tantric principle that imbalances in male and female energies in relationships can cause incompatibilities that you might not even be aware of. For this exercise, consider "male" and "female" to be whatever comes to your mind that defines those qualities. Use the following table to review past important relationships and see which partner has demonstrated more male or female energy, or whether these have been balanced. Rate the degree of male or female energy on the scale by putting a mark on the line closest to the description. Include what your parents' relationship was like and several relationships that have been important to you, even if they have not been overtly sexual. Note in the space provided what happened in the relationship (we broke up, I was dissatisfied, he left me, I left him, we fought, and so forth).

Notice whether you are repeating your parents' pattern (for example, if you are a woman and rated your mother and yourself as extremely "female" and your father and your partner as extremely "male"). Also notice from the chart whether you consistently pick partners with similar energy, and whether they are similar or opposite to the energy you bring to the relationship. Knowing your pattern in important relationships gives you more freedom to choose to change it, either by changing yourself or by choosing another type of partner next time. Notice your emotional reaction to the relationships. Were you happy about or annoyed by the female or male characteristics of a person?

 Tantra Tales _____

Juliette found Damian sweet and attentive during their first dates. But after a while his high voice and tentative manner annoyed her. When he looked at her like a hurt puppy or begged her to come to bed she would snap at him. She found herself longing for her ex-boyfriend who had a much deeper voice and was more strong-willed. She couldn't put her finger on the problem until she realized from doing the Sex Relations Review that Damian was being too "female" (or yin) for her taste, while she rated two ex-boyfriends higher on the "male" scale. In her therapy sessions with me, Juliette realized she had to become more balanced in her own male and female energies to attract a man who was similarly balanced.

The Sex Relations Review: Getting the Yin and Yang of It

Person	Degree of Male or Female Energy				
	A great deal of female energy	Some female energy	Balanced male and female energy	Some male energy	A great deal of male energy
My mother					
My father					
Other significant person					
A partner #1					
Me with partner #1					
What happened in the relationship? (describe)					
A partner #2					
Me with partner #2					
What happened in the relationship? (describe)					
A partner #3					
Me with partner 3					
What happened in the relationship? (describe)					

Seven Ways to Balance Sexual Energy

After you've become aware of your male and female energy from doing the Sexual Relations Review, how do you balance them? All the tantric practices mentioned in this book help you to do that. Be patient; this achievement takes time. Meanwhile, here are several simple ways to balance those energies:

♦ **Nostril breathing.** You can control the balance of your male or female energy by choosing which nostril to block or open. To stimulate more male (yang) energy (active, analytical, assertive), block your left nostril and breathe only through your right nostril. To stimulate more feminine (yin) energy (receptive, passive, nurturing), block your right nostril and breathe through your left nostril. You can also turn your head to the left to activate more male energy; this assists in breathing through your right nostril. Turn to the right to activate more female energy.

♦ **Alternate nostril breathing.** This is a common exercise in yoga classes. Sit quietly. Put your right index finger on your third eye, and rest your thumb and middle finger on your nostrils. Exhale forcefully and then close one nostril with your finger and inhale through the other nostril, to the count of seven. Then close that nostril while releasing the other nostril, and breathe through the open nostril to the count of seven. Without pausing, continue alternately closing and opening the nostrils as you breathe. In more advanced practice, you would contract the PC muscles (see Chapter 6) to create more force in the breath.

♦ **Use different sounds.** Chant "om" to stimulate more male energy and "aum" for more female energy. Then chant the two sounds alternately for several minutes until you feel the sounds are merging.

♦ **Focus on symbols of male or female.** The Star of David, commonly identified as a symbol of the Jewish religion, is actually a mediation design, with the two intersecting triangles symbolizing the male and female, mind and body. The points on the Star of David also symbolize the sex organs, with the penis and vagina at the upper and lower tips, the breasts at either end of the top line, and the testicles at either end of the lower line. Focus on different points at will.

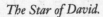

The Star of David.

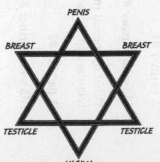

- **Walk a mile in his or her shoes.** In my workshops, I often invite the class to purposefully walk around the room as if they were a stereotypic male and then walk purposefully like a stereotypic female. This often leads to amused reactions and amusing demonstrations!

- **Focus on colors.** Male energy is blue (cool, logical), and female energy is red (emotional, passionate). By surrounding yourself with the desired color, you can focus on that aspect of yourself. Mentally focus on red or blue, look at an item colored red or blue, or purposefully put on red or blue clothing.

- **Move your body.** To draw in more male energy, sweep your hands out from your sides over your head, into the sky. Looking up, imagine calling in the energy from the sky. For more female energy, bend down slightly and scoop the energy up from mother earth into your heart. In a variation of this, use just your right arm to sweep the sky or your left hand to sweep the earth while keeping the other hand on whatever energy center you want to empower.

Getting Past Desperation and Attachment

Part of any spiritual path is to reach a state in which you are not attached to anyone or anything. You might know this feeling of desperation or clinging to a partner. For Janine, it pushed all past lovers away from her. She admitted to me, "They all said I was too needy." One way to ease this feeling of desperation is to understand it. Review in your mind about your past with your parents to see whether they abandoned you (in which case you are still panicked over being left) or suffocated you (so you felt used). These dynamics can make you resist intimacy out of fear of repeating abandonment or suffocation.

Besides understanding, the following two tantric practices might help:

- **Breathe deeply.** When you feel needy, before you do or say something that grasps at someone, take a deep breath, letting the sound come out loudly as you exhale. Let the energy go through your body and out of you.

- **Ground yourself.** Feel yourself rooted to the floor. Stand with your feet comfortably apart, and bend your knees slightly. Bounce up and down (be careful not to put pressure on your knees!), taking deep

Dr. Judy's TantrAdvice

Try this favorite breathing variation of mine: Put your thumbs in your ears and your fingers on the top of your head. Listen to the sound of your breathing. This is one of the wonders I discovered while scuba diving. It accomplishes a womblike relaxation.

breaths that go into your first chakra, the center that symbolizes security. Feel rooted to the ground like a tree. Doing this helps ground you so you feel secure, safe, and more your own person.

When you are breathing deeply and feeling grounded, you won't grasp at a partner.

Purging Panic and Obsessions

Fears and anxieties that can lead to panic attacks, and repetitive distracting thoughts that become obsessions, are not only distressing but take you out of the moment—yet as I've discussed throughout this book, all tantric practices require you to be present in the moment. To achieve this, use the two techniques in the previous section to get past desperation and attachment. Other breathing techniques are helpful, such as exhaling for a longer time than inhaling.

Focus on what is present in the moment. Ask yourself, "What is present now?" "And now?" "And now?" When you catch yourself fretting about the past or worrying about the future, keep asking, "What is present now?"

Tantra Tutorial

Rebirthing is an advanced (and controversial) technique that can help people cleanse the pain during their birth by reliving the experience. People play certain roles (for example, the mother) to facilitate the process and to offer support and structure. In some exercises, the love partner is present. Because the process involves regression and birthing, some practitioners submerge the receiver underwater. Rebirthing should be done only under the supervision of people trained in this process because it can bring powerful emotions to the surface that must be processed and worked through.

More Ways to Clear Blocks

In addition to your mind, blocks can be cleared through working on your physical body! One way to clear blocks physically is through exercise and the practices described in Chapters 6 and 16. You might already know the experience of being able to clear your mind and work out your problems with physical exercise.

Blocks can also be cleared through working on your nutrition. What are your eating habits? There is convincing evidence that food affects your mood. Could you be eating foods that are creating trouble (too much sugar, not enough protein)? Also, evaluate whether you have any food allergies. Investigate eating plans that could be healthier for you. Ask friends, read about nutrition, or consult tantra teachers and other tantra students you meet about what they do.

I have mentioned that some tantric practitioners do a cleanse as part of their health routine, in which they drink only juice for a period of time or follow other eating plans to clear their digestive system. Removing toxins from your system in this or other ways can also help unblock emotions.

> **Blocks to Bliss**
>
> Uncovering emotions should always be taken seriously. Although any loving person can assist and witness, it is important to be cautious. Consult a qualified therapist if you feel you have any distress that persists a few weeks or for answers to your questions.

The Least You Need to Know

♦ Blocks to reaching states of bliss can come from feeling separated from others, storing up anger, and obsessive thoughts—all of which can be eliminated through processes like emotional clearing and tantric breathing techniques.

♦ Misunderstandings and tension between you and a partner can be eased by resolving to spend even short amounts of time together to exchange acknowledgments and blessings.

♦ Simple breathing and meditative techniques can help you balance male and female energy in yourself and in your relationship that cause incompatibilities.

♦ Although many blocks to bliss can be eliminated, it is important to seek professional help when problems are persistent or deep-seated.

evaluate whether you have any food allergies. Investigate eating plans that could be healthier for you. Ask friends, read about nutrition, or consult tantra teachers and other tantra students you meet about what they do.

I have mentioned that some tantric practitioners do a cleanse as part of their health routine, in which they drink only juice for a period of time or follow other eating plans to clear their digestive system. Removing toxins from your system in this or other ways can also help unblock emotions.

The Least You Need to Know

- Blocks to reaching states of bliss can come from feeling separated from others, storing up anger and obsessive thoughts—all of which can be eliminated through processes like emotional clearing and tantric breathing techniques.

- Misunderstandings and tension between you and a partner can be eased by resolving to spend even short amounts of time together to exchange acknowledgments and blessings.

- Simple breathing and meditative techniques can help you balance male and female energy in yourself and in your relationship that cause incompatibilities.

- Although many blocks to bliss can be eliminated, it is important to seek professional help when problems are persistent or deep-seated.

Part 3

Making Major Progress on the Tantric Path

Now that you know all the basic steps toward bliss and have cleared away roadblocks on your journey to joy, you're ready for the "best nights ever"— truly!

Get set for great experiences in this part, as you learn step by step exactly what to do to treat your partner to unforgettable nights of pleasure. Best of all, you'll learn how you can make it last as long as you want using effective practices that lead you to extended lovemaking, more orgasms, and better than that—much more love. This requires a shift in your ideas about sex and orgasm, though; so get ready for some new ways to look at lovemaking. And get fit in the process, as I show you some wonderful workout routines that will make your journey with your partner more fun and keep you physically and spiritually in tune.

Giving Her the Best Nights Ever

In This Chapter

♦ Preparing to please your goddess

♦ What to do on the first of her nights of pleasure

♦ What to do on the second and third pleasure nights—and beyond

♦ What to say and which specific pleasure techniques to use

♦ The possibility of love liquid flow

♦ Giving her what she really wants and needs

It's time for the culmination of all the work you have done in the previous part of this book: his and her nights of pleasure, when the partner promises to be totally present to please the beloved. It's delicious and ever so much fun—and yes, a little scary—but I'll guide you through the steps so that you're bound to have an amazing time and look forward to the next.

The goddess gets her turn first, consistent with ancient worship of the goddess and the Taoist tradition of the male "consort" as servant to his goddess, considering her satisfaction ahead of his own. In this chapter, I speak directly to the man as giver, but of course the woman will want to read closely to see what's in store for her as receiver. In the next chapter, she'll be the one orchestrating his night of pleasure. For now, men, it's your turn to please your goddess.

The Value of Taking Turns at Pleasure

Taking turns at pleasing and being pleased might sound programmed, but the technique has proven successful in many sex therapies. I've recommended it for years, as it is highly effective, particularly because so many women worry, "When is my turn up?" and "Have I taken too much time?" and because many men fret, "Have I performed well?" and "Have I really pleased her?" Taking turns is crucial in some tantric love-making practices to allow full focus on either giving or receiving without worrying about taking too much time, being selfish, or your partner getting tired.

Ecstasy Essentials

Of course, your pleasure time together does not have to be nighttime. It can be any time of day—morning, afternoon, or evening. Whatever suits your schedule!

Ultimately, when the energy of lovemaking is truly flowing, the partners are so intertwined that it's hard to distinguish who is giving and who is receiving. Body parts and souls merge into one and into universal consciousness. The receiver and giver blend into one.

Choose one night when she will be the total receiver and you will be the full-on giver, attending to her every need and delight. Choose another night when it is your turn to receive all of her undivided attention.

What Do Women Really Want?

What do women want? It's the question famed psychoanalyst Sigmund Freud asked, and that men have been asking for ages. When you're a tantric man, you really *know.* Even if you have doubts, you won't after studying this chapter, which shows you exactly how to please your woman. In short, women want care, attention, and love. The tantric man gives that.

How can you be sure this night is different from all other nights? Let's go over the five basic steps to prepare you to receive your beautiful goddess and then to please her.

Step 1: Set Your Intention

"Winging it" on a date can get some good results, but you're better off if you deliberately plan a good time. Write down your intention.

What I want to happen tonight:_____

_____

_____

Go back over your intention and be sure it has some encouraging, positive statements in it, such as "I want to make her feel good." Make your intention even more positive: "I want her to have the most memorable evening ever."

Step 2: Remind Yourself That This Is Her Night

This is one of the most fulfilling aspects of tantric practices. It means that you are totally devoted to your goddess on this night. It's not about your tension at the office, your aching back, and your aroused erection; in fact, clear your mind of those thoughts or worries. Notice how you feel (irritable, nervous, excited, confident) and your physical state (tired, energized) so that you can focus on your role—being there to please her.

Tantra Tutorial

Men who are used to concentrating on themselves have to remember that they'll have their turn on "his night," when he'll be the focus. This is described in Chapter 12.

Step 3: Be Prepared to Serve Your Goddess

For some men, this is the first time they have considered this concept: serving the woman, 100 percent. She will not bring you the newspaper, put your socks in the laundry, or lick your lingam. It's not easy to be totally selfless, but it's worth it to make this night work and to earn your own—and her—deepest appreciation.

Step 4: Face Your Fears

"What if I don't do it right?" "What will she expect of me?" "What if I can't take this much intensity of feeling?" "What if this means I have to be like this or even better next time and I can't live up to it?" These all are natural fears that you need to recognize and face now, so you can be clear of them as you go deeper in your loving connections and sexual pleasuring. Being clear now will allow you both to enjoy the evenings and look forward to more. In true tantric style, let fears

Dr. Judy's TantrAdvice

If you have a terrific night, don't worry about topping yourself next time. Something different and new will always come up that can take you to another place and possibility for deeper connection—whether it is challenging or pleasurable.

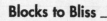

Blocks to Bliss _____

Some men might be thinking, "When do we get to the sex?" Hold on, that's why you're on this path: to relish all the delicious buildup, especially because that's what the goddess wants!

come up, feel any reactions (tight chest, weak knees), and breathe through them. They will pass and the anxiety will transmute into energy, which leads to being turned on. What a wonderful twist!

Step 5: Decide How You Will Call On Her

Notice I use the phrase "call on," a dating term from the 1930s, to purposefully evoke the gentleman style (as gentlemen "came calling"). It works well for this first night of pleasure.

Here are some ideas:

◆ Call her at work and tell her to meet you somewhere first. Pick a romantic spot, or someplace where you know she'll have fun (a concert, play).

◆ Arrange for her to do something that treats her first (like getting a manicure or a massage at a spa).

◆ Tell her to meet you at home (where you will already have prepared a love nest).

Fill out the following to help you prepare for her night of pleasure; then go over your list and picture doing the steps in your mind:

Preparing for Her Pleasure Night
Where you will first meet (for dinner, a show): _____
Where you will end up (in your bedroom, at a hotel): _____
How you will invite and entice her: _____
What you will say: _____
What you will wear: _____
How the room will be set up: _____

Boudoir Basics

Women are bound to be impressed with a man who has put some effort into preparations, especially in the house, making the setting look romantic. Here are some tips to set the stage for romance:

- Follow the instructions in Chapter 8 that discuss setting the stage for a tantric pleasure date.

- Turn both the bathroom and the bedroom into a sensuous seduction scene. Use scents (jasmine, rose, ylang-ylang), soft lighting (candles in purple shades to invoke female energy or blue shades to enhance size), and flowers (rose for female genitals; hibiscus for fulfillment).

- Choose the music you are going to play. It's usually a good idea to pick something sensuous and slow for this first evening (see the suggestions in Chapter 19).

- Set out sensuous food and drink to surprise her during your pleasuring (chocolate Kisses, fresh fruit slices, sparkling water).

Night of Pleasure 1: Promises to the Goddess in the Pleasure Palace

Greet her at the door dressed in your god attire (silk pajamas or silk shirt and slacks), freshly shaved and bathed. During the evening, use words of encouragement and endearment, and reaffirm your enthusiasm. For example, you might say …

- "This is *your* night."

- "I am totally here for you, at your service, devoted to your pleasure."

- "Take all the time you need."

- "Be sure to tell me exactly what you want."

- "I am enjoying tonight so much."

- "It gives me such pleasure to be able to give to you fully."

- "You don't have to do anything for me tonight."

Dr. Judy's TantrAdvice

Women need to be reminded that they can make requests and that their partner is enjoying the role of giver. Keep asking questions such as "What can I do to make you feel good tonight?"

Tantra Tales

In Charles and Caroline Muir's weekend workshops on Conscious Loving, his and her nights are central to the couple's pleasure. The sharing after their nights of giving is heartwarming and inspiring. Many men report delight in serving their goddess. One man said, "I was so proud to make her so happy"; another said, "I never knew it could feel so good to give."

Relaxing Her

Everyone needs to be relaxed before sex; in tantric practice, every step of the way is sacred. Remember that tantric lovemaking is about moving energy through the breath and being present in the body and in the moment. Here are several ways to help her relax to achieve these goals:

♦ Invite her to express her feelings. Encourage her to say whatever is on her mind. She will be ecstatic at that suggestion alone! Invite her to vent about whatever might be bothering her from her day to clear her mind so you can concentrate fully on the good feelings between you. Venting feelings inevitably leads to a release, which produces warm feelings toward the person who witnessed the purge.

♦ Bathe her. Prepare a bath with scented bath oils. Pay particular attention to washing her feet, an ancient tradition that shows respect and service. Bathing also is meant for purification.

♦ Give her a massage. When her mind is at peace, she is more ready to be touched. Ask permission to massage her. Don't worry that you are not a professional masseur, or that you don't know anything about proper techniques. This is about a gift of love through your loving touch; as long as your hands communicate love, the techniques are not important. When giving her a massage, keep these techniques in mind:

  ♦ Always use a *nondemand touch*, which means you are not expecting your touch to lead to intercourse. Touch just for her pleasure of being touched and your pleasure in touching.

  ♦ Never take your hands off the body when you massage; always maintain some physical contact to keep her feeling safe and secure.

  ♦ Focus your attention on your touching, without allowing your mind to get distracted into worries, fears, or plans.

  ♦ Be confident about what you are doing. Don't fret that you are not touching her right; ask for feedback right away so you are reassured that she is pleased.

  ♦ Close your eyes, connect with your feelings, and tune in to her; let your fingers do what you feel her body is asking for.

  ♦ Encourage emotions and be prepared for their release. Giver her permission to make sounds and move in any way that feels comfortable.

  ♦ Pay attention to often-neglected sensuous areas such as the palm, side of the little finger, and base of the spine.

- ◆ Ask her what parts she would like you to pay specific attention to and linger on those parts.

- ◆ Send your love through your hands and all parts of you.

- ◆ Move her energy by focusing your attention to where you feel she needs it (to her heart to be more open, to the power center around the midsection to empower her, to her base chakra at the base of her spine for more security and grounding).

Tantra Tutorial

Prepare your hands as instruments of love. Breathe fully and let out a sound, rub your hands together to warm them up, let energy flow from your heart to your hands, and let your fingers flow along any curves they find.

As I've emphasized, using a loving touch is all that matters in massage, but getting some training in technique can add something extra. Buy books or videos on erotic and tantric massage or take a couples' massage course together.

Massaging the goddess.

Tantra Tales

When Jose and Cecelia came to see me for therapy, they had barely made love since their 3-year-old was born, but just a few sessions of tantric love coaching revived their passion. Jose prepared her night, shopping carefully for a massage oil with a smell he liked, buying roses and spreading the petals around the bed, and stashing away the baby's toys. Then Jose bathed Cecelia, lay her on the bed, and licked her toes. "I fell in love with him again," she said in the next therapy session. "He was exactly what I've ever dreamed."

Night of Pleasure 2: Getting Closer

When something is pleasurable, why not repeat it? On a successive night that you identify as her night, you can repeat the previous steps. Add something extra as a surprise, such as a small gift, new massage stroke, different music, or new outfit that you wear. With each date, you can get more intense about pleasuring her sex center and her sacred space. Remember to do the following:

◆ Hold your hand on her sex center (yoni) and ask permission to enter her sacred space.

◆ If you and your goddess are comfortable with it, use flowery words to label this area ("your love cave," "your flower garden," "your secret love space").

◆ Do the *Double Love Blast*. I use this term because he sends and she receives love from both her sex and heart centers—just what women want: sex with love! Send your love through your hand and into her "sacred cave" (one of the tantric terms for vagina), and through your breath into her heart.

◆ Ask to examine her body all over. Be enthusiastic ("I'm enjoying this") and complimentary ("You look so beautiful").

◆ Use different strokes to touch her sexual area inside and out.

◆ Keep looking in her eyes and encouraging her to look at you. Breathe together to harmonize your energies.

Sending love energy from her sex center and his heart into her heart.

◆ Add oral pleasure. A woman who has gotten over her shame or embarrassment about her genitals can experience tremendous excitement from your lips and mouth on her genitalia. She will feel truly adored and pleased. Be sure to tell her how much you enjoy doing this. Include "polishing the pearl" (a tantric term for oral stimulation of the clitoris) and exploring her sacred cave. Ask her what kind of stimulation she likes.

Sending pleasure by polishing her pearl and pleasing her sacred space while sending energy into her heart center for total love connection.

The tantra man who can bring a woman to heights of oral pleasure is rightfully pleased with himself. As one man told me, "I'm even happier knowing I can please her than when I get satisfied first. Women think we're all selfish, but we're not!"

♦ Before one of her nights, encourage her to pleasure herself; then, on one of your dates, ask her to show you what she does so you know exactly how to please her. It's likely she will concentrate on her clitoris, using motions you should study carefully so that you can repeat them. Reassure her how much men enjoy watching a woman do this.

Ecstasy Essentials

Learn everything you can about the clitoris, as it is an important trigger for a woman's pleasure. Read *The Clitoral Truth* by Rebecca Chalker (Seven Stories Press, 2000) to ease into the conversation about exploring exactly where this pleasure button is, how far it extends into a woman's body, and how it becomes erect (like a lingam) when excited.

The Resolution Phase

In tantric sex, the resolution phase, or cool-down period, is meant to continue the intimacy. Keep in mind that women usually need more of a cooling-down period after intense lovemaking than men do. Of course, you both could be tired and want to sleep; this is fine. But she might want to spend some time dwelling in the moments of pleasure, talking about how she feels or about what happened, and certainly would want you to be awake enough to listen and share. Be sensitive to her needs on these special nights, and resist the desire to fall asleep. (Over time, you can better coordinate your timing in this phase, because you will have learned to control your ejaculation and both of you will be able to continue cycling your energy.)

Some tips to accomplish this phase in ongoing delight:

♦ Assume the spoons position, in which one of you nestles into the chest of the other, so you are essentially back to front.

♦ Continue the synchronized breath so you are breathing in and out at the same time, staying in tune.

♦ Lightly tap on each other's energy center at the base of the spine—not enough to generate a great deal of energy, as you both want to relax now, but enough to keep you both awake and drinking in the delights of your experience.

Night of Pleasure 3: When Love and Love Liquid Flow

Honoring the goddess takes on a special meaning on the night that she is ready to allow you to explore her sacred space freely. Always start with giving her a loving massage and repeat the steps in the instructions for the first two nights. Ask permission to pleasure her and to enter her sacred space. Using your finger, enter her yoni gently, guided by her response. Use your middle finger to make a "come hither" motion to stimulate the sacred space on the front wall of the vagina, one third of the way up (commonly called the G spot, but actually an area, also called the goddess space and sacred sector). The tissue might become a little rougher to the feel and expand, yielding more lubrication. If she responds with pleasure, you can become more vigorous. As her excitement mounts, call out encouragement and quicken your motion.

Always wait for her invitation. Do not enter her until she invites you to do so by words or actions. Then enter slowly, feeling each exquisite sensation. Move to her rhythm. Keep reminding her to breathe. Keep reassuring her that you are enjoying yourself, that she has all the time she needs, and that you appreciate her.

Remember to avoid having expectations about how she will respond. Some men feel challenged to "make" a woman's love liquid flow (have a female ejaculation). Take the pressure off her, just as you don't want any pressure to perform! Although any woman can ejaculate, not all do, partly because the sensation immediately before often feels like the urge to urinate, which confuses women and makes them stop what they are

doing. It's also not as easy as men's ejaculation, because women (except those practiced in this art!) take longer to get exited and have more conflicted feelings about
their sexual expression and letting go in orgasm. Additionally, women really do have
more emotional prerequisites than men for letting go in orgasm.

*How to pleasure the
goddess space.*

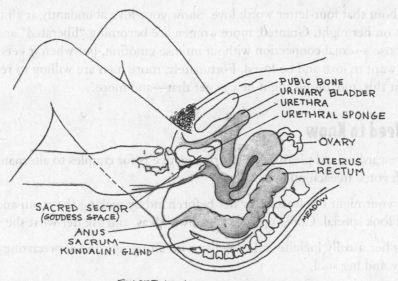

PUBIC BONE
URINARY BLADDER
URETHRA
URETHRAL SPONGE
OVARY
UTERUS
RECTUM
MEADOW
SACRED SECTOR
(GODDESS SPACE)
ANUS
SACRUM
KUNDALINI GLAND

FINGER IN YONI ON SACRED SECTOR

Tantra Tutorial

Some sex therapists are skeptical about female ejaculate. However, researchers
such as Gary Schubach prove the earlier, now-famous research of Whipple and Perry
about the existence of the G spot (see DoctorG.com). The G Spot, or Skene's Glands,
urethral sponge, or urethral glands, is, in fact, the female prostate that completely surrounds the urethra, just as with the male. The nerve pathways are through the pelvic
nerve, rather than the pudental with the clitoris. Schubach's studies of female emission
from stimulation of the area show it is a mixture of fluid from urethral glands and ducts
and the bladder (although definitely not urine). The fluid seeps from the urethral sponge
tissue surrounding the urethra and exits the body from the urethral opening.

The One Thing Women Need Most

In all my work with couples over the years and teaching women to have orgasm, the
one thing women mention as being most important to them is trust. A woman needs
to be able to trust that you care about her and that you love her. Obviously it would

be best if you really do love her—and then profess your love openly, honestly, and passionately.

The One Thing Women Want Most

Yes, it's still about that four-letter word: love. Show your love abundantly at all times, but especially on her night. Granted, more women are becoming "liberated" and even willing to choose a sexual connection without intense emotion, but when it gets down to it, women want to love and be loved. Fortunately, more men are willing to reveal that they want this, too; on his night he can get that—and more.

The Least You Need to Know

- A very rewarding and pleasurable tantric practice is for couples to alternate nights devoted to each other.

- Prepare your night of pleasure for her beforehand by making the room and yourself look special. Come up with your own ideas, and ask her what she wants.

- Pleasing her usually includes relaxing her with a massage and appreciating both her body and her soul.

- Always start by harmonizing your energies and connecting at the heart level before you progress to more sexual actions. A solid foundation of trust, loving, and sharing will open her—and you—to pleasure.

- As you progress in pleasuring her sexually and more intimately, ask her permission and continue to send your love energy into her heart.

- Include oral pleasuring and pleasuring her sacred space, encouraging her to allow the fullest extent of expression, including the possibility of a female ejaculation.

Chapter 12

Giving Him the Best Nights Ever

In This Chapter

+ Setting up many nights of pleasure for him

+ How to help him surrender to pleasure

+ What to do on the second and third nights—and beyond

+ What to say and which specific pleasure techniques to use

+ Moving energy to his heart to create more love

+ Lingam strokes to send him into bliss

She had her night in the previous chapter; now it's his turn! In this chapter, I'll guide you through several nights of pleasure for him. Of course, you can use the exercises in this book to inspire you to design your own night of pleasure. I encourage you to use your imagination—after all, tantra is about you expressing your inner self! Although I speak directly to the woman in this chapter because she is the giver, the man will want to read about the delights in store for him as receiver. (Even though you both did this exercise for "her night," there will still be surprises for him.)

Remember, you are goddess to his god; Shakti to his Shiva. You are the embodiment of all eternal beauty of women, the source of all nourishment, the essential other half to complete his path to bliss. He is the embodiment of all that is eternal strength in man, the source of light, an essential completion of your being on your path to bliss. He is Zeus to your Hera, Lancelot to your Guenevere, Romeo to your Juliet (just the passion, not tragedy, please!).

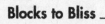

> **Blocks to Bliss** _____
>
> Of course you might be nervous during this evening, doing something new and worrying about getting it right. Don't be! In time you will become more comfortable. It's only important that you are devoted to adding a new dimension to your lovemaking and intimacy.

Night 1: Taking Your Man into Tantric Bliss

The first evening of pleasing your man will be only the beginning of many nights of pleasure. Keep in mind that this night is different from the other nights you have spent together. This night will incorporate the specific tantric rituals you have been learning in this book, including your preparation and what to do during the actual time between you.

Preparing Him for Pleasure

Decide on some surprises for your man, such as where you will meet and how he will get there. Make it original and special. Call him and tell him where to be. For example, tell him to meet you at a restaurant that you know has a romantic atmosphere. Be yourself, or be mysterious and pretend to be a secret admirer. Dress in a way that you know will excite him.

Gather the items you'll need for his night of pleasure so you are prepared (see Chapter 8). This includes music, sacraments (wine, special drinks, or foods), and clothing. Prepare the pleasure den as much as possible beforehand by arranging the furniture, adjusting the lighting, placing candles in the bathroom, and making any other preparations.

> **Tantra Tutorial** _____
>
> Same-sex partners should read this chapter with the references to the woman as the giver and the man as the receiver.

Fill out the following list—just as he did for your night of pleasure in the previous chapter—to prepare for his pleasure night. Go over your list, and picture doing the steps in your mind.

Preparing for His Tantric Night

Where you will first meet (for dinner, a show): _____

Where you will end up (in your bedroom, at a hotel): _____

How you will invite and entice him: _____

What you will say: _____

What you will wear: _____

How the room will be set up: _____

 Tantra Tales _____

Although Patrice and Hank lived in New York for years, they had never taken a horse-drawn carriage ride through Central Park, one of the tourist attractions and a romantic experience. For his pleasure night, Patrice called Hank at the end of his work day and said, "I'm waiting outside for you; come downstairs." When he arrived on the street, Patrice was in the horse-drawn carriage, waiting to whisk him away. As they cuddled under the blanket in the cool air, Patrice promised him the evening was for him—and tantalized him with hints about the tantric pleasures that she had prepared for him.

Leading Him to the Tantric Love Temple

After you've been out on the town, or whatever place your god enjoys, you are ready to go back to the tantric love temple to begin the rituals of pleasure. Your tantric love temple is whatever place you have decided you can have private time to enjoy your tantric love ritual. Of course, you need to spend some time and energy on the preparations.

 Dr. Judy's TantrAdvice _____

If you will be spending the evening at his house or another place, prepare your *goddess bag:* a traveling bag with your goddess clothes and all the accoutrements you will need for his night, including special music, candles, and foods, and of course, safe sex precautions.

Preparing Him for His Night of Love

When your man is in your sacred space, the next stage of your pleasuring begins.

Step 1: Put Him at Ease

Make him comfortable by seating him in a soft reclining chair or laying him on a couch while you go prepare his bath and yourself. Put on music he enjoys to ease his mind; then dress in your goddess clothes. It is always a good idea to dress separately to create surprise when you see each other, just as a bride and groom dress separately before their wedding. Come out in your goddess clothes and pose before him, allowing him to appreciate your beauty.

You can also ask him to prepare himself in his clothes while you wait. Do this even if you will be disrobing him either for his bath or for lovemaking. His dress-up makes him feel the evening is special and delights you when you see him.

Step 2: Bathe Him

As I've pointed out earlier, bathing is an important part of the tantric love ritual. Escort your Shiva god into the bath with your most seductive smile. Tilt your head, expose a thigh, drop a strap off your shoulder. Undress him, admiring every part of his body.

Proceed with the bath:

♦ Suggest that he shave and then watch as he does—or do it for him, if he agrees (carefully, of course!).

♦ Wash each part of his body, including his feet and hair (if he agrees); this is especially erotic.

♦ Tantalize him by washing other parts before you get to his genitals. Run soapy hands up and around his lingam and scrotum area, over the cheeks of his buttocks, and gently around his first chakra (anal area).

♦ Make appreciative remarks about his body parts as you are bathing them.

♦ When you're done, wrap him in a soft towel or bathrobe and walk him into the bedroom or other room designated as your love temple.

Step 3: Enter the Love Temple

Lay him down on the bed, mat, or whatever you decide will be your love nest. Give him a few minutes to relax in the space and get comfortable.

Step 4: Promise Him Pleasure

Tell him a few exciting promises about how the evening will go. Although men are not always verbal—often responding to just action—tantric lovemaking stimulates all the senses, which includes offering verbal statements about your love, what you want to do, and reassurances. Men also often like to be in control, so giving him some cues about what is happening and what will happen will probably make him feel more relaxed. Say just enough to put him at ease but not too much; that would be a distraction or engage his mind. The idea of tantric sex is to feel in the body and quiet the mind.

Use the following four R's as guidelines:

◆ **Reassure him.** Assure him that he does not have to perform or do anything to please you. Say, "You don't have to do anything to please me. I'm here totally to please you tonight" or "This night is totally for you." As the pleasuring progresses, add statements such as "You don't have to have an erection or get excited, just enjoy the feelings in your body."

◆ **Relax him.** Say, "I'm going to massage you to relax you, and you just have to lay there and enjoy the sensations. You can tell me what you would particularly like."

◆ **Relieve him.** Constantly tell him that you are enjoying what you are doing, so he doesn't worry.

◆ **Reward him.** Men (just as women) love to be acknowledged, so tell him how delighted you are with him as a person. Compliment who he is, and tell him what you particularly like about his body.

Now that he feels relaxed and appreciated, you can begin more physical pleasuring.

 Tantra Tales

Michelle noticed that her husband was less enthusiastic about their sex life after only 2 years of being together. She admitted that she had grown more inhibited, spending less time touching him and only allowing intercourse without giving him the oral pleasure he once enjoyed so much. Learning tantric sex practices turned all this around. Michelle committed herself to becoming a better lover, offering to massage her husband all over, experimenting with new ways of pleasing him, following her instincts, and sensing what he would enjoy.

The Tantric Shiva Massage: A Time to Surrender

A massage should always be part of a pleasure night. Nothing is more relaxing or makes a partner feel more open emotionally. Spend at least half an hour doing this. Here are the key steps and points to remember about giving your Shiva a tantrically superlative massage:

◆ Begin by laying him comfortably on his front side on a flat but padded surface. Run your hands smoothly over his body, then rest them along the top of his spine and the base of his spine (this connecting the entire spine). What do you feel? Is he warm or cold in one of those spots? Cooler places might need more of your love energy to warm them up.

Dr. Judy's TantrAdvice

Be aware that as your man lies on his back (in a traditionally "female" receiving position), he might feel vulnerable. Reassure him that these feelings are natural, and expect him to resist. When Kelman protested with all kinds of excuses ("I'm tired," "That's enough"), I coached Joelly to insist they continue. As she rubbed his stomach, he began to cry, feeling never before so open or so loved.

◆ Warm his skin with lots of oil. Use your body as much as your hands, rubbing your breasts against him from his mouth down his belly. Tell him, "You feel so good." Rub his back and legs and turn him over to pleasure his chest.

◆ Keep looking into his eyes and encourage him to make sounds of pleasure.

◆ Open his heart. Run your hands from his sex center (lingam) to his heart, transmuting his sexual arousal energy into loving feelings. This is what you want from him—and what he wants for himself! Send your love through your hands. Always be conscious and respectful that you are moving energy in the massage, bringing his energy from his sex center up into his heart.

Using massage to draw his sex energy into his heart.

Languishing Over His Lingam

After you have massaged his entire body, you are ready to begin concentrating on his lingam. Most men delight in being touched there. After a body massage, he might be so excited when you touch his lingam that he feels the urge to ejaculate. In that case, use the stop-start technique (see Chapter 13) and transmute the energy, so he gets a chance to dwell in the pleasure of this part of the massage.

At this point, reassurance is very important; reassure him he doesn't need to get an erection, only to lay back and enjoy it. There are more than three dozen strokes you can choose from. All the massage strokes that are relevant to the body massage can be applied to the lingam massage. Keep in mind the different degrees of pressure, firmness of your touch, and different touches: from smooth strokes to light, feathery touches and from presses and squeezes to light scratches.

When pleasuring his lingam, tune in to his energy and the degree of touch he wants at any particular moment. Vary your touches to surprise him and heighten the stimulation. Remember that in tantric lovemaking you are not trying to turn him on, get him hard, or make him come; you are playing with and moving his energy. Be attentive, respectful, and aware of the power of this massage act as part of your union.

Consider these lingam love strokes:

- Start by delicately feathering the lingam by lightly brushing your fingers up the shaft and around the tip.

- Do a traditional up-and-down motion, gripping the lingam fairly firmly (ask him what pressure feels good for him).

- Move your hand up and down the lingam with your fingers working their way up in a motion like a spider's legs.

- Work your hand up and down the lingam, pulsing your hand as you move it up a notch.

- Hold your hands with palms stretched out, press the lingam between your hands, and twist the lingam inside your hands as you move your hands up from base to tip as if kneading dough. This stroke is called *rolling thunder*.

- Grip his lingam with one hand at the base—this helps him keep his erection. With your other hand, start at the base

Dr. Judy's TantrAdvice

Many men want women to be more assertive in how they caress their lingam. Ask what degree of firmness he likes. Shift from more yin (light, gentle) touches to more yang (strong, firm) ones, and vice versa.

and run your hand up the shaft and over the top of his lingam, stopping to caress the head in a circular motion, and then run your hand down the shaft again.

♦ Hold the lingam between your hands and gently "toss" it from one hand to another.

Loving the lingam with rolling thunder along the shaft.

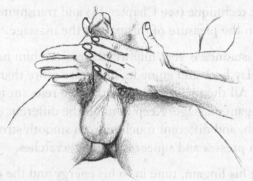

The Second Pleasure Night

Repeat all the steps you've learned so far, but add some variation. Wear a different goddess outfit. Put on different music (see Chapter 19 or Appendix C for some ideas). Make love in a different room or place, or decorate the room and bed differently.

A Variation on Massage

For his second night, repeat the strokes and techniques he liked in the last massage you gave him, then surprise him with new approaches or touches. Some more advanced massage techniques include the following:

Dr. Judy's TantrAdvice

Always remind him to breathe. When he gets excited, he might hold his breath (just as women tend to do). This holding can be helpful only if it is done in the context of a tantric breathing practice in which he is consciously moving his breath to move his energy. Encourage him to make sounds as a way to ensure that he continues breathing.

♦ Don't just use your fingers; use your palms, heels of your hands, your breasts, even your feet.

♦ Insert his lingam between your breasts and press your breasts lightly together. Move them up and down and side to side.

♦ Brush your hair lightly against his body parts.

♦ Use longer strokes that start at the top or bottom of his body and end at his lingam, then trace back to the extremities.

Include More Lingam Strokes When Pleasuring

Here are some advanced strokes to try for pleasuring your partner. Use lotion on both hands to make the movements glide more smoothly and the sensations more pleasurable. Some lotions become too sticky or will irritate the penis, so experiment with different kinds. Vaseline will feel good for him; just be sure not to insert the lingam in the yoni unless this is wiped off because it is not healthy for the chemistry of the vagina.

- **Corkscrew.** Hold the lingam firmly at the base while the other hand slides from the base to the tip with a twisting motion. Change hands and continue the motion. Ask him how tight a grip he likes you to use and how vigorously he would like you to rotate your hands.

- **Heady trip.** Hold the base of the lingam firmly as you caress the tip by making circles. Alternate this caress with pulling the head up and twisting it gently.

- **Polishing the helmet.** Move one hand up and down the shaft as you cradle the head in the center of the palm of your other hand, and move that hand in a circular motion.

- **Palming the crown.** Hold the shaft firmly with one hand and rotate the tip with the palm of the other. Move your hands so they change position.

- **The lingam mudras.** Press two fingers lightly on two different parts of the lingam, scrotum, *perineum* (the space between the scrotum and anus), and anal opening. This runs powerful energy through his pleasure spots.

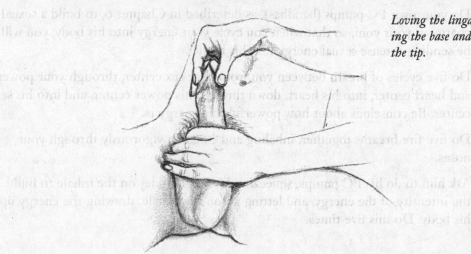

Loving the lingam by holding the base and caressing the tip.

Pleasing His God Spots

In popular jargon the woman has the infamous G spot—the spot inside the vagina that is supersensitive. Similarly, the man has sensitive G spots, hot spots, or *god areas*. On night two, focus on his two external hot spots:

♦ The frenulum, which is the knoblike protrusion on the underside of the penis where the tip meets the shaft.

♦ The perineum, located between the testicles and the anal opening.

On night three, you can get to his internal god area. This can be done only when he is more relaxed and prepared to get more intimate, because this type of stimulation will raise many more feelings in him, possibly even resistance and fear. (For more details, see Chapter 18.)

Building His Sexual Charge

To drive your man wild in tantric sex, build a sexual charge starting in his sex center (lingam) and then assist him in sending this energy throughout his body. The techniques to do this have been described in earlier chapters in this book, but to review them, follow these steps:

♦ Sit together in yab yum position, or whatever position feels comfortable for you. Do the synchronizing breath for five breaths and then the alternating breath for five breaths (as described in Chapter 2) to get yourselves in tune.

♦ Do your own PC pumps (bandhas), as described in Chapter 6, to build a sexual charge in your yoni, so that when you cycle your energy into his body, you will be sending intense sexual energy into his body.

♦ Do five cycles of breath between you from your sex center, through your power and heart center, into his heart, down through his power center, and into his sex center. Be conscious about how powerful this energy is.

♦ Do five fire breaths together, inhaling and exhaling vigorously through your noses.

♦ Ask him to do his PC pumps, squeezing his PC muscles on the inhale to build the intensity of the energy, and letting go on the exhale, drawing the energy up his body. Do this five times.

The Secret to Moving His Energy

As you are pleasuring him, concentrate on directing his energy to connect the sexual charge from his genital area to other body parts, particularly his heart (to create more love). Choose which part of him you feel needs energy or you want to energize. For example, if you feel he needs to be more sensitive at that moment, you can help move his energy to his heart center. If you feel he needs to express something at that time, you can move his sexual energy to his throat center.

While stimulating his lingam with your right hand, move your left hand up the center of his body to his other energy centers. Send your breath into his lingam through your right hand, and trace the breath with your imagination as it goes up his body into the chakra you have chosen, then out your left hand and into your body again. Exhale as you send the energy into his body, and inhale as you draw it into your body to be recharged, creating a cycle. With these chakra connects, you can actually move the energy up by sweeping your hands up his body. Adjust your own position from sitting between his legs to sitting at his left (receiving) side, so you can reach his energy centers easily.

◆ Move your hand to his power center, and gently hold your hand there. Keep your other hand on his lingam. Encourage him to feel any feelings he might have, including any sensations of power.

◆ Move your hand to his throat center, and gently hold your hand there. Keep your other hand on his lingam. Encourage him to feel any feelings that he might have, including his ability to communicate and say what he wants.

◆ Move your hand to his brow center (third eye), and gently hold your hand there. Keep your other hand on his lingam. Encourage him to feel any feelings he might have or see any visions that might come.

◆ Move your hand to the top of his head, and gently hold your hand there. Keep your other hand on his lingam. Encourage him to have any feelings or sensations.

Be aware that as you touch these places on his body, he might feel flashes, bolts of light, or electricity. This is because you are acting as a conductor of powerful energy, facilitating its travel from one place to the other. Experiment with different touches, and ask him what he likes.

The Third Night of Pleasure

On each successive night of pleasure for him, repeat some of the previous techniques. While you are pleasing his lingam, don't forget other areas of pleasure:

- Stroke his inner thighs.

- Stretch his legs apart and squeeze the muscles that connect the thigh with the genital area (the ones that seem to pop out when you stretch his legs). This feels exceptionally good.

- Start at his belly button and "walk" your fingers down his body into his pubic area, pressing his sensitive god spot located in the perineal area (as described earlier in this chapter). Repeat the same steps in reverse.

- Pay attention to his testicles (be gentle!) as well as the lingam.

Entering His Sacred Space

In advanced steps, you're ready to enter his sacred space—the anal opening that most men panic over. They usually have never been touched there or fear the homosexuality they believe it implies. When he seems extremely relaxed, ask him, "May I enter you?" Remember, always ask permission!

If he says no, go back to doing something he was enjoying. If he wants you to continue, rest your finger at his opening. Encourage him to breathe, allowing whatever feelings come up. Cover the area and your finger with lots of oil. Hold your finger steady, and let him push against you, showing his readiness. Entering slowly, he can tense his anal muscles and release them against your finger. Remember to go very slowly. Rest your finger inside in a still fashion, and allow him to guide the degree, speed, and depth with which you stimulate him.

Exploring and Exciting His God Spot

After he is more comfortable with being entered in his sacred space, read his signals about when to be more vigorous and experimental with how you please him there.

- Add manual pleasure with your other hand to his lingam and scrotal area while you are pleasing his sacred space.

- Add oral pleasure to his lingam and scrotal area while you are pleasing his sacred space.

◆ Move the energy with your other hand to his other energy centers as described previously for night two.

◆ Let your fingers explore his sacred space by varying the depth and type of touch. Let your fingers sweep inside his sacred space, imagining a clock inside and sweeping from 10 o'clock to 2 o'clock.

◆ Press your palm against his perineum (external G spot) and anal opening to add pleasure. Use your other hand to stroke his lingam up and down. With the tip of your thumb, gently and rhythmically stroke the frenulum, the sensitive underside at the tip.

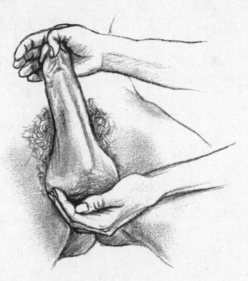

One hand pressing one of the male G spots for pleasure with the other hand cradling the scrotum; between the base of the scrotum and the anal opening is the perineum, another male G spot.

As you do these advanced stimulation techniques, remember to transmute the energy, always drawing it up to his higher energy centers. Lightly "hum" into an area, or blow warm breath onto it. The warmth of your breath and your love will surely warm his heart—in addition to making him excited all over.

The Least You Need to Know

◆ On his nights of pleasure, let him know that you are totally his servant; you are there to please him, and he does not have to do anything in return.

◆ Prepare yourself (what you will wear, say, do) and your space for lovemaking, then be spontaneous and create new delights.

- Build the types of stimulation in several steps so that he is able to receive pleasure comfortably and without fears or anxiety.

- Build his sexual energy by pleasuring his lingam and then direct that energy to other energy centers, particularly his heart, to build more love between you.

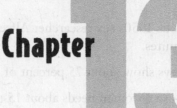

Chapter 13

Make Lovemaking Last ...
and Last ... and Last

In This Chapter

- How tantric sex makes men—and sex—last longer
- Testing your reaction to quickie sex
- Myths and facts about lasting longer
- Pros and cons of delaying ejaculation
- Sexual Kung Fu and other secrets of delaying ejaculation
- What the partner can do to help the man last longer

Yes, men can make love for hours, once they know what to do; this chapter will tell you how. Best of all, it doesn't have to be difficult for him, and ends up being a real pleasure for both of you.

How Long Is He Supposed to Last?

Several dimensions have been used to determine how soon is too soon for a man to reach his peak, or how long he should last before ejaculating. Consider the following:

◆ Famous 1950s sex researcher Alfred Kinsey thought "too soon" was lasting only 2 minutes.

◆ Surveys show about 75 percent of men last between 4 and 7 minutes.

◆ Because a woman needs about 15 minutes to reach an excitement level that takes a man only 3 minutes to reach, he would need to delay himself five times the male average.

◆ The timing is based on the man's ability to control his excitement level, not an actual amount of time.

◆ Is the man (or his partner) upset about his performance? Is his partner satisfied at least half the time? If the answers to these questions are no and yes, respectively, there's no reason to worry.

Here's the tantric take on how long a man should last: both the man and his partner should be satisfied—and they will be, when he learns control. How long you last is not as important as channeling energy between you in a mutually satisfying way. But if you want to last longer, you can—and there are more joys in store for you if you do so. Acquiring the skills found in this chapter will boost your self-esteem sky high and delight your partner—and you can choose to come whenever you please!

Tantra Tutorial

Traditional Taoist belief demands semen retention, claiming that spilling sperm other than for having children weakens the man's health and even provokes anger toward women. Releases are allowed once every three days in spring, twice a month in summer and autumn, not at all in winter, and only 5,000 in a lifetime. But please don't let that you scare you—many modern tantra teachers don't agree!

When It's All Over Too Fast

It's a complaint so many women have, as one woman appearing with me on TV said, "An egg takes 3 minutes, why does my husband?" She was referring to the disappointment women feel when the sex act lasts only about 3 minutes. When the man reaches orgasm so quickly and the woman is left unsatisfied, it has an effect on both partners that can be hurtful to the relationship.

Her Reaction to Three-Minute Sex

Remember that women have a different natural sexual response cycle than men—she needs more time to get to the same level of pleasure. Women are also stereotypically more emotional about sex—they want lovemaking to last longer because they want the intimacy, communication, and closeness, both in foreplay and afterplay (concepts not necessarily consistent with tantric sex, because all of lovemaking is the main act!). If the buildup and cool down are both cut short, as it is when the man reaches his peak in 3 minutes and then withdraws and falls asleep, the woman can have many reactions that are not healthy for her or the relationship.

The following list will help you evaluate your reactions to the length of time spent lovemaking. Pick what best describes how you feel by putting a checkmark next to that item; then think of another possible way you can react and write it under the "Instead, I Can Feel This Way" column heading. The idea is for you to have an alternative way of reacting. Read over your reactions and what you have written as new affirmations.

Her Reaction to How Long Lovemaking Lasts

I Feel ...	Yes	Instead, I Can Feel This Way
Frustrated, unfulfilled, resentful.	❏	_____
Angry toward my partner.	❏	_____
Disinterested and withdrawn from sex.	❏	_____
Responsible (like I don't turn him on).	❏	_____
Less confident.	❏	_____
Abandoned and unloved.	❏	_____
I'm too fat.	❏	_____
I'm not attractive.	❏	_____
Worried that he's having an affair.	❏	_____
He's selfish.	❏	_____
Other: _____		

His Reaction to Three-Minute Sex

Some men and their partners are okay with a short sexual experience. Some women don't like sex much and are relieved to get it over with. This sadly cuts off her potential for pleasure and reveals deeper problems that likely stem from childhood or earlier sexual experiences. However, if you know your partner wants to make love last longer and you're willing to find out how to do this, be reassured that this is possible. Changes in a relationship happen most effectively when both people are motivated.

Even if men defend, rationalize, or joke about "quickies," they are often unhappy about not lasting longer. They might have fears, inhibitions, and past hurts that get in the way. (I'll talk more about those and how to help heal them in Chapter 18.) The man who comes too quickly wonders to himself, "What's wrong with me?" He feels cheated out of a better experience, just as his partner does. Worse yet, he feels out of control, as his body seems to take over, leading him quickly from excitement to ejaculation.

Now it's the man's turn to fill out the following checklist, this time focusing on *his* reactions to the length of time spent lovemaking. Pick what best describes how you feel by putting a checkmark next to that item; then think of another possible way you can react and fill it under the "Instead, I Can Feel This Way" column.

His Reactions to Lovemaking Timing

I Feel ...	Yes	Instead, I Can Feel This Way
I'm a bad lover.	❑	_____
Selfish.	❑	_____
Disgusted with myself.	❑	_____
Frustrated and angry.	❑	_____
Depressed.	❑	_____
Anxious my partner will lose interest in me.	❑	_____
I'm to blame.	❑	_____
My partner is to blame.	❑	_____
I don't want to think about it.	❑	_____
Withdrawn from sex.	❑	_____

Other: _____

Compare what each of you said in your lists. Talk with your partner about your answers to better understand those reactions. Review what you both wrote in the column about how you could react more positively.

Why Men Come So Fast

You can't always blame him for being a "3-minute man." Men essentially train themselves to respond quickly. This stems from childhood, when a young man learns to masturbate quickly, so he won't get caught by someone walking in on him in the bathroom or his bedroom. If he was looking at sexy magazines or an X-rated video in the family VCR, he's even more in a rush—so his "naughty" act won't be discovered. This get-done-quick routine perpetuates even our computer age, when he could get caught checking out sexy websites.

Another reason men peak fast—faster than women—is that they *can*. Messages in the male brain go quickly to the sexual organs, and sperm is released quickly with the contractions of the muscle. After these behavior patterns are established, the man has to be motivated to do the practices that will help him last longer. It takes effort and a change in beliefs. These include overcoming myths such as the following:

- **Controlling ejaculation is not possible.** Wrong. It is possible!

- **Holding back ejaculation is dangerous.** Wrong. You won't explode or "blow a gasket."

- **If he lasts a long time, he won't be able to repeat the good performance.** Wrong. Of course he will!

- **It's not pleasurable for the man to hold back.** Wrong. The answer to "Can I still have pleasure?" is a resounding "Yes!"

No Expectations, Please!

Expectations are the absolute ruination of a man's ability to enjoy sex. If the man thinks he has to last long, his body will be sure to sabotage him and he will ejaculate quickly. Emotionally he will also cut himself off from the pleasure, out of pressure and resentment about how he is supposed to behave. Men typically expect that they have to get it up quick and keep it up. The more a man expects he has to have an erection, the harder it will be to have one; the more he thinks he has to last forever, the quicker he will come.

Dr. Judy's TantrAdvice

There is a place in tantric sex for a "quickie," as long as the couple stays conscious of what they are doing. Have a quickie if you have no more time before work, or get the urge before a dinner engagement, as long as you both feel connected and honored.

Tantra Tales _____

Mick found one night of pleasure so fulfilling, he shocked himself by admitting "I didn't even have to ejaculate at all!" It happened when he was performing oral sex on Noreen and she was sending energy down her body and out her clitoris. The energy was so strong, he felt it shoot throughout his body. He wondered, "How can I feel as good without ejaculating as I feel when I do ejaculate?" He described to Noreen, "I felt bolts of electricity going through my head." Without realizing it, Mick was receiving Noreen's energy and allowing the energy to cycle through him and go into his crown chakra (the reason he felt the bolts in his head). The experience was so powerful, he did not need to ejaculate!

Ejaculation and Orgasm Are Different

The relationship between ejaculation and orgasm is crucial to how long a man lasts. Read the following two statements, and decide whether you think they are true or false:

◆ A man can ejaculate without experiencing an orgasm.

◆ A man can have an orgasm without ejaculating.

Both are true. Understanding that ejaculation and orgasm are two separate functions is crucial to the delight of tantric sex. A man can delay ejaculation or not ejaculate at all but still achieve orgasm—and not just one orgasm, but many. Men can have multiple orgasms, just like women. To understand this, one has to understand the physiology of the man's body.

The mechanism of ejaculation, like an erection reflex, is triggered from the spinal cord (the sympathetic nervous system). The penis responds to stimulation by sending a message to the lumbar portion of the spinal cord (the ejaculatory center) through the nerves. This triggers contractions of muscles in the internal genital organs. Although it all sounds so automatic, the timing of the process can actually be controlled consciously.

The Stages of the Male Sexual Response Cycle

The traditional model of the male sexual response is composed of four stages:

◆ Excitement (increase in muscle tension and sex flush)

◆ Plateau (vasocongestion, pronounced muscle tension, increased respiration)

- Orgasm (reduced muscle control, increased heart rate, involuntary pelvic thrusting)

- Resolution (reduced muscle tension within 5 minutes, loss of vasocongestion, heart rate and blood pressure return to normal)

Other theories have added concepts such as desire, but none has taken energy into account. In my model, the initial stage is one of attraction in which energy is being stimulated. With continued interaction, the sensations build and are felt in various parts of the body and mind. Tension rises in response to the energy. The energy mounts and surges through the body, causing more general physical and emotional alert. Using the tantric transmutations properly (using breath to direct the energy) causes an overall sensation of both relaxation and excitement. In the next cycle, energy can go to either higher or lower levels, depending on how the person and partner play with the energy. The resolution phase is less abrupt than in traditional models, as the energy can be moved into many surges.

Traditional Control Tactics

Traditional ways to help a man overcome premature ejaculation have included the following techniques:

- **Stop-start.** This technique was popularized by the famous sex research team of Masters and Johnson decades ago and is still effective. The man stimulates himself to the point where he feels he will ejaculate and then stops. When he feels more in control, he starts stimulation again.

- **Squeeze.** When he feels the urge to ejaculate, he applies pressure on the lingam where the shaft connects to the head, placing his thumb on the top and forefinger and middle finger on the underside on either side of the sensitive bump (the frenulum). When the urge subsides, he resumes stimulation.

- **The testicle tug.** At the point of no return the man pulls his testicles down—gently— to inhibit ejaculation. This method is tricky and potentially dangerous (don't pull too hard!), so try the others first, please.

> **Blocks to Bliss**
>
> Some critics charge that continual high pressure on the perineum can damage nerves and blood vessels crucial to sexual functioning, and warn that *injaculation* (causing the semen to flow back into the bladder) can force bacteria into the bladder, causing an infection.

The man can do these techniques on his own, or his partner can help. It's best if he learns on his own what works best for him and then teaches his partner, giving precise cues (sounds or movements) about what to do.

Ecstasy Essentials

One traditional technique to find the point of no return is the ladder, in which during masturbation the man pays attention to his level of excitement as if going up and down steps on a ladder, to pinpoint which step comes close to ejaculation (as if on a split screen in his mind). He imagines climbing a ladder, looking ahead, and not falling off the top. While he (or his partner) does whatever is stimulating, he switches his attention from the sensation to another part of his body and asks, "Where am I now on the ladder?" When he is close to the top, he stops stimulating until he goes back a few steps to the bottom of the ladder, where he waits until he is calmer and then starts again.

Certain aids to delay ejaculation that are not compatible with tantric practices (which requires being tuned in to every sensation) include lotions that desensitize sensations in the lingam, devices to trap blood in the penis, or purposefully distracting thoughts (like of baseball scores or other nonsensual subjects).

"Sealing the Penis," or Sexual Kung Fu

The spot located halfway between the anal opening and the base of the scrotum—called the *in between spot* or "million-dollar spot"—can be pressed to inhibit the flow of semen out of the penis. Look for its location on the perineum as shown in the diagram of the man's body in Chapter 6. To find it, feel for a slight indentation where your finger seems to press into a softer area, and press this spot at the moment when you feel the sensation that you are about to ejaculate. Putting two fingers behind your index finger (for more support) is called the *finger lock*. Variations of this practice are called *sealing the penis*, or *sexual Kung Fu*.

Tantric Sex Versus Other Methods of Prolonging Lovemaking

Of course, you can delay ejaculation through these traditional sex therapy methods—sex therapists have been teaching certain ejaculation delay methods for years, since

Masters and Johnson popularized them decades ago. The stop-start and squeeze techniques are effective; however, they can be even *more* effective when you add techniques of tantric sexuality while carrying them out. The secret is encouraging the man to focus on, direct, and channel his sexual energy.

Conscious awareness of sexual energy when performing any of the traditional methods of ejaculatory control is important in tantric practice and makes the man and his partner more attuned to his body's needs and responses. In tantric practice, techniques for ejaculatory control include breathing exercises and other specific actions, which I'll describe a little later in this chapter.

The following table summarizes the several differences between traditional sex therapy techniques for premature ejaculation and tantric sex techniques.

Traditional Sex Therapy Versus Tantric Sex

	Traditional Sex Therapy	**Tantric Sex**
Technique	Uses mind control, such as identifying grades of excitement and imagining steps on a ladder to measure excitement level.	Insists on awareness of energy and directing energy.
Recommended positions	Advises the man not to be on top, but rather the woman be on top, so he can relax.	The man can be on top to move energy more freely; preferred position is yab yum with female in male's lap.
Communicating with the partner	He gives her feedback.	Their energetic connetion helps her sense where he is in the sexual response cycle.
Measuring success rates	Squeeze or stop-start training is 90 percent effective within 10 weeks.	Considers measurement contrary to the experience of energy.

There are also similarities between traditional sex therapy techniques and tantric sex techniques. Both ...

♦ Emphasize relaxation.

♦ Focus on enjoying sensations in all parts of the body (called *sensate focus* in traditional sex therapy).

♦ Recommend practices for the limp lingam, such as *stuffing* in traditional sex therapy (the woman inserts the flaccid penis in her vaginal opening and tightens her muscles to hold it there). This is similar to second chakra connecting or *kareeza*, in which the man is inside the woman feeling their energy co-mingling but unconcerned with how erect he is, because energy can be transmitted regardless of the erection.

Dr. Judy's TantrAdvice

The more a man thrusts vigorously, the more likely he is to feel the urge to come. A good solution: while keeping the lingam in the yoni, sit up in yab yum and breathe together. The change in position will quiet down the energy but still keep it flowing.

The Transmutation Breath

This is the tantric variation of the stop-start—which is a lot more fun! As soon as the man feels the urge to ejaculate, he draws up the energy from his lingam through his spine, up his chakras, flooding his heart. He can do this on his own, or with a partner. Vary the circuits: she can move her hand from his lingam to his heart, sweeping the energy up to his heart, or she can charge it with her own sexual energy by holding one hand on her yoni and sweeping the other hand from his lingam into his heart and then into her yoni and out again, in a continuous cycle.

Moving his own energy from his lingam to his heart.

As soon as either partner feels the man is at the "point of no return," the partner can say, "Breathe, my beloved," "Let's breathe together," or "Imagine my love going into your lingam and your heart and your love coming out to me."

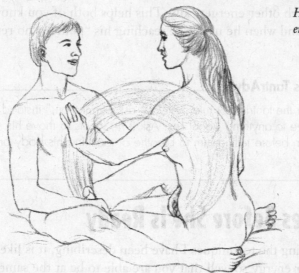

Helping him move sexual energy to his heart.

Tips on How the Partner Can Help

It can be threatening for a man to ask his partner to help him control his ejaculation, but a partner can be very helpful. Here's what you both can do:

♦ Teach her about how ejaculation and male orgasm work, and what it feels like for men in general and specifically for him.

♦ Spend time together "playing doctor" and examining his body. Get over any embarrassment or shame about how you look or what you want. Let her get close. Sit on the bed and shine a light so you can both see.

♦ Show how you respond. Yes, that means pleasuring yourself in front of your partner. Allow feelings to emerge—whether excitement or embarrassment— and consider sharing aloud to help process and clear them.

♦ Give your partner cues and feedback in movements and sounds, even if you thinks she already knows. Needs can change over time, so don't make your partner guess.

♦ The partner should be enthusiastic about the man's discoveries, encouraging him that control is possible, and being appreciative of his courage in revealing himself.

♦ Be careful not to pressure him to come or not to come. Always be sensitive to his needs and where his energy is. Never criticize if he ejaculates, even before you (the partner) have not reached your peak.

◆ Stay with each other energetically. This helps both of you know the level of his excitement and when he might be reaching his "point of no return."

Dr. Judy's TantrAdvice _____

Remember the tantric sex rule, "Always ask permission," instead of assuming that men would agree to anything about sex. Ask if he wants to move his sexual energy or delay ejaculation before telling him to breathe or touching his body on places that aid such delay.

If He Ejaculates Before She Is Ready

If you are practicing the techniques I have been describing, it is likely that you will be harmonizing your energy so well that you are able to be at the same point at the same time often. This makes it more likely that you will reach that experience that many couples want—simultaneous orgasm. However, don't despair if there are times when you are out of tune in your energies, or if he ejaculates before the partner is ready.

If that happens, avoid all the traps you filled out in the checklists earlier in this chapter, such as criticizing, feeling like a failure, or doubting if you are right for each other. Remember that there is always another time for lovemaking, and that not each experience is going to be the ultimate—even though you are attempting these new techniques. If things don't go exactly as you wished or planned, rely on another principle of tantric sex: whatever happens at that time is right to happen; just respect where the energy goes.

The Least You Need to Know

◆ A man's ejaculation is a physical act that is separate from the emotional experience of orgasm—a distinction that makes it possible for men to delay ejaculation but still have pleasure.

◆ Delaying ejaculation is a matter of choice; techniques in tantric sex practice can lead to extended periods and greater intensity of pleasure.

◆ A man can use several methods to delay ejaculation or teach his partner to help; he can last as long as he wants and ejaculate when he wants.

◆ Being sensitive to your energy, and purposefully directing it within yourself or cycling it through your partner, is one of the most exciting and satisfying ways to make lovemaking last as long as you want.

14

A New View of Love, Sex, and Orgasm: The Big TTO

In This Chapter

- ◆ Approaching love, sex, and orgasm in a new way
- ◆ New patterns of sexual arousal
- ◆ New orgasms possible through tantric sex, including the TTO
- ◆ Uncovering secret places of excitement
- ◆ Connecting sound to movement to raise sexual energy

I've been talking about tantric sex throughout this book, but notice the emphasis is always on sex energy to empower love. This is a new view of love. Tantra also requires a new view of sex. Sex is no longer simply an act, nor is it a performance; instead, it is a spiritual transformation. Consistent with this, the *tantric transformation orgasm* (*TTO*) is even better than that "Big O" you've been striving for.

In this chapter, you'll learn about the different kinds of cosmic experiences, including orgasm, that you can have in tantric sex. You'll also learn some exercises to spark your desire and move toward those higher states.

As if I weren't already challenging you to shift your perspective about relationships, here's yet another step I invite you to take: a new view of sex and orgasm.

What's Love Got to Do with It?

The answer is, everything! In my many lectures about sex to diverse groups, even when discussing the latest techniques or the hottest new trends, I always mention that the underlying message is really about how the sex act itself generates love—for yourself, your partner, and even the world.

> **Tantra Tutorial**
>
> Tantric sex energy is harnessed into a force for love. Women have always bemoaned using sex to get love; ironically, tantric sex energy is an adaptation on that theme: sexual energy is used to inspire, create, and expand love.

Although this book is about tantric sex, it really is about harnessing sexual energy to empower your love for yourself and everything around you. Consider yourself as the beloved—reflected in everything. Tantra teachers Charles Muir and his wife Caroline express this concept perfectly as *conscious love* (the title of their popular workshops and book, *Tantra: The Art of Conscious Loving;* see Appendix B). This means making love with keen awareness about what you are doing—and learning to honor each other as beloveds. Tantric sex allows an expanded view of what sex is, the nature of the sexual response cycles, and what's possible in orgasm.

A New View of Orgasm and the Sexual Response Cycle

I remember the early days of sex therapy (only a quarter of a century ago!) when sex experts argued that there were two types of female orgasm: the clitoral and the vaginal, originating from stimulation of those two parts of the women's genitalia. Over time, professionals came to recognize a third type, called *blended,* because although a woman's orgasm is triggered by stimulation of the clitoris, the sensation can also be extended into deeper internal areas or can start deeper and spread to other genital areas.

Traditional views of orgasm for men were even more limited: the one quick release. More modern views revealed that the processes of ejaculation and orgasm in men are in fact separate, as I described in the previous chapter. Orgasm for men is the psychological experience of pleasure, much like for women; ejaculation is the release of sperm. This opens many possibilities of sexual response and pleasure for men. The practices of tantric sex reveal even more thrills for both sexes.

Over time, we are increasingly aware that there are more types of orgasms, based on the locations, timing, and intensity of the experience. This is true for men as well as women.

Not only are there many types of orgasm, but I have postulated that there are two directions of expression of the energy: *outward* and *inward*. Both are powerful, can lead to states of bliss, and can be expressed alone or with a partner. They are different in that …

♦ The outward orgasm can be wild and uninhibited, as you let out emotions or scream and move vigorously.

♦ The inward orgasm can be quiet and subtle; however, it can release as much energy and reveal as much feeling as a more active response. Thoughts are powerful enough to trigger these responses. Imagine inhaling a ball of energy from your sexual organs, up through your body, and back down again. You can experience quiet inward orgasms as explosions that take place subtly.

Dr. Judy's TantrAdvice

Remember that everyone is individual in his or her intensity and variety and self-expression. Appreciate your individuality and allow responses to emerge from all parts of your body.

Traditional views of sex also posed four progressive cycles: excitement, plateau, orgasm, and resolution. However, the results of tantric practice come to a different conclusion: one can fluctuate within these stages and stay in these stages for extended periods of time. In fact, the sky's the limit as far as how high you can go.

Notice the three couples in the following figure. The couple on the bottom line is building sexual energy gradually. The middle couple is generating more sexual energy and building more quickly. The couple on the top is having strong spurts of sexual energy and then resting (or rather *nesting*, as you see the birds in the figure doing!).

The figures are based on tantric practices of couples in lovemaking that are described later in this chapter. By transmuting their sexual energy during their lovemaking, at different intervals and times they blast off or come down to earth, as they want—together!

Most couples think they have to keep at it to increase the intensity of their arousal. You can add more charge by relaxing into a "sexual quiet place" and then doing a fire breath (quick nostril breathing in and out) for even more intense buildup. I recommend alternating your energy in these ways—the process sustains arousal and also brings you to higher states of pleasure, multiple orgasms, and an expanded sense of well-being so that you can control your sexuality and yourself!

Couples riding different tantric waves to bliss.

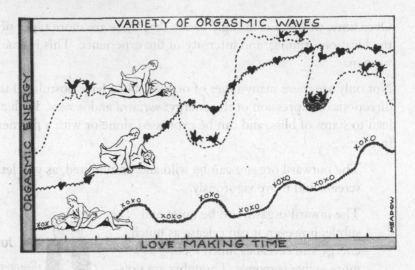

I am always asked about how to have the best orgasms (and have spent years teaching women how to do this). Here's a look at the different kinds of wonderful orgasmic experiences that are possible with tantric sex.

The Cosmorgasm

The *cosmorgasm* is the orgasm that extends out into the universe, or the cosmos. It happens when you alone or the two of you build your energy within yourself and then—when you are fully charged and grounded—extend your energy out the top of your head, through your crown chakra, into the air and sky above.

Blocks to Bliss

Whenever you send energy out your crown chakra for cosmic orgasms connecting beyond your physical body, you have to be sure you are not "throwing it away" or "losing yourself." You must cycle the energy fully and ground it first within yourself.

The Mega-Orgasm

The *mega-orgasm*, like the Energizer Bunny, keeps going and going and going. It continues in an upward direction, increasing in excitement, with small valleys where you linger in the good feeling, and then spurting to even higher levels of excitement and pleasure. Follow the birds in the previous figure to see how the couple on the top line are having a mega-orgasm; they keep going upward for a long time, taking a few rests.

The Clearing Orgasm

The *clearing orgasm* is unleashed from a big release of emotions rather than direct sexual contact—and can be just as powerful. This big release of tension can clear out stuck emotions. Because of this, the release can sound painful, with screams and wails. These reactions might frighten a partner (and will be described more in Chapter 18), but such releases should be welcomed as a sign of freeing the soul, body, and mind. After such an orgasm, you can feel spent, exhausted, and drained; however, the experience is worth it because of the pleasure it brings—and the pleasure it frees you to experience.

Ecstasy Essentials

Hollywood's classic portrayal of a woman's orgasm was Meg Ryan's noisy imitation in the movie *When Harry Met Sally*. My favorite is the scene in the film *Cocoon*, in which Tawhnee Welch (playing an alien) transmits powerful orgasmic energy across a pool to Steve Gutenberg.

Reaching Multiple and Simultaneous Orgasms

The secret to multiple orgasms lies in controlling the level of your excitement through your breath and cycling your sexual energy. This is similar to what I described in the previous chapter on how men can control their release to make lovemaking last longer. When you get to one of your peaks, you both can do a transmutation breath (drawing the energy up from your genitals) at the same time. Remind each other by saying it aloud, "Let's breathe now!" Do this twice and even three times, building your excitement.

Tantra Tutorial

According to ancient Eastern tradition, the male is expected to bring the woman to nine levels of orgasm. Progressively, the woman sighs and breathes heavily, offers tongue kissing, grasps the man with her muscles, has vaginal secretions and spasms, feels the urge to bite, undulates like a snake, grabs the man furtively, desires to bite more vigorously, surrenders, and collapses. Modern views and some tantra teachers point out that the biting response is not necessary and might occur in cases in which women have more unresolved aggression.

The Tantric Wave

The *tantric orgasm* is an undulation that is shaped like a wave. The body flows like a dolphin moves through water, in smooth motions up and down in natural curves that keep coming and coming.

The tantric wave of bliss.

The Stock Market Orgasm

Banking on a quippy analogy of the sexual response cycle and cycles in the stock market (men's erections go down when the Dow dips!), California sexologist Ava Cadell created a new lovemaking system. It combines sexual techniques such as erotic talk, oral sex, G-spot stimulation, and intercourse (in various positions) for men; combined with sensual techniques such as synchronized breathing, body massage, love toys, and the "Venus Butterfly" for women. She calls it the *stock market orgasm* (also the title of her book, published by Peters Publishing, 1999) because there are seven peaks of sexual excitement and then seven dips of sensuality, maintaining a level of arousal for both partners.

Ecstasy Essentials

Valley orgasms do not refer to valley girls, but to continuous orgasms that extend through the time in between your peaks.

The profit that couples get from their investment is multiple orgasms for both people, after he learns how to separate his orgasm from ejaculation. Says Cadell, "The best lovers are those who are long-term investors rather than those who are addicted to quickies."

How to Have the Big TTO

The Big TTO—tantric transformative orgasm—comes from cycling sexual energy, using all the exercises I've told you about up to now (and more to come in later chapters). Since the time I developed this technique, I have taught it to many men and women, with great results. The process includes the ways to amp up or damp down your energy (as described in Chapter 7), breathing patterns (as in Chapter 2), and many other techniques I teach you in this book, including ways to play and have fun (because I think loving should be about fun!). All these help you respond freely and connect with love and a beloved.

Taking Sex Drive to a New Level

A pervasive problem for couples today is complaints about sex drive; this ceases to be a problem when you follow the tantric path. It's all about building peaks of sexual excitement, but not leaving it there. When you got the energy going, the practices invite you to move it. This process is called *transmuting* the sexual energy (a process I refer to often in this book and one I teach extensively in workshops because it is especially effective in connecting love energy to sex).

The following exercises show you how to do that. You can do any of these exercises by yourself or with a partner. When you do them with a partner, it's a good idea to face each other, sitting knee to knee or in the more intimate classic yab yum position, with one of you in the other's lap.

The Shiva Shakti Mudra

One of my favorite exercises is called the *Shiva Shakti mudra*. It connects energy from the earth and sky, bringing it inward to the heart area, then directing it outward to a partner or to the world. You can also add words to the exercise.

Here's how it's done. Stand with your feet shoulder width apart and knees slightly bent. Take several deep breaths. On the inhale, sweep your arms up from the earth, scooping up energy from mother earth, and bring the energy into your heart area. Feel the warmth, security, and love of earth energy going in to your heart. Exhale. Inhale again, this time reaching up to the sky and gathering energy from father sky. Sweep your arms down, crossing your hands over each other as you pass your face and into your heart area. Feel the energy of enlightenment and vision going into your heart. This exercise is called Shiva Shakti mudra because it connects the mother earth/female Shakti energy with the father sky/male Shiva energy. It's a good exercise to do when you are tired, to give you more energy in general.

Variations on the Shiva Shakti Mudra

To do this with a partner, stand facing each other. After bringing the energy into your heart as described in the previous exercise, exhale and extend your arms and hands out toward each other. On the next round, the two of you can extend your arms and hands out to your sides, sending your collected love energy out to others or to the world in general.

The Shiva Shakti mudra: bringing strength and vision into your love, getting help from the earth and sky.

Make up your own dedication and say words about your blessings while doing this exercise. For example, say, "I bring all the love of mother earth up into my heart and send it out to you, my beloved, and I bring down from the sky all the inspiration and vision and vastness of the universal love and send it into you, my beloved." When extending your arms out sideways, you can make a dedication, "I send all collected love energy out to the world, to heal all those who are suffering or who are not as fortunate to feel the love we have, so that they may share in our bliss."

Connecting the Sexual Energy to Other Energy Centers

Here are some exercises to send sexual energy to other parts of the body to empower through breath, sound, and movements.

Using Movements to Send Sexual Energy

Put on music with a powerful drumbeat, and sway your hips to the music. Start with side-to-side movements, then forward and backward, and then circular motions.

Using Sound to Transmute Sexual Energy

Remember that all sounds are associated with different energy centers, or chakras. You can send your pooled sexual energy to different energy centers by chanting the sound of the sexual center and then connecting it to the sound of any of the other chakras. In the following exercise, breathe in through your nose; on the exhale, open your mouth and let the sound come out. Allow the breath to pool in your belly and then exhale like a bellows to get the maximum energy from the sound.

◆ **The ooo-ahhh exercise: Opening the heart.** This is another favorite exercise, both to do and to teach. "Ahhh" is the sound of the heart center. Connecting the sex and heart center is one of the primary techniques of tantra. Use it to prepare yourselves for lovemaking. Build the energy in the sex center, and feel it bolting through your body as you thrust your pelvis forward, saying "ooo" (sounding like the "ou" in the word *you* but with a more rounded mouth). On the inhale, arch your back as you say "ahhh." Your chest will thrust forward; the action itself opens your heart center. In addition, the "ahhh" sound opens your heart. Do this repeatedly; after a while, as the flow of these two sounds and the movements build, they will take you on their own ride, without any effort on your part.

> **Tantra Tutorial**
>
> The ooo-ahhh exercise is particularly important for men, who often separate sex and love. Chanting these two sounds brings sexual energy up to the heart center, making a man more open to feeling his love energy and more able to create an emotional connection with his partner. It is magical how doing this exercise can open—and melt—a man's heart.

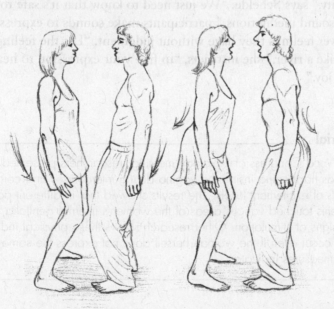

The ooo-ahhh exercise.

◆ **The ooo-ehhh exercise: Freeing the throat.** Do this exercise the same way you would the previous one, but use the sounds "ooo-ehhh." Sending sex energy to the throat chakra is also a major part of tantric sex so you can express yourself freely. Too many women—and men, too—are inhibited about speaking up at all; particularly about making sounds during sex. I have heard so many men complain that women lie too quietly during sex and how they wish women would "talk dirty" (use raunchy words), which many women consider unrefined or demeaning. Free expression during an erotic encounter is essential for ecstatic freedom of sex.

Dr. Judy's TantrAdvice

The sex and throat centers are closely connected; once you open the throat to make noises in sex, you'll be surprised how much more responsive you are sexually. I'll say more about this in Chapter 19.

◆ **The ooo-uhhh exercise: Grounding more security.** Do this exercise the same way you would the ooo-ahhh exercise, but use the words "ooo-uhhh." Move energy generated by pelvic thrusts from your sex center into your base chakra or anal area. As you emit the sound "uhhh," feel yourself getting more and more rooted into the ground like a tree. This grounding stops distracting thoughts and worries that invariably intrude in your intimate interaction.

Sound healer Karin Schelde teaches workshops on freeing up the voice. "Every sound and every part of the body has a vibrational energy that has tremendous healing capacity," says Schelde. "We just need to know that it's safe to be heard." In Schelde's "sound meditations," participants make sounds to express and release whatever feelings they have without judgment. "Let the feelings flow through you like a river," she instructs, "to free your expression to heal but also to experience joy."

Tantra Tutorial

At a recent World Congress of Sexology meeting, researchers presented photographs of what was happening inside the vagina during intercourse, and corresponding measurements of excitement levels. The results showed that in different positions in intercourse, the penis touched various areas of the women's internal genitalia, all of which registered signs of stimulation. Other research shows these physical indications of excitement can occur even if the woman herself does not express the same level of excitement as the measures indicate.

Where Do You Feel the Big O? Alphabet Orgasms

More modern views of orgasm have expanded not only the types of orgasm, but also the places that those delicious sensations occur. Many letters of the alphabet are used as shortcuts for the names of the spots on the body in which these responses occur.

The G Spot

Sex researchers now know what was called the *G-spot* is actually the female prostate gland, which surrounds the urethra, just as in the case of the male prostate. It can be accessed internally at the area on the front wall of the vagina, one third of the way up where the tissue feels more corrugated than the surrounding smooth tissue, or (less easily) externally by pressing deep behind the pubic bone. Its stimulation makes some women at first feel discomfort (numbness, pain, the urge to urinate); others feel intense pleasure and can even release female ejaculate.

> **Blocks to Bliss**
>
> Some women find that stimulating the cervical area is painful, especially during their menstrual and hormonal cycles.

The X Spot

This spot is deep in the vagina around the cervix. Although it does not have many nerves, stimulation can tug on the internal walls and cause radiating sensations. Taoist views of orgasm propose that the tip of the penis and the cervical area both correspond to the heart, explaining why stimulation of this area would be pleasurable to the woman. It can be stimulated manually by inserting several fingers and encircling the cervix at the end of the vaginal canal.

> **Tantra Tutorial**
>
> Names for the female prostate include **sacred spot, G-spot, g-space, peri-urethral glands, urethral sponge,** and **Skene's glands**. Information on the female prostate is posted on www.DoctorG.com by Dr. Gary Schubach, who has done extensive research on this subject.

The AFE Zone

The *anterior fornix erogenous (AFE) zone* is the area from the back of the vaginal canal downward about two thirds to the opening. As with other areas, some women find stroking this pleasurable; others do not.

The PFZ Zone

The *posterior fornix zone* (PFZ) is similar to that described in the previous section, but on the opposite wall.

The Anywhere-in-Your-Body Orgasm

This is probably the best news of all: by practicing tantric sex, every cell in the body can be orgasmic. The orgasm does not just happen in the genitals; you can send it anywhere in the body and make it accessible within seconds.

 Tantra Tales

After learning tantric sex, Nancy found, "I can have an orgasm in my wrist! The energy just explodes wherever Michael touches me. It's like my body is on fire. I can send breath anywhere in my body, and make those cells come alive, and then as soon as he touches me there, it's like a light goes on and he feels the fire, too."

The Least You Need to Know

- Practicing tantric sex requires a new view of sex in which sex is a transmission of energy within oneself or between two beloveds.

- Orgasm, like sex in general, can be a new type of experience through tantric practice, in which energy that is pooled in the sex center is sent, through the breath, to other parts of the body.

- There are many places on the body and inside the woman's genitalia that can be experienced as orgasmic.

- Through tantric practices, any couple can achieve high states of sexual ecstasy in addition to a mixture of physical, emotional, and spiritual bliss. Connecting sound to movements helps direct energy and heightens sensation.

15

Getting Fit Together for Tantric Sex

In This Chapter

- ◆ How exercising together can pump love muscles
- ◆ A yoga routine to do together
- ◆ Workouts that also work your sex energy
- ◆ How emotional issues are worked through during workouts

I told you about the important role that being physically fit plays in pleasurable sex in Chapter 6. Your body is your temple of love, and now you're ready to share it with your partner.

Review the steps in Chapter 6 and do them with your partner. Then you're ready for this chapter, where you'll learn more physical routines and movements you can do together to honor your body temples—and to have some fun!

The Importance of Physical Activity Together

Research proves exercise is an aphrodisiac. In one national survey, 8 out of 10 exercisers credited their workouts with boosting self-confidence, 4 in 10 felt more sexual arousal, and 3 in 10 made love more often. Physical activity is energizing (important for sex), forces you to focus on the body (heightening sensual awareness), builds strength and endurance (for sexual positions and staying power), and releases pleasure chemicals in the brain.

Working out with your lover has immediate payoffs. Your adrenaline is already pumping, and you're already feeling better about yourself. Chemicals will flow in your body, such as the love chemical endorphin and the cuddle chemical oxytocin, prepping you for pleasure in love and sex.

The Love Muscle Exercises for the Man and the Woman

It is important to contract and exercise your pelvic muscles on your own, but you can also do this together. Sit facing each other, look deeply into each other's eyes, and breathe in and out rapidly through your nose (as in the fire breath described in Chapter 2).

Hold your breath and pulse your pelvic muscles 10 times. Relax the muscles and do the fire breath again. Repeat several times. Remember that you both have more than one set of pelvic muscles; one set is around your urethral opening and another set is around your anal opening. As you do this together, don't worry about technique until you get the hang of it; then you can inhale at the same time, hold your breath, and pulse your muscles in unison.

Pulsing PC muscles while you're breathing together does a lot to turn you on to each other. It synchronizes your energy more powerfully than just breathing together, and it sends supercharged sexual energy up your spine, which you then can cycle into each other. Deliberately knowing that you are doing this in the same moment makes you feel very connected, adding intimacy to your excitement.

Partner Pelvic Thrusts

Pelvic motions are the most powerful generator of sexual energy. I've already emphasized that they are important exercises to do on your own; now you're ready to do them with a partner. Put on music that gets your blood going. Stand side to side, or better yet, face each other. (Later you can let loose and move around any way you want.) You can start from a standing position, gradually thrusting at lower heights until you're thrusting while lying down on your back on the bed or floor (knees up); or start on the floor (knees up) and progress to a standing position. Follow your mood; ending up lying down can leave you in a good position for more intimate contact, while ending up standing could make you want to move around for more active play.

Just thrust your pelvis forward and backward. Sounds simple, doesn't it? But that might not be so easy, considering that for many of us, our pelvis is stiff! Stand with your feet shoulder width apart, your sacrum tucked in. Thrust forward and backward in a steady motion, picking up speed. The trick for the best effect is to keep your upper body straight and isolate your hips. Feel the energy surge through your body, and send it out to your partner. Use your hands to guide the energy out to your partner by making a sweeping motion into his or her pelvis and then up into the heart.

Ecstasy Essentials

Add sound to intensify your energy and excitement. In unison, say "ooo" as you thrust forward and "ahhh" as you arch back.

I Could Have Danced All Night

Dancing is a wonderful workout that exercises all kinds of muscles and frees your spirit in the process. It's a powerful way to activate your entire body and move sexual energy through your body—even to the point of sensing orgasmic highs for both men and women. That makes the activity a perfect warm-up for when you want to get more interactive. Use your motions together in dance to express your attraction and desire. I'll explain more about different kinds of dances you can do to express and experience your pleasure together in Chapter 16.

Pace your dance for your desired heart rate, doing slow, sensuous movements and building to faster, more free-flowing motions. Let yourself go into a frenzy, allowing your limbs to fly where they will.

An Eight-Step White Tantra Twosome Routine

White tantra refers to personal practices, including yoga poses, that connect to the chakras, or energy centers. Each time you make a pose, it is meant to stimulate one or several of the energy centers and the emotions or issues associated with those centers.

Follow along as I describe a wonderful tantric yoga routine for couples, and you'll see what I mean. This practice was designed by tantra teacher Carla Tara as a result of her practice with a beloved. It was so effective, she decided to include it in tantra classes she teaches around the country. "Most couples finish their day too exhausted from work or taking care of the kids to enjoy sex," says Carla, "but if they do these physical poses together, they can flood themselves with such a river of sexual energy that they won't even remember they were too tired for sex."

These twosome yoga poses benefit your relationship by ...

♦ Establishing deep trust because you depend on each other for the movements.

♦ Creating balance because you have to physically balance on each other and adjust to the other person's weight to get into and out of the poses.

♦ Requiring and reflecting genuine cooperation because you have to figure out how to get into and out of the poses together.

♦ Providing an example of how you communicate through your bodies, which is a metaphor for how well you can communicate emotionally.

Tantra Tutorial

Adjust every position to accommodate your sizes and ability; never strain. Remain in each position for as long as you want or as long as you feel comfortable.

♦ Giving you a chance to support each other in developing the physical strength and resolving any emotional issues associated with these chakras.

♦ Giving you a chance to laugh and have fun together!

The following sections describe the suggested poses, all demonstrated by Carla and a partner.

Couple Connect

Start your session by being fully present to one another. Sit facing each other and looking into each other's eyes. With knees bent, place your feet comfortably in front of you with his feet on the outside of hers. Encircle each other by stretching out your arms to hold on to your partner comfortably on the sides or under the shoulder. Inhale and exhale together to synchronize your energies. Do this for about seven breaths, or longer if you like.

Circling Couple Celebration

Stay on the floor opposite each other. Stretch your legs out as far as possible with your feet touching or overlapped at the ankles (as comfortable). Hold hands as one partner leans toward the other and the other leans backward. Reverse this.

Do alternating breaths (breathe in as your partner breathes out). Make circles moving to the left together, stretching your right sides, and then the opposite sides. Reverse directions. Make smaller and larger circles. Be spontaneous, guessing which way each of you wants to go, and have fun! Feel more looseness in your base and sex chakras, which will help you in sex.

Couple connect.

Circling couple celebration.

Squat-to-Stand Support

Help each other into a squat position, still grasping each other's wrists. Bounce gently, feeling your lower energy centers getting stimulated. Lift up to a standing position slowly, playing as you balance each other. Lower down and rise again, synchronizing your breath to inhale as you rise up and exhaling as you lower. (Be careful not to strain your knees while doing these movements.)

Squat-to-stand support.

Partner Pelvis Press

Stand close together facing each other, pressing against each other's pelvis for balance as you lean back and lift your arms toward the sky, looking upward. This opens your heart center, but because your pelvis is the seat of power, by pressing your pelvis together you are giving each other strength (from the pelvic energy center) to love. On the exhale, make noises, making the sound come from your pelvis, heart, and throat.

"If I lean too close to my partner, he could fall back, but if I don't lean back enough, he will fall on top of me," explains Carla. "Because we are responsible to not let each other fall, we have to balance male and female energy in the way required in tantric sex."

Dangling Duos

Bring your hands together from the pelvis press and step apart gradually, guiding each other to droop downward and hang like a tree (being careful to go slowly and lowering the spine one vertebrae at a time). Relax your neck and shoulders and allow your head to hang loosely.

Partner pelvis press.

Dangling duos.

The Couple Cobras

Lie fully extended on your stomach with your heads touching. With your hands under your shoulders, slowly lift your upper body, opening your heart to each other and stretching your head and neck upward and curving backward, opening the throat chakra. This will enable you to speak honestly to each other. Lower down and rise up again, inhaling and exhaling at the same pace.

Couple cobra.

Lovers' Table

This is a wonderful experience! One partner kneels on all fours, keeping his back straight and creating a table over which the partner can lean backward and drape her own body with outstretched arms, opening all chakras and feeling trust in the partner. Reverse places if your weight allows.

Lovers' table.

Couple Cuddle

This is the typical resting pose in yoga, but with one partner cradled over the other. Breathe together and feel the energy, connection, trust, and love. Change places.

Couple cuddle.

All these balance postures relate to relationship skills, explains Carla. Notice whether you have trouble with any of the poses (not just physically), which might indicate you are afraid to open your heart, speak up, or trust.

Bedroom Bodybuilding

As a yoga teacher and former professional athlete, Rundy Duphiney worked out every day until his constant cross-country trips from California to Ohio to see his beloved interrupted his fitness routine. He panicked until he realized that making love with his beloved was a workout in itself. Currently also a sex coach, Duphiney developed a sex workout routine to help himself and other men stay physically fit while also creating new highs with a lover. The routine works all the major muscle groups (even several at a time) to build stamina and strength essential for great sex. The exercises include these:

◆ Stand face to face in the shower or bedroom. Warm up by looking into each other's eyes while rolling your head from shoulder to shoulder, and stretching your upper body by leaning in one direction and the other.

◆ With your partner, rotate your arms and hips in synchrony while facing each other, as if looking in a mirror.

◆ When you're both feeling excited, she can turn her back and lean over as he guides her pelvis into and away from his body. This creates thrusting for her that works out her hips and develops strength in her thighs, and resistance for him to work out his stomach, arms, gluts, thighs, hips, and quads.

◆ In the partner push-up, he lies on his back, lifting his hips in the air, thereby working his lower back and abs while she leans over him, supporting herself with straight arms and hands on the bed, lowering and raising her body as if doing push-ups over him. This can also be done in reverse positions, with the man on top doing the push-ups over her.

Push-ups on your partner.

◆ With the man on his back, knees up, the woman squats on top, facing him. He lifts his upper body and grabs her buttocks from underneath, pulling her forward and backward on his wand of light. This has the effect of doing bicep curls, working his biceps, forearms, chest, and shoulders.

◆ Sit up in yab yum position. Grasp each other's wrists and with his lingam still inside her yoni, lean slowly backward together and pull each other up again to sitting position, creating a back pull for several repetitions.

The body stores a distinct memory of the movements, explains Duphiney. "So after you've done this love routine," he says, "I guarantee you'll never be able to work out in the gym again without picturing your partner in the same positions of pleasure.

Tantra Tales _____

Francisco and his girlfriend Nicole had already been doing the pelvic thrusts and partner push-ups before realizing their favorite sex positions doubled as fitness moves. "Thinking about how I'm getting in shape during sex makes me move my muscles more," explained Francisco. "So my body looks buffed and I act like a stud, making Nicole twice as turned on to me." Purposefully exercising during sex can benefit the woman equally. Nicole said, "Francisco and I always loved my legs high in the air and the push-up position, but thinking of them now as formal exercises is a double payoff, because we both need the bodywork. Now I know I'll also do better pelvic thrusts in Pilates class, thinking of his delighting lingam going in and out of me!"

Yogaboxing

"She's the most powerful and persistent woman I ever met," Joshua Smith told me about his then girlfriend, "so I could never say no to her. I'd give in until I got so mad that I wasn't speaking my mind that I'd escape to my own house, avoid sex with her, and think about having an affair." The handsome, outwardly confident 38-year-old fitness instructor is not unlike an increasingly number of men today who, although strong themselves, when faced with an "assertive" woman, can become intimidated and withdraw sexually and emotionally. Smith decided to strike out his feelings—at his punching bag. As he released his anger, he had a brilliant brainstorm. A long-time practitioner of martial arts, T'ai Chi, trance dance, aerobics, and yoga, Smith came up with a new workout now offered by Butterfly Workshops called *Yogaboxing*, a synthesis of yoga and boxing that clears anger and also brings sexual energy into the heart to renew love.

A highlight of the hour-long routine is a yes/no exercise, in which participants face each other and shout a series of commands that are refusals ("no," "get out," "hear me now") and then affirmations ("yes," "yes I can") while extending fists in martial arts motions. The steps sound like those taught in self-defense classes, but the routine can be as effective for intimate relationships as for attacks from strangers.

It worked for him. "After doing the exercise myself over and over," Smith explains, "I realized that rather than staying angry with a partner and sabotaging the relationship and sex life, I could give myself permission to refuse her requests, ask for what I needed, and expect her to honor that. For example, if she wanted to talk but I was not ready, I could say, 'I need some time to myself and after that I can listen to you.' The result is that I can feel better about myself and even more turned on and passionate toward her."

Ecstasy Essentials

A psychological and developmental benefit in Smith's Yogaboxing is called "setting your boundaries"—saying what you will or will not do—which proves to yourself and others that you are in control of your life. This overcomes childhood problems in which Smith and men like him have grown up sensing yet fearing the extent of their own power, and learning to express that power without fear of being destructive. The physical benefits involve the combination of gentler yoga movements with more vigorous boxing, which infuses the muscles with oxygen-rich cells, stimulates the endocrine glands, and aligns the neck and spine—all of which helps retard aging without putting undue stress on the body.

The workout starts with stretches that reach upward, as the group imagines reaching for their strength and stretching to speak up. Many exercises are done in pairs, to simulate confronting a real partner, such as the tug-of-war, in which each holds an end of a handkerchief, saying "yes" and "no" alternately. After each exercise, the partners share how they felt and whether they were able to act as strongly as they wanted. Who pulls the handkerchief harder? Whose voice is more convincing? The participants are invited to associate the exercise with experiences in their relationships in which they have disagreed about even small things, such as what movie to see or where to go to dinner.

The combination of movements and verbalizations, such as those in Yogaboxing, establish a powerful connection between your sense of power and your throat, allowing energy for self-expression to flow more easily to the sexual area. "After such a workout," Smith promises, "a guy can get really turned on because he knows he can speak up to a woman, so he feels safer being more vulnerable—the very combination of qualities that women really like."

Yogaboxing tug-of-war.

Next time you're mad as hell and won't go near your partner, grab a handkerchief and engage in a tug-of-war—then enjoy the spoils of good sex afterwards.

The Least You Need to Know

♦ Working out together activates more sexual energy between you, which sparks your attraction for each other and empowers your union for more pleasure.

♦ Yoga poses that you do on your own can be adapted to do with a partner.

♦ Facing your partner, you can do love muscle exercises, pelvic thrusts, dances, and more complicated white tantra routines.

♦ Exercises that might seem merely physical can actually have deep emotional components that trigger emotional issues and can deepen your relationship by creating opportunities to establish balance, trust, communication, and support.

Part 4

Going Deeper: Tantric Aids and Techniques for More Love and Better Sex

By now you've progressed beautifully on your path to loving passion and you're ready to add more advanced practices, experience more delight in giving and receiving love, and integrate this more deeply into expanding your consciousness. As you become better at moving your energy in new and exciting ways, love becomes more fulfilling and sex more magical.

In this part, it's time to really let go and explore your body, mind, and soul. You'll learn different kinds of erotic dances to entice your mate and discover new erogenous zones and positions. As you expand into exploring how to move your energy, stronger feelings can emerge, so I'll reveal some effective ways to heal any past sexual pain, releasing you to have more intense orgasms and greater overall bliss.

Making It Juicy with Magic and Play

In This Chapter

- The importance of play in good sex
- Dancing for each other
- How food can spark passion
- Toys, gifts, and games to please each other
- Making sex magic
- Tantric events that encourage joyful joinings

Are you having fun yet? Remember that tantric sex is built on a principle of pleasure. I am an absolute believer that you should enjoy loving—and your life! If something feels not quite right, please stop and change the energy so you are experiencing, and sharing, pleasure (unless you're purposefully using the experience to heal, as I discuss in Chapter 18).

All tantric workshops include time for play. One of the most enjoyable aspects for me in the workshops that I lead is creating new and exciting experiences for the participants. I love when the whole room is energized and having a good time! In this chapter, you'll learn some ideas for playtime that you can share with a partner. More important, let your spirit soar and come up with fun ideas that spontaneously occur to you. There are infinite ways to play together; part of the joy is to discover those ways.

The Spirit of Play

Remember being a child—with no fears or inhibitions about what to do to entertain and amuse yourself? Sadly, we develop many fears as we grow up, usually as a result of negative experiences, punishments, and messages telling us "don't do this" and "be careful about that." Tune in to the spirit of yourself as a child. What would you do on your own or with a partner? Give yourself the permission to be that sweet, trusting, uninhibited, playful, charming child.

How Much Juice Is There?

How juicy are you? "I feel the juice between us." "This experience is really juicy." When you say these words, can you feel the succulence? Referring to someone in tantra as "juicy" means that person is being uninhibited, expressing true sensuality, and allowing himself or herself to be turned on and excited. His or her energy is flowing in an excited, sensuous way. Women also are called juicy when they are lubricating, reflecting their excitement—and they're especially juicy when they have that female ejaculation, emitting a flow of love liquid (also called *amrita*).

Dr. Judy's TantrAdvice

Although being called juicy is a big compliment, as with other terms, be sure a woman or man likes being identified this way.

The Importance of Play in Sex

The value of play is endless, both physically and emotionally. Research has even shown that happier people have stronger immune systems and that couples in a happy union live longer than those who are not so content. It has even been proven that smiling lifts your spirits and that a cheerier mood leads to better physical health.

Affirmations About Joyful Sexual Union

When you consciously decide what you want, you are more likely to get it. Speaking out loud what you want, or writing it down on a piece of paper is even more helpful. Read the following affirmations aloud and breathe deeply while you say them, to fix them in your being. Imagine yourself in a sexual union while feeling these emotions and states:

+ I deserve to have joy in my sex life.

+ I enjoy every moment of pleasure.

+ I feel good about myself.

+ My beloved cheers me on in lovemaking.

+ I have fun in sex.

+ I give off an inner and outer glow.

+ I delight in myself and my beloved.

Notice that these affirmations are written in present tense so that they feel more real and create the sense of being "present" that is typical of tantra.

Ecstasy Essentials

One tantra practitioner tells a humorous (made-up) story that scientists have found that all problems can be solved by opening the clown chakra, located in the belly. All you have to do is intentionally give a big belly laugh and you are cleansed of your troubles and ready for joy with your partner!

Laugh Your Way to Better Health

It is well known that laughter improves the immune system and therefore makes you healthier. It also has infinite benefits from an emotional point of view. Laugh aloud now and see how it changes your mood. Laughter opens you to more love—the goal of tantra.

One of spiritual mystic Osho's favorite courses is "Mystic Rose," in which participants spend three hours a day for a week in a room laughing (at nothing in particular, just laughing). In fact, the experience becomes contagious, so that even if you don't feel initially like laughing, someone else's laughter inspires you to laugh, too.

In this exercise, face your partner and make eye contact. Clap at each other while chanting "Ho Ho Ha Ha Ha." Repeat until the laughter becomes more natural, then keep it up for a few minutes.

Dancing for Each Other

Dance is a revered part of the art of love according to ancient Indian texts on the subject. How right they were! Dancing moves strong surges of sexual energy within you and toward your partner. Let your body speak your love by taking turns dancing for each other. Dim the lights. Decide who will dance first and who will be the audience. The dancer gets to put on his or her favorite music—it could be a salsa, jazz, or even heavy metal. Dress for the occasion in an outfit that makes you feel sexy and that your partner will find sexy, too. Here's the challenge: you have to put aside your self-consciousness.

I promise if you just take a deep breath and start doing it, keeping your eyes on your partner's enjoyment of your display, your self-consciousness will go away. Let any fearful thoughts ("I look silly" or "I can't dance") come up and then drown them in your mind by concentrating on the music and looking into your partner's eyes. Feel the music in your body, and let your body move with it. Now switch, and let your partner choose the music and put on a sexy outfit to dance for you.

Dancing for each other.

Guys might need extra encouragement to do this, because usually they have convinced themselves they can't dance. Give him extra reassurance. Help him prepare before you do this practice by going out dancing; he should let her lead and copy her moves, getting close and grinding his groin to her rhythm.

California relationship coach Francesca Gentille teaches couples sacred dancing. "Lead your partner's attention with your hands," she advises. "Move them in front of your heart area to stimulate your partner's concentration on the heart and therefore your loving feelings. Or, to turn up the heat, rub your hips and thighs."

Tantrika Marci Javril, a dancer herself, suggests a woman can benefit from watching a stripper perform. Go to a club with him, if you're comfortable with that idea, or watch it on videotape, emulating her moves to be just as provocative.

Tantra Tales

Lori was tapping away on her computer until late in the night when Lance turned her chair around and began to slither in a winding motion, putting on a dancing show for her. Lori was embarrassed at first, but she was soon delighted at his display. "It seemed like something a woman would do for a man, and here he was doing it for me—and I really liked it."

Mirror, Mirror

Dancing together is an activity you can do in the privacy of your own home. Just put on some erotic, sensual music that moves you and let your bodies flow to the rhythm. Moving together in a free-flow improvisational dance will lead to more stimulation, better orgasms, and higher states of ecstasy together. Mirror each other's motions to synchronize your mood, erase any sense of separation, and turn you on to each other.

Mirroring each other's movements.

Men should watch how a woman channels intense sensual energy through her body, follow her, and then take the lead. Bend her and let her melt in your arms—good practice for what you want to happen when your genitals are locked in a similar dance. Gaze into each other's eyes, and breathe together as you gyrate; when you're ready to reach higher states of ecstasy, fall on the floor or couch on top of each other and continue the action.

The Hand Dance

In this exercise to do with your partner, put up your hands and let them "dance" together. Let one partner be the leader first and the other follow the steps, then switch roles. See how it feels to be the leader or follower. Which feels more natural? If you felt more comfortable being the leader, purposefully be the follower again. If you were more comfortable being the follower, force yourself to be the leader and direct your partner's actions.

Using Your Body Parts

Stand back to back and dance against your partner's back. Play the same leader/ follower game as in the previous exercise. Try using different body parts to connect: your hips, your elbows, whatever you like. Have fun choosing which one, or switch from one to the other. Get your whole body into the action!

Belly Dancing

You might think you could never do those belly rolls and graceful hand motions that belly dancers do, but what if you tried it? Even if you can't dance at all, you have to give it a try to be a true tantrika (men can try it, too). The secret lies in isolating the body parts that belly dancers shake (head, shoulders, arms, hands, rib cage, hips, and belly), and particularly in moving the pelvis (the key to tantric energy, which is what makes tantric sex practice and belly dancing so compatible).

"Belly dancing is an ecstatic celebration of feminine power, creativity, and sexual energy," says Christina Sophia, a tantrika who teaches a form she calls *sacred-erotic belly dance*. "It is also an excellent way for both men and women to connect with their sensuality and cultivate their sexual energy in a fun, sexy way. Slow, sensual, snakey movements are grounding and help us to feel our connection with the earth. In this dance we are directly working with earth energy, cosmic energy, and the breath as we move. It is a moving meditation, as is lovemaking, where we focus completely on the body and energies moving through and around us. In this meditation, it becomes easy to feel our connection and oneness with spirit, and thus experience the sacredness of our body and sexuality. One can gain a sense of balance within of masculine and femi- nine, earthly and divine."

Some dancers says that the pelvic motions mimic the birthing process, further con- necting the dancer to the source of all life.

 Tantra Tutorial

Belly dancing beginners learn a variety of pelvic and rib cage movements, creat- ing geometric designs (circles, diamonds, triangles, figure eights, undulations); correct posture; steps (to the side, front, back); and arm, hand, and head movements. To find belly dancing classes, check local dance instruction studios in the telephone directory, or ask the tantra teachers listed in Appendix B for teachers in your area.

The benefits are extensive, including increasing flexibility, strength, circulation, and muscular and internal awareness of the torso and pelvic regions.

Dance is a joyful form of exercise and creative expression that you can do on your own, by looking in the mirror to appreciate your body and gracefulness, or enjoy with a partner. The body awareness and spontaneous creative inspiration from the dance can easily flow into blissful and expansive tantric lovemaking.

Sophia's tantra co-teacher, William Florian, says belly dancing brought more aliveness and arousal into their sex. "Men will enjoy learning to move this way," says Florian, who also provides original singing at weekend workshops. "It will improve a man's ability to move and flow with his female partner's body during sex, which she will love, and which will make him enjoy everything more and therefore make it easier for him to last longer." Sophia says, "We may think of belly dancing as feminine and a woman's dance, but men all over the Middle East also dance. Many of the movements are similar, but the men dance them in their masculine way with their male energy. In this way, it can be a turn-on for the men, too, as they get more in touch with their eroticism through these kinds of movements."

Ecstatic Dance

A premier dance instructor, musician, and teacher who runs workshops around the world, Gabrielle Roth teaches students a moving meditation and workout she calls *ecstatic dance*. It consists of five essential rhythms: flowing (a fluid circular motion), staccato (stops and starts), chaos (wild and free), lyrical (trancelike), and stillness (inner movement). Dancing to these rhythms takes you through stages of sexual arousal. Music is an essential element to create these progressive moods; use Roth's customized CDs or create one of your own.

The Temple Dance

The temple dance, which starts with a ritual bath, is an erotic version of trance dances done in exotic islands like Bali. As in ancient times, instead of following certain steps, you channel your energy according to what your partner needs. In this way, your dance is not only for pleasure, it's also for healing.

Sit facing your partner and look into his or her eyes. Watch his or her body language and movement. Observe everything about your partner and sense what he or she is feeling and desiring. Then sway to the mood and the desire you sense. Let your self-consciousness fade away. Allow yourself to change your movements when you sense a change in your partner's mood.

Next take more of the initiative, and purposefully entice and seduce your partner with your movements and undulations. Raise his or her energy and interest. At first, tantalize from a distance, then move closer. As you feel tingling and waves of energy flowing through you, transmit those to your partner through your movements, glances, and gestures. Let the dance go where it will, perhaps leading to a massage or more, then switch places and let your partner dance for you!

> **Tantra Tales**
>
> Romance keeps love alive and is an integral part of tantric play. Tantra teacher Francesca Gentille, a talented tantric dancer, knows how to do it well! As she says, "My beloved John and I were both raised in families with a culture that values beauty and romance every day. It's like Sacred Sexuality Italian style. Every day we light candles and play music during dinner. Whoever gets home first throws the kids' toys into baskets, lights incense and starts a great meal, because of course cooking is part of love and romance. We take time to compliment and appreciate each other for the way we dress, how hard we work, or whatever we can think. I had great teachers—after 50 years of marriage, my parents still hold hands and look adoringly into each other's eyes."

Feasting on Your Love

I have long recommended a healthy way for couples to use food to spark passion. In a sensuous supper, every aspect—what, how, where, and when you eat—awakens all your senses. The experience follows the curve of sex from foreplay (shopping and cooking together, serving each other), to a peak (consuming the meal), to lingering in afterplay (relishing tastes and even enjoying cleaning up).

> **Ecstasy Essentials**
>
> To use food as a turn-on for sex (called sitiphilia), choose foods with pleasing smells, suggestive shapes (cucumbers, artichokes) and colors (red tomatoes symbolic of her ripeness), and stimulating textures (peaches that remind him of her skin).

Tantric lovemaking takes the use of food for pleasure or heightening sensuality to a new level, where you also become the table! A highlight of tantra seminars run by Butterfly Workshops, is the *Gate feast* (meaning "to go beyond" in Sanskrit). In this erotic banquet, you prepare seven courses of foods that are visually appealing, taste good, and can be easily eaten from various body parts (such as salmon mousse, juicy fruits, and ice cream).

Make abundant portions to create the sense that you can have it all, says workshop leader Laurie Handlers. Use no utensils and feed your lover with your hands or mouth, or offer up courses on any part of your body for your partner to feast on. The experience invariably leaves everyone laughing, loving each other, and wanting to taste more.

"If you go slowly and savor the experience of giving and receiving pleasure in each sample and swallow," explains Handlers, "you go into a dreamy state, making you feel sexy."

The erotic Gate feast.

Games Lovers Play

Tantric sex celebrates games. After all, that's what kids do, and they embody the spirit of joy and delight. The word *game* has taken on a derogatory connotation, as often it is used to refer to single men and women playing games with each other to trap them into relationships. (I have always advised in my dating workshops that you should never play games!) Redefine the word to have a positive meaning, to represent release, freedom, and joy. Here are some tantric games you and your partner can enjoy together:

◆ **Make up a story by taking turns adding different themes and events.** Let the story go in any direction it takes, without censoring yourselves or worrying about what it means. You can speak into a tape recorder or write the story down, so that you can read it back to each other at another time.

◆ **Picture your love.** Make a collage of your love for each other. Collect items that are significant both for yourself and for your partner and then create your collage together.

◆ **Bring out the animal in you and your partner.** Animals are uninhibited when it comes to following their desires. Play a game in which the two of you are animals. Get down on your knees, close your eyes, and use smell and sound to find each other. See what you do with one another. See which animals you choose to be! Are those animals compatible?

Tantra Tales

In constructing their collective collage of their relationship, Mae collected CD covers and Greek recipes because her beloved is a musician who likes to cook; he brought used airline receipts and seashells because she likes to travel and walk on the beach. When they finished, they told each other how they felt about their respective hobbies and interests, and how warm they felt about being acknowledged for their interests.

◆ **Play a tune on your partner's body.** Professional musician Paul Ramana Das not only plays piano like a virtuoso, he plays music on the body of his beloved. This can be wonderful play for you and your partner. Pretend you are the musician and play a rhythm on any part of your beloved's body. You don't have to be a musician or know music to do this, as long as you let yourself feel what you want to express through your motions.

Tantra Tales

Ted surprised his beloved—and himself—by penning a love poem. "The words just came out of me," he explained. "I just sat quietly, thought of Caryn, and started writing." Like Ted, let yourself be inspired by the feeling without any second-guessing or judging. Don't worry about style, rhyming, or even making sense! Ted's poem expressed how relieved he was to allow himself to love again without being hurt. A verse reads:

My whole body radiates with the warmth and joy of my love and our love,

It streams from my smile for all to see and glistens in the glow of my eyes ...

My body is relaxed and my mind is peaceful, calm and free;

Never again will I give up my love to protect from feeling hurt.

Creating Sex Magic Through Tantric Sex

Sex magic is an advanced art of tantric lovemaking. Of course, any part of your union can be magical; however, the phrase technically refers to creating what you want through tantric union and practices. Sex magic involves several steps:

◆ Create a vision of what you want to have in your life (more love/abundance/ happiness). Lie relaxed with soft music playing. Hold your partner's hand if you like. Let your mind wander until an image of what you would like to manifest comes to you (more love, happiness, even world peace!).

Ecstasy Essentials

The Art of Sexual Magic (Tarcher/Putnam, 1996) by recognized tantra teacher Margot Anand includes lots of ways you can create sex magic in your relationship.

◆ Imagine sexual energy fueling your idea. Draw that energy up through your body using what you've learned in this book (concentrating, imagining, feeling, and directing your energy to move).

◆ "Feel" your goal silently, or state it aloud to yourself or to your partner. Have your partner repeat it to you to strengthen the energy of your desire. Think about that vision when you are in the highest states of pleasure, such as at the moment of orgasm.

◆ Cry out "yes, yes" together to heighten permission for the dream to come true.

Creating sex magic.

Sex magic is possible through tantric practices because you can visualize what you want while in a heightened state of bliss, making it more likely that this will happen. This is based on a valid scientific theory that the brain does not know the difference between what is imagined and what is real; therefore, the more you imagine something desirable as happening, the more you condition your mind and body to move toward that reality.

You can do sex magic by yourself through the steps previously described. If you have a partner, you can take turns doing sex magic individually, or do it together (having a joint image of what you want).

Toys for Tantric Play

In tantric sex, the best toy is your imagination, and every part of your body and soul as well as that of your beloved. However, because tantric sex is about fun, you also can use many real toys. Tantric sex toys can be used for men or women, alone or together. But their use has special requirements different from just any sex toys or love aids:

> **Blocks to Bliss**
>
> Sex toys can carry bacteria unless you keep them clean. Tantrika Cynthia Taylor Lamborne recommends disinfecting sex toys after use by wiping them with a solution of nutribiotic grapefruit seed extract (available at health food stores) and water (use 10 drops of extract to 1 cup of water).

- They should facilitate the process of cycling your energy through your chakra centers.

- They should encourage sensuality more than sexuality.

- They should never distract you from the real focus of your attention: your energy exchange with your beloved.

- They should help you get in touch with subtle energies, not distract or rush you.

- They should help you have greater pleasure and joy and hopefully contribute to your physical health.

- They should bring you increased calmness or excitement as desired.

- They can also be used under special circumstances for sexual healing.

Some suggestions of sex toys include the following:

- **Crystal onyx massage egg.** Stronger, healthier vaginal muscles add more erotic sensation and sexual energy. The egg is meant to help develop these muscles, like doing isotonic exercises. The woman inserts the egg inside her vagina and pulses against it. "Such skills help a woman master the ancient eastern art of *pompoir* (also called *playing the flute*), in which she stimulates the lingam just by her vaginal muscle movements," says Cynthia Taylor Lamborne, creator of the egg and other tantric tools for play and healing.

◆ **Crystal Wand.** This 10-inch curved clear Lucite wand can be inserted in any sexual opening for men or women. It has different sizes at each end to stimulate either the woman's G spot or man's G spot (prostate). The "S" shape makes it easier to reach these areas than with your own fingers.

◆ **The Honey Dipper.** This latest version of the Crystal Wand is slimmer (the thickness of a woman's baby finger), with three ridges like a honey dipper on one end. Changes were based on feedback from male customers (using it for prostate massage) but women users now give it high ratings. Says Lamborne, "Use of it has revealed that it stimulates and releases blocked energy in the vagina that reflects points connecting to every organ and part of the body."

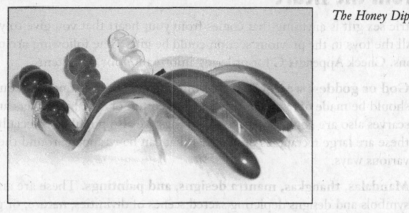

The Honey Dipper Deluxe.

◆ **Natural rabbit fur massage mitt.** This soft mitt fits over your hand and feels soft as you glide it over a beloved's or your own skin.

◆ **Lubricants.** These applications make sexual activities—from touching to intercourse—flow more easily and can be crucial for women with problems lubricating (from lack of stimulation or hormonal troubles). Also, gliding motions prevent damage to delicate tissues during prolonged sexual contact. Perhaps even more important, they feel good and are just plain fun!

Lubricants should taste good and glide easily, without feeling gummy or sticky. They should also be made out of natural ingredients. For example, some preparations of glycerin are made from 100 percent pure vegetables and are water-soluble and edible. Never use anything that disrupts the chemical balance of the vagina (such as baby oil or cooking oil, which some people reach for in a rush or when unprepared).

◆ **Videos.** As tantric sex becomes more popular, there are more videos on its practices. These are chock full of helpful tips (for more about these, see Chapter 18).

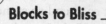

♦ **Vibrators.** Vibrators come in all colors, sizes, and shapes, just like real genitalia. Rather than be threatened that you are not providing enough stimulation for your partner if he or she wants to use a vibrator, see it as a help to spark for pleasure for both of you. The constant motion can be stimulating for men as well as women, on all areas of the body.

Gifts from the Heart

A tantric sex gift is anything that comes from your heart that you give to your partner. All the toys in the previous section could be gifts. The following are other suggestions. Check Appendix C for ordering information for such items.

♦ **God or goddess wear.** Choose clothing that is loose-fitting and comfortable. It should be made of natural fibers, such as cotton or silk, but velvets and beaded scarves also are popular. Pareos or sarongs are also popular, especially for men; these are large rectangles of material that can be wrapped around the body in various ways.

♦ **Mandalas, thangkas, mantra designs, and paintings.** These are artwork of symbols and designs depicting sacred scenes of divinities, nature, or geometric forms meant for meditation, as described in Chapter 3.

♦ **God and goddess figurines and statues.** Many gift shops that specialize in Nepalese and Eastern artifacts offer these.

♦ **Books or videos on tantric sex.** These can be instructional as well as stimulating. I particularly like the ones that add imagery of historical erotic art, like the book *Forbidden Art* by Miss Naomi, or the video *Hot Sex in Erotic Art* from Access Instructional Media.

♦ **Adornments such as earrings, necklaces, or bracelets that evoke tantric sex or that have the yin yang symbol.** In tantric sex, men also wear jewelry as adornments and symbols of power, just as they did in ancient times. These include rings, bracelets, necklaces, and even earrings. Tantric adornments also include *bindis* (beaded designs that are affixed to the third eye), toe rings, and beaded straps that fit around the second toe and around the heel.

♦ **A can of Kama Sutra body dust.** Smell is a powerful sense in attraction, and this powder smells wonderful!

◆ **Pleasure promise coupons.** These are pieces of paper printed with statements of what you will do for your partner; for example, I will give you a massage, do a chore for you, take you to a romantic dinner, please you in any way you want for an hour. You can make any pledge that strikes your fancy. These coupons are available in stores, in my book *The Complete Idiot's Guide to a Healthy Relationship* (Alpha Books, 2001), or you can make up your own.

Where to Find Tantric Love Toys and Gifts

Of course, there are sex shops that might carry some of the toys that fit the criteria for tantric sex practice; however, there are also vendors who specialize in such aids. You can find them …

◆ On websites for tantra teachers.

◆ In the resources listed in Appendixes B and C.

◆ By recommendation from friends who practice tantra or tantra teachers.

◆ At tantra workshops, where there are usually tables of tantra-oriented items.

The Least You Need to Know

◆ Tantric sex practices are meant for your pleasure and joy; you deserve it.

◆ Be creative about what you do. Let your imagination go, sense your energy, and let yourself follow your feelings.

◆ The best sex toy is your own body and that of your partner. If you purchase a sex toy, be sure it's safe and respectful.

◆ Give gifts to each other to increase your fun and pleasure.

What Makes a Technique "Advanced"?

Chapter 17

Advanced Tantric Lovemaking Techniques

In This Chapter

♦ What makes a tantric technique advanced?

♦ Examples of advanced tantric lovemaking rituals

♦ Magical love rituals

♦ Advanced white tantra poses

♦ Aids for advanced tantric use

Now that you've mastered the basics, had a wonderful time on his and her "best nights ever," and discovered some new ways to play together, I am sure you are curious about what could come next. There are endless levels of training and practices in this tradition, as in many other paths.

In this chapter, I will give you a taste of some advanced practices—practices that will take you deeper into sacred love and the wonders of expanded consciousness.

What Makes a Practice "Advanced"?

It takes time and practice to become proficient at any skill, and tantra is no exception. Because moving energy in tantra is a powerful force, you need to respect the process and not rush. But after you've mastered the practices as I have described them in these chapters, you're ready for the more advanced exercises. These are characterized by the fact that they ...

- ◆ Use breathing patterns in more complicated ways.

- ◆ Generate more intense energy.

- ◆ Coordinate more steps.

- ◆ Clear deeper emotions.

- ◆ Direct energy in more diverse ways.

Be prepared for powerful rushes of energy that will catapult you to higher states of consciousness.

A Slow Ride into Timeless Love

Some advanced practices might seem simple on the surface, but truly are more advanced because more skills are required to move energy in a new way. *Relaxing into ecstasy* is an advanced practice that California tantra teachers Steve and Lokita Carter discovered to be so effective in their lovemaking, they adapted it for students in their various classes at the Institute for Ecstatic Living. It is advanced in that it requires extreme sensitivity to very subtle movements of energy that elicit intense sensations. "We call it a 'slow ride into timeless love,'" explains Steve, "because it includes *micro movements*, where the partners connect with tiny motions that are no more than half an inch, yet the results are exceptionally intense."

Here are the five steps:

1. **Ritual.** Start your lovemaking session by telling each other what you love most about each other at this moment. This creates a feeling of safety and trust.

2. **Communication.** Agree to try something different. Tell each other how you feel about it and what you are afraid of.

3. **The experience.** Do whatever you enjoy to get aroused. After you are inside each other and have made love for some time, slow down. Resist the temptation to have an orgasm. Melt into each other, and move your pelvis ever so slightly

toward your partner's pelvis, in those in micro movements, while looking into each other's eyes.

When you both feel ready to do something different, contract your pelvic floor muscles a few times. Do this at the same time or alternately. Focus on these small movements, allowing the awareness to increase sensitivity in your genitals. Play with the speed and frequency. Tell each other what it feels like.

After a while, come to stillness. With open eyes, let your breathing and the contractions of your pelvic floor muscles carry you into timelessness.

Include the micro movements, stillness, and contractions in your lovemaking. Move faster, then return to the stillness. This creates a slow wave of ecstasy.

4. **Sharing.** After you have made love like this, share your feelings:

   ◆ Did you feel relaxed?

   ◆ Were you able to feel your ecstasy in the relaxation?

   ◆ Did you feel connected to each other?

   ◆ Is this something you would like to try again?

5. **Closing.** End your lovemaking by thanking each other and bowing to each other.

Tantra Tales

Tantra teachers Richard and Antoinette Asimus have been together 30 years but deepen their love daily, spending 3 hours every morning in ritual practices. In their new course, "Sexual Spiritual Joy," they coach couples to stay with worshipping, blessing, gazing at, touching, and pleasuring the lower part of the body for 1½ hours for 60 days. "Do this not with expectation, but with the spirit of experimentation, being curious and watching how your inner and outer world change without forcing or controlling it."

The Magical Maithuna Love Ritual

In Parts 2 and 3 of this book, I introduced you to various rituals in tantric lovemaking. The *maithuna* is the most elaborate of these rituals and includes many steps. At one of Bodhi Avinasha's teacher-training courses for Tantrika International, Seattle tantra teachers Kirby Jacobson and his co-teacher Radhika demonstrated this ritual.

"It is to be done with reverence," instructs Jacobson. "The power of the maithuna is revealed when the couple believes that each movement is a dedication to themselves, each other, and the universe."

Here are steps in this ceremony:

1. Prepare the lovemaking space in the shape of a yantra (magical geometric design).

Tantra Tutorial

Maithuna refers to the coming together of god and goddess with the acknowledgment that everything is sacred, from food to acts of orgiastic proportions. The ritual is an elaborate performance using specific items as part of the sacred ceremony.

2. Purify and seal off the space with blessings in each direction, including the corners of the room, ceiling, and floor.

3. Prepare special powders, light lamps with special igniting substances (called "ghee butter"), make offerings to chosen deities, and massage each other's chakras.

4. Use hand movements and mantra chants to invoke and connect energy between the partners.

This ritual could go on for days!

The Snake Dance

When you really follow your intense energy, it can feel like a snake coming up your spine. Kundalini is the name of the famous serpent power that lies coiled up at the base of the spine. After it is awakened (through your practices), this energy travels up the spine. If you go with its flow its journey can take you into new intense sensations!

Intense power surges of this hot kundalini energy rushing up the spine can literally make you shake—with fear, fury, enthusiasm, or ecstasy. Lack of preparation can lead to a panic called a *spiritual emergency,* but with responsible practice, you can follow the inner snake to where it takes you, ending up dancing primitively, seeing visions, feeling outside your body, or experiencing inner knowing.

If you feel uncomfortable, read the book *Spiritual Emergency: When Personal Transformation Becomes a Crisis* by Stanislav Grof and Kristina Grof (Tarcher/Putnam, 1989), call the Spiritual Emergence Network for a referral, or contact me for expert help understanding these experiences.

Following the kundalini rising for an ecstatic experience.

Advanced Tantric Yoga Twosome

Physical practices—yogic poses to move energy—complement your sexual practices, as I discussed in Chapters 6 and 15. As you progress, these poses can become more advanced.

Here are two exceptional advanced poses, developed by tantra teacher Carla Tara:

◆ **Earth to sky salute.** Stand facing your partner with enough space between you so you can bend down without bumping into one another. Take a few breaths to center and connect, then clasp your own hands behind your back with your index fingers pointed out. Bend over slowly (one vertebrae at a time), dropping your head down as far as you can go comfortably and touching the back of your head. Lift your arms behind you as straight as possible with your index finger pointing up to the sky. Breathe and feel the energy of the two of you creating a channel connecting earth with sky (Shakti with Shiva). Lower your arms and come up slowly, taking care with your spine, and do a backward bend to balance. Repeat three times, then do the following pose.

◆ **Tantric twosome trestle.** Sit in front of each other with your legs outstretched and slightly bent, with the soles of your feet pressed together. Reach forward to clasp your partner's hands, and interlock

Dr. Judy's TantrAdvice

Remember that every pose has a purpose and moves your energy in specific ways. Also, always do preliminary poses in a routine; this prepares your body for more physically demanding ones.

your fingers. Keeping your body straight, raise your legs at the same time, keeping them between your straightened arms (or outside your arms if that's easier). Do five fully synchronized breaths together while looking in each other's eyes. Notice how you maintain your balance in this position and how that is reflected in your relationship.

Earth to sky salute.

Tantric twosome trestle.

Advanced Passion Positions and Acts

The Kama Sutra contains many positions and acts, many of which are shown on various videotapes that you'll read about in Chapter 19 on aids for tantric pleasure. But tantra teachers and students often come up with new possibilities from their own practice; you can do this, too. The only pre-requisites to be sure these fit the tantric tradition are that they ...

♦ Connect chakras (energy centers) to move energy.

♦ Include breathing patterns.

♦ Are part of a practice rather than an isolated act.

♦ Honor one another.

♦ Use the intense energy for a higher purpose.

Dr. Judy's TantrAdvice

To come down to earth and re-enter the real world after such intense energetic experiences, you must do closing ceremonies, such as releasing spirits, acknowledging your partner, or saying a closing prayer.

A sexual position is not just an acrobatic achievement. In tantra, it is the passageway to divinity, allowing you to be and see the god/goddess. After you can arouse a forceful pool of kundalini energy at the base of your spine, intensifying it in your sex center and then circulating it through your body, you can then send it rising out through the top of your head in a unified spiral together, reaching higher states of consciousness, to the point where you sense an expansion of this unified mass merging with the universe in outer space. There are no boundaries. You have become divine and merged with the divine to know true and intense god/goddess consciousness.

Enflaming of the Dragon Goddess

I love this position because it invokes the dragon, the Chinese symbol of heavenly power conferred on man. The two steps allow the fulfillment of the ultimate purpose of positions: to connect with divine energy in yourself, your partnership, and all that is.

"This position and practice just came through me, and I knew my advanced students would love it," explained Carla. Lie on the bed or floor on your back (head on a pillow for comfort and to maintain eye contact) with your feet to each other's head, base chakra pressed against each other, and thighs interlocking. Carla explains, "In this position, my partner kisses my feet, an act that opens up my appreciation and energy so much that I want to do anything to please him. I hold his lingam in my hands, and guide it to make circles at the entrance of my yoni. Then we make small circles with our groins pressed together, to move the energy."

Enflaming the dragon, first position, connects sex centers.

Carla continues, "We help each other up into the classical yab yum sitting position, with his lingam still in my yoni, so the penetration is deeper. We undulate while we do the fire breath and then draw the energy up into our hearts and the back of the brain. Then we hold the breath, press our heart centers together, and visualize spirals of energy and fire connecting us and lifting us higher, while our hearts expand and merge together. Exhaling, we make the sound 'ahhh' and allow the energy to come back into the genitals, visualizing a golden energy coming down from the universe, flushing and enlivening all the cells of our physical body. In this way, we experience a nonejaculatory body orgasm. Then we go into a meditative state and repeat the building-up process three times before the man decides to go into an ejaculation."

Enflaming the dragon, second position, connects heart centers and aids in visualization of the divine connection.

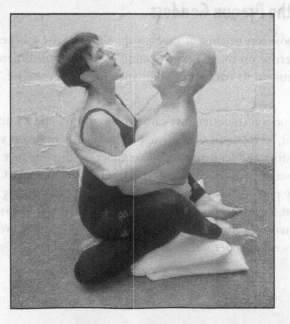

The Kabazzah

It's no wonder that the sexual skills of the Japanese geishas gained such mystique with American GIs during World War II. The women practiced an ancient sexual art that allowed the man to lie blissfully passive. The secret: the *kabazzah*, in which the woman mounted the man and moved only her internal muscles to bring him to climax.

The Full Stop

In the *full stop* technique, you freeze in a position in the middle of lovemaking (take turns giving the signal) for 1 minute—becoming aware of thoughts and sensations instead of ongoing compulsive activity. Many Easterners believe that only with such valleys can the peaks be higher.

The Two New Erogenous Zones

The man who is advanced in tantra knows the full art of "polishing the pearl" (pleasuring the woman's clitoris). One way to do this is the *Kivin method*, in which the man stimulates the woman orally on two erogenous points on her genitals to bring her to orgasm within 3 to 8 minutes. The method requires pressing one point (between the vaginal and anal openings) while applying pressure with the tongue on other points located on each side of the clitoral shaft.

Tongue Fu

In a Taoist practice, a woman strengthens her tongue muscles by pressing her tongue against an orange or a grapefruit using various motions, side to side, or up and down along the fruit. These practices are described by Mantak Chia in his book, *Tao for Women: Cultivating Female Sexual Energy*. Similar routines are described in Chia's corollary book for men, *Taoist Secrets of Love: Cultivating Male Sexual Energy*.

Ecstasy Essentials

The middle finger has more direct, intense energy than the fourth finger or pinky. Be conscious of which you use with yourself or your partner. Touch each other with different fingers, in different combinations, and on different body parts. Feel the sensations of each.

Mudras

Mudras are positions of the arms, hands, and fingers that connect the energy centers. There are many combinations of mudras; they can be placed externally on many areas of the body, on outside points correlating with inner points, and even reached internally. Every finger that is used communicates a different energy, which you must learn to become skilled in sending energy patterns to your partner.

Advanced Visualization in Tantric Sex

Imagery sets pictures in the mind that the brain cannot distinguish from reality, so you are likely to act on these. Taking advantage of this, sexual visions can inspire physical actions that lead to blissful union when practiced in a meditative, disciplined way. Here are two examples:

♦ **The tantric triangle.** Visualize yourself as a male godlike being with a triangle of white light at your third eye that points downward (the symbol of the female yoni), with the lower angle pointing toward the back of your tongue. The angles become the three doors of liberation, opening to the wisdom of great bliss.

♦ **The Shakti shine.** Visualize the goddess Shakti with blue lights radiating from her body that enter your body through your genitals and melt a blue radiance throughout your body.

Advanced Tuning In: You, Too, Can Be Psychic!

People in love who are having great sex seem to really know what each other wants and needs. Everybody dreams of being so tuned in to a lover that you can read each other's minds—so you don't have to say what you want because your partner just does or says the perfect thing. (Like Nicole, who was ecstatic when her new lover was walking in the street with her and blurted out, "I'm so proud to be with you." It was exactly what she always dreamed of hearing. Or like Pam, whose beloved Jim whispered huskily in her ear during intercourse, "You're the most beautiful woman I've ever known. I'll never leave you." That was heaven to her ears.)

The desire to be known so well is one of the reasons people go to psychics, but the truth is, you can tap into your own intuitive powers. If you get calm and focus, you will be surprised at what you can accurately sense about your partner. Doing this deliberately is called a *psychic* (or *energy*) *reading*. I have been to many tantric weekends and massage workshops in which we did a psychic reading of each other. Everyone is always so surprised at how it is possible (after several preliminary exercises) to read another person's energy (without really knowing him or her before) just by putting our hands close to the other person's body. Once when I did this exercise with another tantrika, I felt sparks jumping out at my hands at even 2 feet away, telling me how much energy (and power) she has!

Do a simple energy reading with your partner. Sit in yab yum and breathe together for a few minutes to get attuned. With your eyes closed, let your hands go to a certain place on your partner's body and say aloud whatever comes to your mind. Don't censor your words! You'll be surprised how accurate you can be. Say what you sensed that he or she needs. For example, Fred was reading his partner June and heard her (energy) saying, "I need you to hold me tightly like I've always wanted." Some couples feel so in tune after doing a reading that they feel like being closer and making love.

Eight Steps in Deity Yoga

In Chapter 5 I introduced you to many deities and promised to tell you about techniques to bring their energies into you. *Deity yoga* does this. In this exercise, you can use your favorite gods and goddesses from that chapter—the ones you most identify with—or experiment with others. Follow these eight steps to actualize a particular deity to achieve a certain state of being within you:

1. Set your intention. Meditating on any deity should always be toward the goals of wisdom, compassion, and service to others.

2. Sit comfortably in front of a picture or statue and focus. Relax, close your eyes, and let the image appear in your mind's eye. After a while, the image will become a radiant being of light. You will feel inspired and blessed; realizations will come to you.

3. Request the deity bestow blessings on you.

4. Picture the deity as light energy entering your head, allowing it to descend and then rise through your spine, dissolving into your heart. Feel the essence of the deity becoming one with you.

5. Focus on yantras, geometric forms that are associated with the deity and trigger desired energies.

6. Look at geometrically shaped mandalas with the deity's image that triggers certain imagery or emotions.

7. Listen to music invoking such energies. (See listings in Appendix C for some ideas.) Choose CDs whose titles imply the energy, such as *Ecstatica* or *Trance*.

8. Perform mantras, prayers, and ceremonies associated with the deity and characteristics you desire. These can be simple or very elaborate.

The practice of "deity yoga," meditating on the divine to realize a desired goal.

Base Chakra Pleasuring

I will talk more about base chakra stimulation in the next chapter with regard to male sexual healing, but such exploration can also be a source of pleasure. Be aware that many partners will cringe at the thought, which can arouse shame, embarrassment, and fears (especially for heterosexual men, who may associate the act with being gay). Yet the presence of many nerve endings around the anal opening can lead to arousal. Always respect your partner's boundaries, go slowly, and follow your partner's cues about when, where, and how to touch.

Tantra Tutorial

Although you can learn about tantra and deities on your own, such study is best under the guidance of an experienced teacher.

As I described in Chapter 2, the base chakra is associated with issues of safety and security; therefore moving energy from the base center to the heart, throat, or sex centers brings more solidity to expression in that area. Bring the energy there by sweeping your hand in that direction and then holding a hand on each of two areas to connect them.

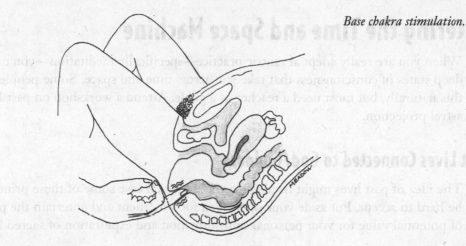

Base chakra stimulation.

Advanced Aids in Tantric Play

Just like toys are rated for use with age groups, sex aids are appropriate for different levels of lovers in their practices. Although there is no rating system, trust your intuition about which ones could be above your head (restraints, anal beads) for the time being. By all means surprise your partner with new sexual pleasures, but when it comes to some activities you know might be a stretch, discuss readiness together.

One such aid is the *Pearls of Delight*, a long strand of washable pearls (costing about $12.95), that can be worn around the neck but also inserted inside the vaginal or anal canal and pulled out slowly. "Surprise your partner," says Cynthia Taylor Lamborne, a California tantrika who sells them. "Wear them when you go out for dinner as a signal of what's in store for your love play when you come home that evening."

Pearls of Delight.

Entering the Time and Space Machine

When you are really adept at tantric practice—specifically meditation—you can enter deep states of consciousness that take you across time and space. Some people can do this naturally, but most need a teacher as a guide. Attend a workshop on past lives or astral projection.

Past Lives Connected to God/Goddess

The idea of past lives might be alien to you, in which case some of these principles might be hard to accept. Put aside your skepticism for a moment and entertain the possibilities of potential value for your personal transformation and exploration of sacred loving.

 Ecstasy Essentials

Some advanced practices require supervision or guidance of a teacher; seek that out freely.

The principle of past lives is intrinsic, although not essential, to tantric loving because the gods and goddesses come from a tradition that is traced back to the beginnings of time. Becoming one with the lineage of all these deities helps you unite with all that is, all that has come before, and all that will be. This merging of time helps you reach the state of bliss within yourself and realize that you are complete without any partner.

Astral Projection

Advanced tantric sex partners can send love and sensual connections through the airwaves, across space and time. This transmission is obviously useful for long-distance lovers, forced to be in different locations because of jobs, schooling, or other reasons. People who don't think they have psychic powers can find themselves able to do such projected communication—by deep concentration and "sensing" the other person.

The Least You Need to Know

♦ As you master the preliminaries as presented in this book, there are ever-increasing levels of information and practices to study.

♦ Practices become more advanced when they add more elements and intensify the energy cycled and emotions that can be triggered.

♦ Advanced practices include rituals; white tantra poses, positions, and visualization; exploring past lives; and connecting across time and space.

♦ Allow yourself to come up with new practices and variations. Trust yourself to experience new dimensions.

Sexual Healing to Set You Free

In This Chapter

- The power of sexual healing
- Who can be a healer?
- What happens during a healing?
- Guidelines for the healer and the receiver
- Healing the pain of abuse
- The effects for the healer and the healed

Up to this point, I have concentrated on telling you about practices that bring pleasure. However, in the process of arousing powerful sexual energy, strong emotions may arise that trigger past pains. These can be handled through the emotional release exercises described in Chapter 10, in psychotherapy, or in specific sessions called *sexual healings*. In this chapter, I will tell you about sexual healings, how they happen, and what you need to know to participate in this most powerful experience.

What Is a Sexual Healing?

Everyone has been hurt emotionally in some way by a relationship. These hurts unintentionally get stored in the first chakra (where feelings of insecurity and lack of safety are lodged) and in the second chakra (where feelings of shame and inhibitions are stored) in men as well as women, blocking the free flow of energy, emotions, and joy. The blockages can come from past painful relationships, abusive sex, physical conditions (such as a hysterectomy), emotionally charged experiences (abortion, miscarriages), shame and embarrassment, body hate, intimacy and commitment fears, religious prohibitions, or parental punishments.

Ecstasy Essentials

Love has healing power. At a recent conference of scientists, visionaries, and healers (called the Prophets Conference), scholar Gregg Braden reported on research that showed that the human expression of love actually changed the molecules of water. This proves that emotions can change surrounding matter. Find out more at www. greatmystery.org.

A sexual healing involves specific rituals to assist someone through an experience to clear these pains or blocks locked in the body. It is important to distinguish these healing sessions from the nights of pleasure we discussed in Chapters 11 and 12. The healing sessions entail more ritualized interaction in which the healer and receiver have very distinct roles, with the focus on uncovering and releasing any blocks in the receiver's sexual responses.

When you heal your own past wounds in this way, your newfound wholeness extends beyond just you. In fact, you are healing all beings on this planet. And when you are the healer, you represent many divine beings who have healing powers. Your actions help heal everyone suffering from similar pain and heighten joy for everyone.

Who Can Be a Healer?

There are two types of healers. Your loving partner is a healer every day, soothing a beloved from the stresses of the day. However, taking on the serious role of healer requires training. Hawaii-based tantra master Charles Muir has proven that couples can learn to do this for each other in a weekend course. "Men can learn in one weekend how to free their goddess to be expressive and enjoy sex, even after years of fears have been locked in her vagina from past mistreatment by men," he says. "And women can learn how to heal their god from any past pains he may have suffered from her, or other experiences in his past."

Other healers are highly trained dakas and tantrikas, some of whom have completed Muir's and other extensive training courses. The trainings require a several-year commitment of retreats, assisting at various introductory weekends, and producing case reports. Some women and men who decide to be sexual healers and offer services to the public advertise on the Internet. Some do hands-on healing, using phrases such as "goddess spot massage" or "male sacred spot massage."

> **Blocks to Bliss**
>
> Just as there are good or bad therapists and licensed or untrained health practitioners of all kinds, there are responsible or untrained sexual healers. Be careful when choosing someone to whom you are entrusting the most vulnerable places in your body and soul. Use the same criteria as you would in selecting a good therapist. Do research, network with people experienced in tantra, and check out tantra websites. Ask respected tantra teachers for referrals. Interview healers intensely about their experience and check references.

What Happens in a Healing

To set the stage for a healing, the healer creates a safe and comfortable space. He or she might spread out a pretty sheet or soft blanket, light candles, and ensure privacy and confidentiality. For example, a healer would say, "I give my word that I honor your sharing with complete confidentiality. Whatever happens stays between us."

Start with a ceremony that sets both the healer's and the receiver's intentions. Hold hands and speak a dedication. The healer might say, "I devote myself to you and am here for you with the best of love and intention for you to have the most healing experience you choose." The receiver might say, "I thank you for being here for my healing and intend to be fully present for myself in whatever comes up so that I can be healed. In doing so, I will heal others who are similarly suffering."

Healing the Goddess

Invite your goddess to lie down and relax. Ask permission to give her a massage. A healing massage has a different intention from the relaxing and pleasuring massage. Massage her thighs and entire pelvic and stomach area. When she is ready, put your hand over her pubic area and stay still. Put your other hand over her heart (if you feel she needs to feel your love) or over her power center (if you feel she needs to feel stronger). Make small movements around her pubic area.

Releasing painful emotions opens the potential to receive more pleasure, in more places, for longer periods of time. As a result, even not intentional, the sexual healing ceremony can actually heighten arousal, from relaxation, trust, and release. Be aware of the receiver's potential escapes from intense emotions by ending the session, switching attention to the healer, or changing the energy to lovemaking. Gently invite the receiver to return to the emotion that was happening before the withdrawal.

Ecstasy Essentials

As tantra teacher and professional bodyworker Marci Javril describes, "Tantric touch in sexual healing massage is a special way to approach intimacy and genital contact. Complete compassion and attention gives the receiver a chance to really feel into the emotions held in the physical body and to release tension, frustrations, and anger that could have been stored for years."

Encourage her to focus on the sensations and not worry if there is burning or numbness (typical signs of emotional pain being brought to awareness), and encourage her to stay with any feelings or expression (crying, yelling, thrashing about) that might arise. Tell her you are there for her, and reassure her she is safe and loved.

When she says that she is ready to go further, ask permission to enter her sacred space. Go slowly and move your fingers gently, because a particular spot might trigger a reaction. Keep reminding her to breathe, as the breath is crucial to the expression of the motions and ultimately of pleasure at the other end of the pain.

The yoni massage.

Each healing session can be different. One time the receiver might be calm and even joyous; another time deep pain and anguish can be triggered. Never consider any reaction bad or dysfunctional.

Healing the God

Men can achieve sexual and emotional healing, too. Although we expect that men are the cause of hurt in relationships more often than women, men also suffer pain from sexual rejection and emotional upset that needs healing. Sexual healing helps the man learn to appreciate intimacy rather than just genital sex and become more open. Female partners are very appreciative when men express emotion and demonstrate trust by doing so.

The man's healing can center around his base chakra as well as his sex chakra. Muir's healing techniques for the Shiva involve stimulation of the prostate gland (a male hot spot for arousal similar to the woman's G spot). Some men are uncomfortable with this, and some critics challenge the process, but Muir has many examples of men who found it helpful to heal hurts, release pleasure, and increase their capacity to love.

Tantra Tutorial

A healing session with internal stimulation does not have to be painful can lead to pleasure and even a female ejaculation, as described in Chapter 10.

Overcoming the Two Major Hurdles in His Healing

During the session, the woman prepares the setting and herself as healer in the same way described earlier for healing the goddess. There are two major hurdles to overcome in men's healing:

♦ The man has to surrender. Lying on his back in the more traditional female position makes him feel additionally vulnerable, because men generally prefer to be in control. Continually encourage him. Say, "Allow yourself to surrender" or "I know this is difficult for you."

♦ As I mentioned in Chapter 12, most men are uncomfortable about being touched or entered in their anal area. A major reason is that it arouses homosexual anxieties (although some heterosexual men have discovered great pleasure in stimulation in the base chakra). To overcome this resistance, the healer must go very slowly, resting a finger gently at that area and waiting for him to invite entry.

Instructions for His Healer

His healing, like hers, should always start with a body massage to relax him. After the general massage, pleasure his lingam using the techniques described in Chapter 11.

Reassure him that he need not have an erection but should just lay back and enjoy it. Vary the strokes; use those previously suggested or make up your own. Include pleasuring the testicles. Use all your body parts (fingers, side of the arm, breasts).

As Muir instructs, move the energy from his lingam to his base chakra by stroking the lingam and gliding your hand to his base. Rest an oiled finger at his opening, and wait for him to push against it to show his readiness. Ask, "May I enter you?" Remind him to breathe and allow whatever feelings come up, and invite him to heal. Enter slowly, inviting him to tense and release his anal sphincter muscles against your finger.

Blocks to Bliss

Don't interrupt a receiver's process by saying, "Don't worry about that" or "Don't cry" because that stops the process. Also be careful to not interrupt because you are frightened or threatened; only do so if you feel the person is in too much emotional distress to continue.

Ecstasy Essentials

There are four male G spots. The two external ones are the frenulum (knoblike protrusion on the underside of the penis where the tip meets the shaft) and perineum (space between the testicles and anal opening). The two internal ones are inside his anal canal in a slight indentation (reached by curling a finger toward the front wall in a come-hither action) and higher inside the anal canal (rubbing around or on the prostate gland). Just as with the woman, this sacred space can house past pains and memories of either real or imagined hurts, rejections, intrusions, or abuse.

Doing a male sexual healing by stimulating the prostate through the base chakra.

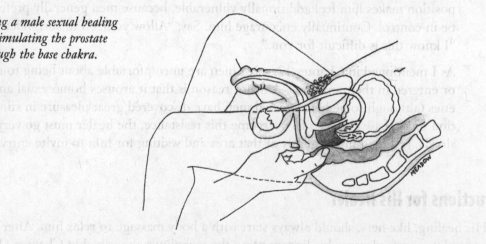

Expect him to deny feeling anything. Or he might have strong emotional outbursts (as with the woman when she receives) that could include anger at you. Don't take these personally. Keep encouraging him to express whatever comes up. Keep reassuring him: "You're doing great," "I'm here for you." Go only as far and as long as he wants. You can reassure him of safety by breathing with him and reminding him to breathe; this is reassuring when he is deep in the process.

Preparing the Pelvis for Pleasure

The pelvis needs healing more than other areas of the body, says California tantrika and professional bodyworker Marci Javril. This is because of many taboos and physical and psychic toxins stored in the tissues there. Javril suggests empowering the pelvis to allow more vitality in three steps:

- Activation, by doing the pelvic floor (PC muscle) pumps, described in Chapter 6
- Cleansing, through pelvic massage
- Balance, by a sexual healing experience with conscious touch that has no agenda

Healing the Pain of Abuse

Sexual healings can have dramatic effects in cases of abuse. Sadly, many women have suffered from sexual abuse of one sort or another, causing them to feel violated or taken advantage of. For example, many women I have counseled have been extremely traumatized by past abusive experiences with men in which they feel they were pressured into having sex or performing a certain sex act—even without force—and afterward felt "used" and angry. These feelings build over time—even years—creating low self-esteem and distrust of men.

Tantra Tales

A sexual healing can feel like a miraculous release for a woman who has been abused. I have witnessed many such healings; for example, in one teacher training demonstration, Muir worked with a woman who had been abused by continually offering encouraging instructions like "Breathe" and "Stay with the feeling," while using expert hand movements inside her. After initial resistance, she screamed as if re-living a past attack. But this time, she told off her attacker. This empowerment was essential to her healing. Afterward, her body and facial expression relaxed and showed signs of pleasure. She later reported that she felt as if a huge block had been removed from her insides and from her soul.

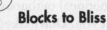

> **Blocks to Bliss** _____
>
> When sexual abuse is uncovered in a healing, further help should be arranged by support groups (of others with similar experiences) and professional therapists, to help the person work through the trauma.

It is important to note, however, that men also have been sexually, physically, and emotionally abused. Our society is just becoming sensitive to this. One man I know, Carlton J. Buller, had the courage to write a book about his experiences suffering from sexual abuse and the steps he has taken to recover, called *Stolen Innocence: The Autobiography of a Lost Soul* (Fair Weather Publications, 2001).

Handling Emotions in a Healing

Of course emotions can come up naturally when you have sex! I have certainly heard enough stories from women or their partners in which the woman has cried hysterically during or after sex, much to both their panic or surprise. Or she might break out in laughter, causing him to think, "Am I doing something funny? I didn't think so!" I always offer reassurance that these are natural reactions, from powerful pools of energy that are stimulated and being released in a big burst. Crying, I always explain, does not always mean pain; as I mentioned in Chapter 11, it can be the result of release from pain or the contrast between present loving and past hurt.

Rules for the Healer

Effective healing requires careful attunement to the person's energy. For this reason, you need great skill to do a healing and should only perform one after you have been to a workshop with a qualified tantra teacher. There are certain conditions for the healing session to be effective for the receiver as well as the healer. The healer must …

♦ **Create a safe space physically.** The receiver must be able to relax and feel safe. This starts from the simple provision of privacy and quiet (phones off the hook, locked doors) and extends to an energetic feeling that he or she can trust the receiver and let go in this setting.

> **Blocks to Bliss** _____
>
> A healer, like any therapist, must not use someone for his or her own sexual or emotional gratification or needs. This is both unethical and criminal.

♦ **Beautify the space.** A person feels more at ease when the setting is clean, peaceful, and lovely. Dim the lights or light some candles. Put flowers and other items that invoke natural elements around, such as a bowl of water and some rocks (for earth energy).

◆ **Take care of whatever you have to, so you can be fully present at the moment.** This means get clean, make any necessary phone calls, and go to the bathroom, so that these things are not on your mind during the session. Ground yourself beforehand, so you are not in your own head and can be aware of the receiver's needs. Be aware of whatever problems, conflicts, or needs you have (anger at your partner, frustration, being turned on), as these could influence your reactions to the receiver's process. Set these aside, so you don't bring them into the session and project onto your receiver.

Dr. Judy's TantrAdvice

Be kind to yourself as the healer. If something is too much for you (the emotions are too high, for example), it is better to let the receiver know than to proceed and muddy the experience.

◆ **Set intentions.** Verbalize to yourself what you want to have happen. Speaking your intentions makes them more likely to happen. Say, "I intend this session for (the receiver's) highest good, keeping my own needs out of it."

◆ **Be respectful, especially of personal boundaries.** Remember that you are always equal, even if the receiver seems in pain now. Pay attention to how the receiver feels; what his or her needs and limits are; what is okay or not okay for you to say, do, or touch.

◆ **Be empathic.** This doesn't mean feeling pity; rather, it means putting yourself in the receiver's place, as if inside his or her skin.

◆ **Don't take anything that happens personally.** The receiver might get upset about something that happened between you, but often these emotions can be traced to earlier traumas and feelings. Never defend, judge, correct, or criticize.

◆ **Follow the receiver's energy.** Of course you might have some techniques in mind, such as those I have introduced you to in this book, but follow what the receiver wants and needs. This allows him or her, not you, to be in control of what happens and when.

Rules for the Receiver

There are equivalent requirements for the receiver as for the healer, as shown in the following list. This follows the tantric principle that both people are creating a circle of energy and are equal. The receiver is also healer and vice versa.

◆ **Commit to being present in the moment.** Avoid distractions, and keep your mind focused on the here and now.

◆ **Respect yourself.** You're not a victim with a sexual dysfunction but a beautiful being who wants to be fully released of anything that holds you back from experiencing the full potential of your love.

◆ **Prepare your body.** Take a bath, or brush your teeth. Dress up in something that makes you feel wonderful. Ground yourself to be in your body, not in your head with worries, anger, and disappointments.

◆ **Set your intention.** Verbalize to yourself what you want to have happen. Speaking your intentions makes them more likely to happen. Say, "I intend to relax during this time and allow myself to experience whatever happens for the highest good of myself, my healer, and all involved."

◆ **Set your boundaries.** Let the healer know what your limits are. Are there any parts of your body that you do not want touched? Any actions you do not want him or her to take?

◆ **Make requests.** Say what you want from the healer, accepting the healer's boundaries, too.

◆ **Appreciate the healer.** It is a big responsibility for someone to undertake a sexual healing for you; that deserves your gratitude.

At the End of a Session

After a powerful experience, a person needs to be nurtured and held. Cover the receiver with a blanket, or better yet, ask if you can hold him or her, and how he or she would like to be held. A good position is a nurturing one, either spooning the person by laying against his or her body from behind, or lying over the receiver's chest area (because the heart is very open and vulnerable now).

A sexual healing is a powerful experience, whether you laugh, cry, or think nothing much happened. Much *did* happen—because a strong intention was set, and because you both directed intense energy in some way. Sometimes the effects might not be felt for days, weeks, or months. Share what you experienced and ask for feedback if you want to, or be silent and allow the experience to be integrated into your being.

Be kind to yourself after a healing, recognizing that you have been through a powerful time. Don't just jump up and go about your business. Instead, you might want to …

◆ Take time to allow the experience to sink in and be absorbed into your being. Stay still, lying in bed quietly. Breathe naturally. Let your mind and body rest.

- Drink water. Even if your body didn't move much to the outside world, it moved a great deal internally. As after any intense physical exercise, drink water to replenish your hydration.

- Take a shower or bath; water soothes the soul and washes away some of the intensity of the emotions and helps you transition into daily life.

Comforting and caring after a healing.

Are Healings Effective?

There is little formal documentation to show the effects of healings. I did the first research on the effects of tantric sex trainings to date, which I'll talk about in Chapter 25. I have witnessed many powerful sessions in which men and women have purged present and past pains. Many men and women who have either been trained in tantra or had private sessions, or couples who have taken weekend workshops, attest to positive and desired changes. Some even feel profoundly transformed.

People often want to know whether there is ever a point at which they can say, "I am healed." It's the same question men and women who go through any other kind of therapy ask. Here are some ways to measure progress in sexual healings:

> **Ecstasy Essentials**
>
> The process of facilitating someone else's healing can also heal the healer. While energetically and empathetically connected to the other person, the healer might go through equally intense experiences. As a result, the healer might want or need to process whatever comes up for him or her. Decide on the best time to do this.

◆ Decreased intensity of emotional pain

◆ Increased feeling of trust

◆ Increased ability to experience joy

◆ More feelings of giving and receiving love

◆ Less physical pain upon touching various parts of the genitals

◆ More freedom in sexual expression with a partner

The experienced healer will also be able to tell whether there is reduced trauma in the genitals and more joy in the person in general. Muir has said that the healed goddess feels more moist inside, her body moves more freely, her vaginal tissue is softer, and her vagina is more open and welcoming. The vaginal muscles become more elastic and responsive to the lingam, able to pulse and massage the lingam, expanding to receive him, and contracting to embrace him. She will look younger, make more joyful noises, and even smile more!

Some people might require many sexual healing sessions, especially in cases in which there has been abuse of any kind, and particularly sexual abuse. Others might feel the need for only a few such sessions.

Some tantric partners request a sexual healing when they are feeling stressed and want to concentrate on releasing some inner blocks, even if they are not feeling a serious problem. You can request such a session at any time. Remember, it does not have to start with or lead to pain. Joy can motivate healing, too!

The Least You Need to Know

◆ A sexual healing is a powerful session that should be taken seriously; it can lead to intense results whereby stored-up or even fleeting pains and blocks can be released.

◆ If you do a sexual healing on your partner, it is best to have training from an experienced tantra teacher at a special workshop or private coaching.

◆ Appropriate conditions should be set for the healing session, including creating safety and setting boundaries.

◆ The receiver of a healing has a responsibility to tell the healer what he or she wants and needs.

◆ People who advertise themselves as sexual healers should have extensive training by a professional; you should inquire about their background and experience.

Chapter

19

Aids to Tantric Pleasure: Sexsense, Song, and DVDs

In This Chapter

♦ The importance of music to set the mood

♦ CDs to spark your tantric thrills

♦ Videotapes and DVDs that tutor and tantalize

♦ Tantra on the silver screen, over the air, and on the Internet

Tantric lovemaking is about arousing the senses and includes even more exquisite attention to detail than other sex traditions. That means stimulating your aural as well as visual senses. These senses are important in your tantric practice, so in this chapter, I give you some suggestions about which CDs and DVDs can help your love life (see Appendix C for how to get these materials). Some of the videos have great tips that even I enjoyed—and I thought I'd seen and heard it all!

Tantric Music

Music is key to setting the mood of your tantric sessions. In this chapter, you'll learn how to use sound to spark your mood and some music that is the best for your practices. List your favorite music for lovemaking in the exercise in this section. Ask your partner to list his or her choices, too, and see if your choices overlap. Put your choices in order, as if you put them in a five-CD changer. Be sure to identify the mood the music evokes, as that will determine the tone of the love-making experience and give you some clues about whether you and your partner will be on the same wavelength.

Music for Our Tantra Love Date

	Artist	CD Title	Specific Cut	Mood
My choices:				
1.	_____	_____	_____	_____
2.	_____	_____	_____	_____
3.	_____	_____	_____	_____
4.	_____	_____	_____	_____
5.	_____	_____	_____	_____
My partner's choices:				
1.	_____	_____	_____	_____
2.	_____	_____	_____	_____
3.	_____	_____	_____	_____
4.	_____	_____	_____	_____
5.	_____	_____	_____	_____

I have my favorite tantric music handy to load into my CD changer or to take with me when I lead tantric seminars or teach tantra at workshops or conferences. The mood that the music evokes varies and so applies to different tantric practices; for example, meditation, massage, yoga, or dancing up a storm (as in the Shakti Shake or Dynamic Meditation described in this book). I have favorite artists in the hard rock, grunge, and even heavy metal style, and others, like the classic Barry White, that are undeniably meant for seduction. There's an increasing library of music that is specifically designed to be compatible with and facilitate tantric practices and moods. These are designed to open the heart and stir progress from sensuality and tenderness to tantalization and erotica to a crescendo of ecstasy and bliss.

My favorites include:

♦ *Spirit of Love* by Awakening Heart. It has a great song called "Give Yourself to Love," which I play over and over at classes.

♦ *Journey Into Love* by Sophia, with another terrific song I play all the time in classes, "Heal Me With Your Love."

♦ *Sex 'n' Violets* by my good friend and brilliant Maui musician Jaiia Earthschild, whose song "Learning How to Love" is beautiful for intimate settings. Other songs speak of honoring the goddess or the environment.

♦ Raphael and Kutira's *Music to Disappear In*, which sweeps you into an ecstatic, quietly peaceful state. All their music invokes beautiful prayers and rituals, such as "The Calling" and "Prayer."

♦ Gabrielle Roth's *Waves*, although others of hers are equally exciting, such as *Bones, Trance, Totem,* or *Ritual*. Some of these have one of my favorite music styles, what I call "techno tribal trance." Roth's music takes you through various stages of activity and sensuality.

♦ Robert Frey's *Opening to Love* is a classic in the tantra world for heart-opening, inspiring healing, and personal growth (also used by midwives, churches, and hospice groups). Tracks 6 and 7 are especially valuable at the end of a tantric meditation or lovemaking session.

What Makes Tantric Music Special?

Certain themes are emphasized in tantric music to facilitate your practices. These include choruses that create harmony between lovers, rhythms that are consistent with breathing patterns, hypnotic repetitions to still the mind, and tribal sounds to activate the body.

Tantric songs imply blessing the beloved, as in "Blessed One" written by Robert Frey and Ashana Lobody:

Love so divine, love so compelling
Love with a radiance that outshines the sun
In your divinity I see my reflection
In your tender glance I find my heart

Chorus: Woman and man there is no separation
Goddess and God are one and the same
Children and elder united together
All rejoice at the sound of your name

Tantric songs also invoke honoring, as in this wonderful message from Jaiia Earthschild:

> I have to feel honored by you, That's what it comes down to.
> You speak to me with words of love but I feel incomplete.
> Words are fine—should be enough but I listen with my feet.
> To my feet love is a verb. It's what you do that will be heard.
> I have to feel honored by you, And when I feel honored by you
> Then I will unleash my passion for you.

Some tantra teachers have made tapes that talk you through a transformative tantric experience. Good ones in this genre include Raphael and Kutira's *Tantric Wave*, *Oceanic Tantra*, which guides you through the steps of ecstatic lovemaking from breathing to sensuous touch, heart opening, and sex magic. Another is Robert Frey's *Sacred Inner Marriage*, a guided meditation that evokes inner male and female energies and brings them together in a progressive visualization process to create relationship harmony.

Tantra Tutorial _____

Not surprisingly, many magical tantric musicians come from the island of Maui on Hawaii, the land of gods and goddesses, and from San Francisco, known as a city that experiments in all realms of exploring consciousness.

Dr. Judy's TantrAdvice _____

Make a special CD for your lovemaking. Take turns being the disc jockey during a lovemaking date. See what moods each of you likes to create.

Let the Music Flow Through You

Tantra is flow of energy. Performing tantric music, like tantric breathing techniques, is always attuned to the energy of the moment. The most gifted musicians know that they are in the flow, feeling the music from the inside. I knew that magical feeling when I played in a band; I loved playing the same sets over and over, and really getting into the flow of the music. Musicians "feel" the music. Keyboards virtuoso and daka Paul Ramana Das puts himself in an ecstatic state and lets his fingers flow over the keyboard. He calls his music and performance "vibrational engorgement" and "tantromatic" because as he says, "I attune myself to the piano as a feminine divine entity. I approach the keys as 'her' senses, and respond to the inner flow with appropriate melody, rhythm, flow, and passion." He uses the same approach to "play" on his beloved's body as the instrument!

Sounding Chakras

In Chapter 3, I described the sounds associated with certain energy centers. Chanting these sounds evokes their energies: lam, vam, ram, ham, yam, ooo, oomm. Voice and sound healer Karin Schelde suggests using your voice on your partner's body to evoke energy. Put your mouth close to your partner's chest and make any sound at first to express yourself; then make the "ahhh" sound of the heart chakra. It is fascinating in Karin's workshops to see how some people cry when this is done, feeling touched in their hearts. Her audiotape *Classic Sound Healing* takes you through the chakra sounds to achieve releases.

Ecstasy Essentials

Tantric music might sound "New Age," but it's not always slow and melodic. In fact, some tantric exercises described in this book have chaotic rhythms and fast beats, intended to create faster breathing and activation of the body. The Osho dynamic meditation is a good example of a chaotic action, meant to energize, progressing to quiet meditation states. Gabrielle Roth's *Bones* CD is a good example of music cuts that progressively move through the stages of relaxation, arousal, and resolution in a typical lovemaking sequence.

Chants That Charge Your Connection

Have you ever heard a song that you can't get out of your head? When that happens you are no longer the singer; the song is singing itself. That is how chants work. As a form of mantra, a chant puts you in a meditative state by simple, repetitive, and memorable rhythms. Often about love, but never sad like the blues, chanting assists you in the journey to joy and peace. Lyrics can sound almost like a tantra lesson, invoking god/goddess, grace and beauty, and choruses that hypnotically still the mind and move the body. Often they inspire tribal movements and are done at tantric gatherings, either in circle or free form.

Henry Marshall, master of chants in CDs such as *Mantras, Magical Songs of Power*, offers mantras for different purposes. The mantra to attract a partner evolved from Marshall's own problems and solution to finding a mate. First, he found himself chanting. "As I continued

Ecstasy Essentials

Tantric songwriter Michael Stillwater, who holds ChantWave Celebrations in San Francisco, describes using song and singing as "movement that carries awareness into the field of the ecstatic open heart, using song and chant as the vehicle."

chanting, I began to feel that the mantra was sending a signal from all levels of my being to my soul mate, and I knew I'd find her." After considerable practice chanting and imagining sending the signal, he began to hear from friends about some woman who seemed to meet his expectations. With more chanting, their paths crossed repeatedly and they eventually got together for a date. "Success takes at least 40 days of this practice," Marshall explains, "but you must sing from the heart 108 times every day or else start from scratch." Marshall also tells the story of a man who was estranged from his wife and began chanting. After a while, he had a vision of his wife as a beautiful goddess, and they got back together.

Mantras can also be sung to a beloved, to heighten the love energy. Frey's songs are sung at many tantra gatherings because the lyrics stimulate loving feelings and are meant to be sung to others (not to mention they're repeated over and over, making the words and tune easy to remember!):

> I behold the beauty in you, I know you are divine
> I am inspired by your Light, Shiva Shakti am I

Another beautiful chorus to sing to a beloved is this one from tantric musician Sophia:

> I open my heart to you
> and let your love flow through me.

Tantric Videotapes and DVDs That Tantalize and Teach

What you see is as important as what you hear in tantra. Instructional sex videos are becoming more and more popular in the market of sex-oriented videos. Tantric sex videos and DVDs usually cost between $19.99 and $39.95, but they're worth it. You can watch them more than once and even use them as background inspiration to your lovemaking without paying specific attention to what's playing.

Tantra Tutorial

Reportedly, more than 10,000 new titles in the adult video category were released last year, with rentals totaling more than $3 billion. Obviously there's an interest in seeing the subject of sex on celluloid.

Of all the hundreds of instructional sex videos I have seen over the years, most of those geared toward tantra are appealing and interesting. Some have captivating tantric soundtracks; gorgeous tantric imagery; and visual depictions of goddesses, colors, and special effects that evoke the visions of blending energies dissolving into bliss.

Research by professional sex therapists has shown the value of *Video Assisted Therapy* (*VAT*) in helping couples overcome inhibitions about sex, learn specific techniques to solve sexual issues (premature ejaculation, anorgasmia), and learn healthy sexual functioning. Toronto-based psychiatrist and sex therapist Frank Sommers has couples watch videos at home or in another room and then discuss what they saw.

Many tantric videos contain valuable lovemaking tips; for example, techniques for the man to delay ejaculation by contracting his PC muscles firmly and frequently, and innumerable skills for couples to spark desire.

Don't believe the myth that men are visual and women are not. Women can be just as sexually stimulated by what they see as men are. That's why the tantric man dresses up for his goddess on her night and dances for her—to give her a visual delight. Research even shows that women are renting erotic films in increasing numbers.

Watch videos on your own or with a partner. Watch them before lovemaking or during breaks. Watch a video or DVD on your TV screen, or prop your laptop in a convenient place. Use the videos for enjoyment, or as a way to learn about yourself and your relationships. Here are some key questions to ask yourself:

◆ What scenes made me excited or anxious? What is going on in those scenes that relates to my life and relationships?

◆ What can I learn from the video? Would I feel comfortable acting out a scene I liked?

◆ How comfortable am I letting my spouse know that I am watching these videos? Can I talk to my partner about what we see?

> **Ecstasy Essentials**
>
> Access Instructional Media's video *The Amazing G Spot and Female Ejaculation* shows an inside view, as never before seen on video, of the inside of the vagina during stimulation of the G spot and female ejaculation. Seeing the moist lining and coloring of the internal female organ provides a positive image that can help raise self-esteem.

The *Kama Sutra* Series: Videos with a Tantric Twist

Some companies specialize in sex videos and have a long history of such involvement. A few such companies are even run by trained sex therapists who have spent years in the field, studying and teaching about sexuality. One of these is Dr. Michael Perry, the sexologist who did some of the original research on the G spot. Perry's company, Access Instructional Media (www.sexualintimacy.com), has a number of videos perfectly suited to show you what other people do sexually. These couple-friendly films have just the right mix of instruction and stimulating erotica. The *New Lovers Massage* video presents clear instruction on giving and receiving sensual pleasure. *Sexual Massage* is much more explicit, showing actual massage strokes for the erogenous zones, including the G spot.

Real couples demonstrating tantra, Tao, and Kama Sutra positions and lovemaking on video.

The *Kama Sutra* series combines ancient secrets and modern techniques you're learning about in this book. The set includes *Kama Sutra, Tantra and Tao: The Ancient and Erotic Techniques for Incredible Sexual Pleasure; The Ecstasy of Exotic Sex: The Joys of Total Sexual Ecstasy;* and *Kama Sutra: Hot Sex in Erotic Art.* The latter is like taking a trip around the world reviewing sex in ancient and modern times, by having couples re-enact sexual positions and situations from famous erotic paintings and statues. Perry quotes the Kama Sutra, saying, "You can have health, wealth, and spiritual well-being, but without good sex you have nothing."

Honoring the Goddess on Video

You can read about how to honor the goddess, but seeing it happen with beautiful imagery can give you extra inspiration. Charles and Caroline Muir have made a beautiful film about tantra and female ejaculation. *Secrets of Female Sexual Ecstasy* contains detailed instructions and is erotic and visually exquisite, with gorgeous Hawaiian scenery, original tantric soundtracks (including by Jaiia Earthschild), and original tantric artwork that is a sight to behold in itself. The film is explicit but not X-rated, and shows sexual loving infused with intimacy and caring. The video includes secrets of erotic kissing and touch, techniques to achieve male ejaculatory control, and instructions about how to do the female sacred spot (G spot) massage and achieve female ejaculation (a topic on which the Muirs are truly experts).

A scene from the video, Secrets of Female Sexual Ecstasy.

Other Videos

Intimate Secrets of Sex and Spirit: How to Worship Each Other in Bed shows lovemaking tips and demonstrations by mature couple Paul Ramana Das and Marilena. A powerful lesson is the use of music in lovemaking and humming on the yoni.

Ancient Secrets of Sexual Ecstasy for Modern Lovers includes comments from many of the top teachers, book authors, and workshop leaders in tantra, including the Muirs, the Ramsdales, Nik Douglas, and Margot Anand. Informational sound bites from these experts are interspersed with staged but sensuous scenes of five couples demonstrating tantric techniques such as breath control, ejaculatory control, goddess spot stimulation, lovemaking rituals, full-body orgasms, and simultaneous orgasm. Lori Star's expert demonstration of breathing techniques is very helpful (in case you can't get to a workshop and learn it in person).

Sluts and Goddesses is by Annie Sprinkle, who has worked as a porn star, sex counselor, and workshop leader. Her very risqué video is presented like a "transformational workshop" that is visually fun, very entertaining, and full of exercises for women to bring out their inner goddesses and allow wild expression. Her suggestions include penciling your eyebrows to look like an Egyptian; playing with wigs; decorating your body with jewelry; changing clothes to change your consciousness (high heels, biker boots, or Victorian bustier); posing for sexy shots; and experimenting with crystals, vibrators, feathers, and rattles. Sprinkle mentions every possible trick of the trade, some of which are very racy.

Kama Sutra II: The Art of Making Love from *Penthouse* magazine's video collection is 60 minutes of an extensive and excellent lesson on sexual positions. The scenes are sensuous, and the words used have a tone that's consistent with tantra. There are scenes in which the woman controls the activity tantrically so the man can last longer. The narration starts with foreplay, learning about each other, taking time to touch and caress, letting partners know what to do to give pleasure, and progresses to oral sex and intercourse.

Positions include those Kama Sutra–like titles, such as *Twining of the Creeper*, in which the woman rests her head on the man's stomach while looking up, and he gazes lovingly into her eyes; *Mixture and Season and Rice*, which entails encircling each other completely with arms and legs; and *Milk and Water Embrace*, in which she sits on his lap and he embraces her from behind.

> **Blocks to Bliss**
>
> Some of the positions in these videos are complicated and require agility, as in the Kama Sutra itself. Kneeling for a long time can also be a strain for most people. Only do what's comfortable for you. Work your way up to these positions. Although many videos do use "real" people, don't feel like you have to look like the beautiful couples in these videos.

Let your touch travel all over your beloved's body. Include light, gentle touches and "pressing of nails" (an essential tantra technique that sends shivers up the lover's body). Start at the neck and run down the body to the hips. Go up the chest and down and up the arms, around the shoulders, and down the chest to the hips, making circles. Travel down to the pelvis area and massage and pull at the thighs between the legs. Keep coming back to the chest (breasts) to heighten feelings of love.

Tantra-Related Workouts to Watch

An increasing number of fitness experts who practice tantra have developed workout programs that are compatible with tantric sex principles and practices. *Stephanie's Tantric Toning* combines the physical practices of yoga, T'ai Chi, chi gung, and light aerobics with guided imagery that invokes tantric meditative states. At the end is a color light meditation that reinforces self-esteem. *Chakra Yoga* with Toronto-based yoga teacher Gurutej Kaur shows an interesting exercise program of very gentle poses (mostly sitting) that balance each of the energy centers (chakras). The 16 poses come from the kundalini yoga tradition.

Related Videos and DVDs on Sex

Educational videos about treating sexual dysfunction were first produced in the 1970s, and the numbers keep increasing. My cabinets are already full! Some classics in the field present a variety of proven therapy techniques for sexual dysfunction, are hosted by top educators and therapists, and are used by many professionals over the years. They include the *Better Sex* series (with titles like *Sharing Sexual Fantasies*, *Sex Games and Toys*, and *Advanced Sexual Techniques*) and the *Great Sex* series from psychiatrist Sommers, who has done extensive research to prove the effectiveness of using videos to help couples' sexual and marital life.

The latest trend is that women are producing sexy videos that are meant to present sexuality from a woman's point of view. Candida Royalle is a pioneer in this effort. Through her company, Femme Productions, she has produced many videos that depict women's fantasies and realistic scenes where women are sexually respected and pleasured by men. "Many of my films are highly erotic and show very exciting fantasy sequences," says Candida, "but there's always some relationship, not just rushing to some sex act." Titles bespeaking the female spirit include *Christine's Secret*, *Sensual Escape*, and *Rites of Passion* (the most tantric-oriented selection, in which a woman discovers ancient lovemaking secrets from a "mysterious, Adonislike master").

Tantra in Mainstream Print and on Radio, TV, the Silver Screen, and the Internet

Tantra is becoming an increasingly popular word, in large part because of mainstream media mentions and coverage.

"Tantra is the latest word in sex," said a *San Francisco Chronicle* article. *Esquire* magazine said tantra "makes sex the best it's ever been." Even the *Wall Street Journal*, covering the business angle, touted the "teaching techniques aimed at putting extra zip into sex."

Shows and story lines are increasingly being aired about the topic on radio, TV, and in the movies. For example, tantra was a routine in the movie *Go!* Tantra was also featured in the film *American Pie 2*, a coming-of-age movie in which teens dealing with adolescent angst end up in a perfect world where all the women are gorgeous and available and every guy gets his dream come true. As expected, tantra is portrayed as a mystical Eastern trip to perpetual orgasm.

Tantra Tutorial

Celebrities also make household words of whatever they practice when they reveal it publicly. Likewise with tantric sex, with which several celebrity names often are associated, such as Sting, Woody Harrelson, and *L.A. Law's* Jill Eikenberry and Michael Tucker. Tantra comes up whenever people talk about men being able to last for hours in sex.

A Hollywood feature film has even been produced about one of then-Muir's tantra workshops, with particular focus on the story of a woman and her young HIV-positive lover who travel to Hawaii to learn the techniques in hopes of deepening their connection. The gripping drama whose title, *The Best Ever*, refers to the phrase Muir uses to describe the lovemaking that results from particular tantra practices, follows the blossoming and then breakup of their relationship. A movie released years ago, called *Bliss*, starring Terence Stamp as a daka, was supposedly based on Muir's work. Other tantra teachers have been approached by producers to make movies about their work; some of these projects are being pursued.

The popular TV show on HBO called *Real Sex* often airs segments about workshops run by tantric teachers. And HBO's popular series *Sex and the City* included a subplot in which one of the girlfriends attended a tantra workshop, fearing something was wrong with her sexually because her boyfriend had fallen asleep during sex!

Popular musician Sting told Oprah on her TV show that he and his wife, Trudie Styler, practice tantric sex. (He also spoke of his practice in an interview I did with him for my *LovePhones* radio advice show, and he even graciously did the heart hold with me—proving he knew what he was talking about!).

Over the many years I've studied tantra and hosted call-in advice shows on the radio, I have talked extensively about tantra. My co-host Chris Jagger and I even did one show in which two friends, Carla Tara and Sasha Lessin (who are tantra experts), demonstrated the techniques of pleasuring the goddess, in which the tantrika had a female ejaculation, thanks to the daka's expertise (a classic *LovePhones* radio show that many people still ask me for a copy of—get in touch with me if you want one). Of course, we had to do a running commentary to describe what was happening, because it was radio after all, but it was vivid enough that listeners could hear the yelps of joy and celebration.

Like everything else, tantra is expanding on the Internet. I've addressed the subject many times online, and there are an increasing number of sites on the topic—something I discuss in more length in Chapter 26.

The Least You Need to Know

♦ Your tantric evening of pleasure should have music to reflect and set your mood. Pick anything that appeals to you, but try CDs especially made for tantric love-making that can be particularly conducive.

♦ Music tones vibrate similarly to the chakras, so you can control energies you want to stimulate with the music.

◆ The value of videos that show couples in loving interactions has been proven by research; it can be healthy to watch educational videos about lovemaking with your partner.

◆ An increasing number of erotic films are being produced that are specifically made to demonstrate tantric practices and sexual positions.

◆ One measure of how much a topic is becoming part of the popular culture is how often it shows up in the media. This is happening with tantra, as more shows include the theme in their broadcasts and projects. The Internet also offers a wide opportunity for sexual topics to be discussed.

Part 5

Dating and Mating Tantra Style

Hopefully you're convinced by now of how good love and sex can be—or have had an experience of "the best ever." Now what about the impact of doing these practices on your relationship? What if you're excited about this new path but your partner is not? What if one of you finds someone else to share with? Or perhaps you're enticed about what you've been learning in these pages but don't have a partner to practice with.

All is not lost! Yes, on any powerful new path such as this one, things can get rocky. But there is always a solution to any problem. In this part, I'll help you find those solutions. If you're looking for a tantric partner to practice such delicious loving with, I'll give you suggestions about how to find one and manifest the love you want! Deep, passionate, exhilarating love *is* possible—you'll see that in some amazing stories about couples who are sharing the tantric path, tying the knot, and doing it in grand tantra style! The beauty of their love, and what is possible for you, will be inspiring!

Chapter

20

Singles Enjoying Tantra

In This Chapter

◆ You are the beloved: loving yourself first

◆ The search for Mr. or Ms. Tantric Right

◆ Attracting a tantric mate

◆ The two love lessons you should know

◆ Safe sex when practicing tantra

Now that you've been reading all these undoubtedly compelling things about tantric sex, you must be excited about the potential experiences. The good news is, you can do this even without a partner! In this chapter, you'll learn just how to do that. I'll tell you how singles can enjoy tantric sex alone—but also how to approach that search for your beloved and where to go to find like-minded singles interested in pursuing the tantric path.

You Are the Beloved

Whether or not you are with someone, always remember that you are the beloved; this is a basic principle in tantra. Repeat this phrase, "I am the beloved." I have my patients do this, with great results. Whether you have a new boyfriend or girlfriend, a mate you have been with for a short time, or a lifetime partner, you are still whole within yourself. The first step in tantric sex is to create that wholeness within yourself—the union of male and female energies and all the qualities that implies, as outlined in Chapter 3. Tantric sex gives deeper meaning to a statement you are likely familiar with: You have to love yourself before you can love anyone else. So look in the mirror and fall in love—with *you!*

Fall in love with yourself as the beloved.

One of my favorite exercises to help people develop self-esteem is to take yourself out on a date. That means you treat yourself as well as you would like to be treated by someone else. In Chapter 8, I described how to prepare for a tantric date with a beloved. Refer to that chapter and do all the steps described there, but for yourself! In summary that means ...

- Clean up your house as if a special someone was coming to call.

- Take a bath or shower, and shave or put on makeup, as you would if you were about to go out with someone special.

- Pick out a special outfit that you've been saving for that special someone to appreciate. Choose something particularly sexy or alluring. Remember that tantric clothes are flowing, comfortable, and enticing.

- Choose a place to go that you would take a special someone. Go out to dinner at a wonderful restaurant on your own! What movie do you want to see with someone you could cuddle up to? Go with yourself!

◆ Take that special walk, gaze at the moon, or whatever romantic, fun, or exciting thing you would do with that special someone.

Remember that *you* are that special someone. The more you practice loving yourself and treating yourself well, the more you will create that loving aura around you. People will notice and be drawn to you. You might even have noticed that as soon as you stop looking for that special someone (and appearing desperate), that's when he or she appears in your life. Check out some great ways to build your self-esteem in *The Complete Idiot's Guide to Dating*.

Meeting Your Match

Looking for that perfect mate has traditionally been referred to as the search for Mr. or Ms. Right. In recent years, the slang term for this has been *hooking up*, which actually means anything from meeting someone you really enjoy being with, to sexual interactions with that person (and even then, the term includes anything from kissing to a one-night stand to seeing someone regularly).

In tantra, the phrases for meeting your match are different. To me, they sound more spiritual, more flowery, more respectful, and more honoring. The most common word used is *connecting*. A phrase that expresses attraction is, "I feel the energy between us." These words are meant to express the energy between two people, which is intrinsic to the tantric way of life and implies not only a sexual interest, but also a deeper spiritual attraction.

Conscious Flirting

In tantra, everything is done consciously. That means you are aware of your actions and have only positive intentions, which results in the best outcome for all. Francesca Gentille and her partner John Mariotti led workshops in what they call conscious flirting. Participants are asked to identify their intentions when meeting someone new. Knowing this intention also helps if you are "striking out." "If you flirt to make yourself feel good you won't be as successful as if you do it for the others person's good," Francesca says. Being conscious of your behavior and intention allows you to look at what you might want to shift, making you more effective.

Other exercises include role playing how you flirt to see more objectively how you come across and decide whether you like what you see in yourself and how you make the other person feel. (Some people are shocked at what they see!)

Mariotti, an expert gardener as well as martial artist, notes two exercises that particularly empower men to choose whether to follow up an interest or nurture the chi/ energy coming from a woman. Using gardening as a metaphor for love, he invites men to think of a smile, an offer of assistance, or a light compliment as an initial planting of the seed of intention. Plant too hard and deep, and the seed will never come to fruition. Plant too light, and it will blow away without taking root. A gentle, consistent, and positive approach is the best. And remember, women, like plants, thrive on the consistent nourishment of attention.

Tantra Tutorial

Tantra demands respect for other's boundaries. Being careful about approaches is important in today's society. Be aware what is acceptable according to different cultures and be alert to approaches that are unwelcome and therefore subject to being considered sexual harassment.

In a sports analogy, men can think of women as potential teammates (not opponents) in the game with a goal of pleasure and joy. The team wins when both players succeed. Of course you'd make your pick on more than looks, and you'd be sure your teammate can receive a pass before you send it. See flirting and dating as try-outs for long-term relationships. Set a winning strategy, giving rather than making demands.

Who Is Mr. or Ms. Right?

In tantric sex, your whole idea of the perfect mate can change as you look beyond the superficial values at who the person really is. This means seeing the god/goddess divinity as opposed to thinning hair or size 14 dress. Be open to the possibilities. You could be surprised who shows up in your life—that someone special could be someone you never imagined!

Remember that the basic—and beautiful—spirit of tantra is to look beyond the physical being to see and connect inner souls. Remember, one of the basic exercises is to look into the eyes of another to see the god/goddess within that person. Look into his or her eyes and see beyond age, race, height, and any of your preconceived notions of whom you should be with. It is striking how different this concept is from our culture, which is so rooted in our stereotypical images and so bound to the physical to the point where 8 out of 10 men in surveys today still rate a woman's looks as the first thing that attracts them.

Yet in tantra, when you truly look beyond the physical, you find new love matches. In my book *How to Love a Nice Guy*, I wrote about how women can find the true love they seek if they look beyond their usual love criteria—beyond a dashing Armani suit, flashy Mercedes, or shiny platinum card—to assess instead whether he's a nice guy who will really treat her well.

Of course, there are factors that make a couple more compatible. There are lots of tests you can take of your compatibility in my book *The Complete Idiot's Guide to a Healthy Relationship.* The bottom line is that couples are more likely to get along when they agree on several important dimensions of a relationship: how to raise children and spend money, what kind of sex they like, what kind of lifestyle (quiet country dwelling or bustling city life) they want, and basic values to follow. But here's my general rule: you can make any relationship work, if you really want it to work—if you both are really committed to getting along, and you deeply love and respect each other enough to work out any differences. Yes, you might have to work at the relationship to get past your own or one another's prejudices, but you can make it work if you want to.

The Beloved Shows Up in Surprise Form, If Only for Now

If you walked into a room of couples doing tantric sex workshops, you might be very surprised. You might see married couples or singles who connected for the first time who don't fit a classical mold of the perfectly matched couple. Why is that? Because people following the tantra path are drawn energetically to each other and fall in love based on deep emotional connections that have nothing to do with mere physical attraction.

Tantra Tales

Frances is 54 years old, 5'2", with gray hair, and admittedly 20 pounds over-weight. In one tantra workshop she sat next to Octavio, a 21-year-old, 6'4" Brazilian man whose stunning looks turn women's heads. When asked to energetically find someone to pair up with for the next exercises, they turned to each other and ended up doing an emotional release process together. From that time on, Frances curled up into Octavio's arms during the rest of the workshop. "She's beautiful," Octavio told me. "She's certainly not my typical type—I date tall, stunning, Spanish-looking models. But I need to be with a real woman here who is kind and who can help me grow."

Over-50 Pauline, a fiery, outgoing Italian woman, met 26-year-old Lee, a quiet guy of few words. Pauline was well into her career and owned a house; Lee was still in school and lived at home. But Pauline fell for him; as she explained, "He was kind and faithful and I could count on him for everything. He would always come when I needed him. He set up my computer. He listened to all my worries. Best of all, he learned all the tantric sex practices with me." They were inseparable for several years, but even Pauline herself knew that it was not forever. "I had been hurt so often by so many men, and Lee was safe. Being with him taught me how to trust again." Pauline's new boyfriend is her own age. "Lee was my training for love," she explains. "Often there are relationships that prepare us for the next true love."

Quiz: Are You Ready for Your True Tantric Sex Partner?

Answer the following questions about what qualities your tantric partner might possess. Add more questions, if you like.

Can Your Tantra True Love ...

	Yes	No
1. Be much younger than you?	❏	❏
2. Be much older than you?	❏	❏
3. Be of a different race or culture?	❏	❏
4. Have less money than you?	❏	❏
5. Have dark hair instead of blonde hair?	❏	❏
6. Be balding?	❏	❏
7. Be a different religion from yours?	❏	❏
8. Have children from a previous relationship?	❏	❏
9. Be a night owl when you're an early bird, or vice versa?	❏	❏
10. Dress differently from the way you do?	❏	❏

If you answered *Yes* to six or more questions, you are open to love without being tied to convention or preconceptions about whom you should be with. If you answered *Yes* to fewer than four questions, your concept of who is right for you could be preventing you from making a wonderful connection. Go back over your answers and see what it would feel like if you answered differently.

Sensing, Not Scoring

Whether you consider being a sex object as politically incorrect, or even enjoy it for a momentary thrill, tantric sex practice will shift your mind from that to a whole new attraction. Even women who have been more aggressive in scoping out men for reasons of sexual desire find themselves using new attraction criteria. As one woman, Marcy, put it, "I used to walk into a room and decide who I was going to hit on, which hot guy I would take home for the night, but now that I've been practicing tantric sex, I realize that's empty. My body is my temple now, so I don't want just any man."

Now that she doesn't just zone in on hot guys for sex romps, "the pickings are a little slimmer." Indeed, for Marcy and other men and women practicing tantric sex, the choices for partners might seem slimmer because they are more discriminating. On the contrary, there are more possibilities of partners when you look beyond the obvious and into someone's inner being. As another woman said, "I don't care how old or rich he is, I just care if he's big enough to hold my energy, to accept my anger, and to invite my love." Quoting singer Sheryl Crow's song lyric, "Are you strong enough to be my man?" Another woman said, "I want a man who gets who I am, instead of having some Barbie doll fantasy of what a woman should be like."

Similarly, men want a woman who sees beyond their income potential or the kind of car they drive. As Andrew said, "I'm sick of women who just want a rich guy." And Joe wanted to know, "Where are all the women who want nice guys instead of all those guys who treat them badly but they think are cool?" Fortunately, as a woman matures, she more often goes for the nice guy. Any woman can learn to pick these more loving men; I've laid out a 10-step plan to do this in my book, *How to Love a Nice Guy*.

Dr. Judy's TantrAdvice

Because the lingam and yoni are energy transmitters, it is wise to be discriminating about having sex with someone, because doing so invites their energy into your body and soul.

Finding Your Soul Mate on the Tantric Path

Of course, after you've committed to a tantric way of being, it can be wonderful to find a like-minded person on a similar journey. This makes life easier because you understand what each of you is striving for, in yourselves and in a partnership. You're on the same wavelength because ...

- ◆ You already have a common language. You know what she means by "chakra" or what he means by his appreciating your "Shakti" energy.

- ◆ You encourage each other in your practices and remind each other to do the breathing exercises or yoga practices.

- ◆ You support each other in your affirmations.

- ◆ You accept all parts of each other, even at difficult moments.

- You trust that you will strive to treat each other with respect and honesty.
- You create sex magic together, knowing the steps to do this.

- You give each other space to grow.
- You know the feeling of being "one" together and with all that exists.

Most people are searching for that perfect soul mate. Some experts on the topic say there are only a few perfect soul mates, twin souls or twin flames. More optimistically, it is possible to develop a relationship that feels deeply intimate and touches your soul with a partner who might not fit the previous characteristics.

Practicing tantric sex offers even more hope, because tantric sex means connecting—not on the superficial level, but on your soul level. Also, in tantric sex, every person is considered a divine soul. As a result, you can connect with his or her divinity if you open yourself to it. According to this point of view, you might find more soul mates out there than you thought.

Astrological readings to connect spiritual singles are consistent with tantric respect for the heavens and balanced matches. There are dating services based on what's called "Indian vedic astrology," a particular system of interpreting the effect of the planets on your life that promises profiles specifically geared toward earthly gods and goddesses on the tantric path. (One such site is www.tantric-soulmate-connection.org.)

Getting Ready for the Beloved

Of course you have to be prepared for that special beloved to enter your life. That means you have to clear any conflicts about being in a relationship and problems you might have stored up from past relationships. I have encountered many men and women who say they want commitment but who are unsuccessful at meeting people. If you are not attracting a partner, look inside yourself to be sure you really want a commitment and are not unconsciously sabotaging your efforts to meet someone. Also, confront the limiting beliefs you might have about finding a tantric match, such as …

♦ There are no good ones left; they're all taken.

♦ Even if I find someone, it'll turn sour anyway.

♦ I can never be happy in love.

♦ Whenever you have sex with someone, it always ruins the relationship.

♦ I always get hurt in the end.

♦ I'm destined to be alone.

♦ I'm better off being alone.

♦ Tantric lovers are always prone to affairs anyway, so I'd never have someone to myself.

♦ It didn't work out last time, so what can I expect now?

Catch yourself in these beliefs. Read each one and turn it into a positive affirmation that states how possible this type of love is for you. For example, change the phrase "I can never be happy in love" to "I *will* be happy in love." Feel how much happier you already feel when you say it the new, more positive way!

Bringing In the Beloved

Tantra practices are all designed to open you to love; therefore it is not surprising that some singles have found true love after starting their tantric sex studies. As Celia told me, "I finally realized that even though I was complaining I didn't have a man, I was closed off emotionally and angry at men for using me in the past. Once I got over that anger and learned to love myself and my yoni, I was open to Bill when I met him and I could let a man touch me deeply inside and out again."

Because tantric sex involves rituals, some people do rituals to draw in the energy of a partner. You might think of these as witchcraft or black magic; if anything it is white magic, as we are talking about bringing in love—not doing harm to anyone.

A ritual to bring in a beloved might involve this process: look at the moon, especially when it is full. Invoke spirits (of mother earth and father sky, god/goddess, grandparents, those who love you) to be your aides. State a desire clearly, such as "I declare that my beloved will come to me by next week." State what qualities you would like. End with assurance, saying "It is done" and an affirmation that "It is for the good of all."

Bringing in the beloved.

Where to Go

So many people ask me, "Where do I go to meet someone?" My book *The Complete Idiot's Guide to Dating* is chock full of advice about where to go (and what to say and tests about who is right for you). From all that, my favorite advice is: go to places where you will enjoy yourself. This works for several reasons:

- ◆ You will be happy; therefore you will glow and people will be attracted to you.

- ◆ People with similar interests will be in the same place.

- ◆ You'll be so involved in what you're doing that you won't seem like you're look- ing for someone (which can be a turnoff).

- ◆ Even if you don't meet anyone, you will have had fun!

Here are some concrete suggestions about where to find tantric soul mates:

- ◆ Tantra seminars, parties, and introductory events.

- ◆ Classes in yoga, T'ai Chi, and related Eastern fitness programs.

- ◆ Spirituality conferences and retreat centers.

- ◆ Flyers posted on bulletin boards at spirituality bookstores, health food stores, and meeting places.

- Stores that sell Eastern items or gifts.

- Bookstores, in the section that sell books on tantra and related spiritual practices.

- Workshops on related topics (relationships, personal growth, spirituality) through organizations that specialize in personal and spiritual development.

- Events and retreats related to spiritual leaders (Osho and others).

- Personal ads posted in magazines, newspapers, or on the web.

- Through friends and people you meet while participating in tantra. (You never know whether the person sitting next to you on a plane could be your next tantric beloved. That has happened to at least two women I know who almost gave up on finding their beloveds.)

- On the web. Surf for sites related to tantric sex (just type "tantra" in your search engine or start at www.tantra.com), join tantra newsgroups, and join in on chat rooms. Set up your own website and include your interest in tantra.

- Refer to the listings in Appendix B.

Dr. Judy's TantrAdvice

Instead of waiting for the perfect tantric mate, you can develop loving friendships with tantra buddies. These are platonic friends with whom you share some practices but who understand that you are not romantically committed partners.

After you go to one of these events, you will become networked into the tantra community and more resources will naturally come your way.

Two Love Lessons You Wish You'd Learned When You Were Young

Wouldn't it be nice if you didn't have pain in relationships, and if you didn't feel you wasted your time trying to make something work that was wrong all along? Colorado tantra teacher and psychologist Shavana Fineberg suggests the following two lessons to keep in mind to prevent those problems. "These can save you a lot of aggravation," she says.

- Just because you're incredibly attracted to someone doesn't mean it's a good match. Lust and looks can be deceiving, whereas real energy between people is more lasting and genuine.

♦ If the amount of energy you're putting into a relationship isn't the same as what you're getting back, don't pursue it. A female friend of Feinberg's handles dating wisely; if someone is not really interested in her, she doesn't have to force herself to resist calling him like so many other women—she is genuinely not interested. As she says, "I have enough problems, so if the other person doesn't want to be with me, I don't want him with me, either!"

Safe Sex When Practicing Tantra

Some experts estimate that there is a risk of sexually transmitted diseases (STDs) in the tantra community because of the accessibility of intimate contact between men and women, men and men, women and women, and even groups. Partners might be misled into unsafe sexual contacts because of the expectation of "trust" surrounding the practices. This expectation could lead to unwise assumptions and prevent someone from quizzing others about their sexual past and present health status.

I have been invited to lecture about the importance of safe sex at some tantra seminars, as it is crucial to address this subject. One fact that should be emphasized to prevent the spread of disease is this: even if you don't notice any symptoms, you can still have an STD and pass it on to someone else (as is the case with herpes and early stages of hepatitis C). I implore all tantra initiates and experts to pay attention to this issue!

Blocks to Bliss

Tara had unprotected intercourse with a new tantric lover who proclaimed that he did not have any diseases, but she contracted a yeast infection from him. Find out what a person means by "disease." Also be aware that men as well as women can transmit infections. And of course, always use protection!

Be aware, too, that some people with an STD that stays in the body (such as herpes) do not admit this, living in denial or rationalizing that they are not contagious because their energy has no intention to do so. When Lara found out that Don had herpes but insisted he would not spread it because he had no such intention, she was understandably furious about not being informed.

Be vigilant about asking, and telling, your partner about your sexual health history and risks before you engage in any intimacy. Always practice safe, protected sex to protect against STDs and unplanned pregnancy.

Keeping Confidence

My advice to singles throughout *The Complete Idiot's Guide to Dating* is to enjoy life and keep confident that love is possible—and everywhere and at any time. Tantra teacher Joan Heartfield, co-founder of Conversations That Matter for singles, agrees and says, "Your love relationship is waiting for you at each unique moment." Always remember my favorite phrase, "You are the beloved." When you feel that way, others will be drawn to you—and you will be happy anyway.

The Least You Need to Know

- ◆ You can enjoy a tantric sex lifestyle even if you are single. There's no need to wait for the beloved; you are the beloved!

- ◆ When you see the divinity in all beings, you can expand the possibilities to find someone to love.

- ◆ To find other singles who are interested in tantra, go to events for tantra, search the web, and talk to other people about your interest.

- ◆ Two love lessons are best learned early: real energy between two people is more important than a mere physical attraction, and the amount of energy you and your partner contribute to the relationship should be about equal.

- ◆ Like any sexual activity, always practice safe, protected tantric sex to protect yourself against STDs and unplanned pregnancy.

21

Tantric Ceremonies for All Occasions

In This Chapter

◆ How tantric ceremonies differ from traditional ceremonies

◆ Dedications that couples make to each other

◆ Personal stories from tantric brides and grooms

◆ How couples continue to affirm their love

◆ Some surprising occasions marked by tantric celebration

Particular experiences or a connection with a partner can be so intense that you want to celebrate with an occasion. Tantric ceremonies integrate the intention and rituals that have been presented in this book.

These ceremonies can mark any important occasion or shift in life circumstances, from a wedding, to birth of a child, graduation, new house or job, or even illness, separation, or death. "Even life's difficult occasions can be honored, infused with poignant meaning, and freed with love," says Richard Asimus, a minister and tantra teacher who, with his beloved partner Antoinette, conducts many of these. These ceremonies can be exquisitely original and elaborate, even theatrical, with music, dance, special dress, and eloquent declarations of love. They can be private or attended by hundreds of guests. In this chapter, you'll meet people who have created such events. I know you'll find these stories touching, interesting, and even inspiring.

The Unique Aspects of a Tantric Marriage Ceremony

Every culture has its beautiful—and idiosyncratic—rituals for important events such as weddings. Greeks dance with handkerchiefs; Jews lift the couple into the air on chairs; I've even witnessed two Christian weddings where the couple was wrapped in a braided rope to symbolize their union. Tantra, too, has its special rituals.

Bridal magazines and books today are filled with wonderful ideas on making the ceremony special. There's even a trend for couples to be quite original—such as marrying while scuba diving, sky-diving, or hot air ballooning! Tantric ceremonies are equally creative, although they vary from traditional weddings in some ways:

Dr. Judy's TantrAdvice

A tantric wedding ceremony needn't be elaborate or expensive to be profound. The rituals, dedications, and guest participation can be just as moving as my $30,000 wedding with eggs made to look like penguins and a Viennese dessert table that could fill a bakery.

♦ The wedding does not have to be legal. The couple might never get a state license, or they might get one at another time. Declarations of devotion often will do to mark the couple's commitment and honor their union—for themselves and for friends and family.

♦ The only people who need to be present for the marriage are the tantra bride and groom! Vows can be said that feel binding without anyone actually presiding over or witnessing the ceremony.

Many tantric wedding ceremonies have similar elements that mark the occasion. These include the following:

♦ **Symbolic places to make vows.** The choice of locale is influenced by the elements the couple would like to call in. It might be a forest for its earth connection, as a symbol for being grounded with each other; a mountaintop at dawn for more visionary, sky energy; or a secluded cave, dusty desert, or other holy place where spirits abide. Ceremonies near water are always magical and consistent with tantra's emphasis on cleansing.

♦ **Creative dedications.** Tantric weddings have no boilerplate, so partners can be totally free with what they say to each other.

◆ **Being in the moment.** Tantra teaches you to be present in the moment, so it's no surprise that some couples unite on an impulse. In tantra, couples can be even more spontaneous than a Las Vegas quickie, deciding to unite at a beautiful moment, walking on the beach at a particularly beautiful sunset, during a party where friends are already present, or sitting together in their bathtub!

◆ **Picking an auspicious time.** Some tantric couples wait for a particular day, consistent with the tradition of correct timing (as with Chinese philosophy where certain times are more auspicious than others and predict a happier future for the couple). The determination often rests on the moon's shape or the particular alignment of the planets.

◆ **Specific references to uniting male and female energies.** Because tantra is based on the balance of opposites, tantra marriage ceremonies often include references to the coming together of male and female energy.

◆ **Acknowledging that we are the world.** Tantric consciousness reaches out to the world, so activities and spoken words in the ceremonies reflect this universal consciousness.

◆ **Including more than two.** This is an advanced idea in tantra. Because love can extend to several people, more than two people might want to create a ceremony to testify to their love for one another.

What to Wear

Be as traditional as you like, or let your imagination go when it comes to your special event. What matters in what you wear, as in what you say, is that you feel good and that you dress to celebrate your inner expression of divine self, either feminine or masculine. To do this, close your eyes, breathe, go into your heart, and see what images or sounds come up. A good guideline to keep in mind, given the theme of sacred love and divinity is to dress as a goddess and god. That could mean flowing materials that are soft against your skin and regal jewelry. To be consistent with the tantric principle of union, coordinate your outfits so the two of you are in the same theme.

Feast for the Tantric Wedding

The food served at tantric marriages is purposefully chosen to be consistent with the tantric principle of sensuality. Choices include foods that stimulate all the senses with scent, taste, and color, such as strawberries, chocolate, and avocados. Celebrants might offer food to each other as a symbol of offering love.

Music for the Tantra Marriage

The music for tantric weddings is often original, performed by musicians who practice tantra themselves or make original music consistent with tantric practices. Some of these musicians and their work are listed in Appendix C. It is common to have drummers who drum passionately for hours on end. Guests are often welcomed to play drums, shake rattles, or participate in any imaginative way.

Who Officiates

Priests and priestesses who preside over the ceremony do not have to be traditionally licensed; they could be friends given the honor to perform the role. Sometimes the couple's tantra teacher officiates.

Interfaith ministers are good choices, as they are familiar with the use of ritual and sacred prayer and can also legally solemnize your vows. New York–based interfaith minister Reverend Laurie Sue Brockway unites couples of all backgrounds and faiths, working closely with the couple to create a personalized ceremony using ancient love stories and poetry and traditions of divine consorts (see Appendix B). The consulting room of this wedding officiate, who is trained in all the world's religions as well as in tantra, is filled with statues and images of divinities from all traditions from the Hindu Shiva and Shakti to Mother Mary and the Greek goddess of love, Aphrodite, and her male equivalent, Eros.

Says Brockway, "When two people come together and truly awaken to the depth and the power of their commitment, I can literally sense the gods, angels, ancestors, and spirit guides filling the room, there to help the couple feel the power of the moment, bear witness to their promises, and guide them in coming years. For that reason, the wedding ceremony is a true rite of passage that takes the bride and groom to the next level of their love, and gives their relationship a strong foundation to build on over time."

Ceremonies for All Occasions

These same rituals can be adapted at any stage of your relationship when you want to formally acknowledge your devotion to each other—often called a re-commitment ceremony. Depending on the occasion, adapt the words and vows as appropriate to the stage of your union.

Tantra Tales _____

When wedding officiate Laurie Sue Brockway and her beloved, Vic Fuhrman, a businessman and also a minister, got engaged, they went to their favorite beach on a full moon, created a special altar on the sand, then went to the water to pray to the goddess to cleanse them and ready them for married life. Then they scattered rose petals in a circle around them and recited poetic verses and personal vows to each other. In a sand ceremony, they poured red and green sand, symbolizing passion, heart, and healing, into a heart-shaped container that held their promise to marry. Experts in deity consciousness, they proclaimed their love in honor of the goddess Lakshmi (Hindu goddess of fortune) and her consort Vishnu (known as the Great Pre-server). Laurie's engagement ring has four diamonds, symbolizing the goddess Lakshmi's four arms, and three sapphires for the holy triad.

In a subsequent ceremony with Laurie Sue's close female friends, each said a blessing while pouring water over their hands.

Guest Participation

Friends are often given roles in tantric marriages. Like priests and priestesses in a temple, they might say dedications or perform dances for the delight of the couple and the other guests. Guests are encouraged to bring original songs to sing or poems to recite.

Special Ceremonies for Tantric Lovers

I'm honored to share with you the wedding ceremonies of several friends in the tantra community (who are also tantra teacher teams). They really know how to celebrate their love! Blessings to them!

Christina and William's Tantric Marriage Ceremony

I introduced you to Christina Sophia and William Florian in Chapter 16 when you read about their advice on the joys and benefits of belly dancing and other dance. Christina and William's wedding was exquisitely tantric in its elaborate attention to ritual. Both Californians, they decided not to get a state license because, as William said, "We do not recognize the importance of involving the state in our commitment to each other." Many friends were invited to play a role and also to serve as witnesses.

Tantric wedding rituals often begin the night (or even days) before the actual vows, either in rituals the couple does alone, or that the guests do together. The night before their ceremony, William and some of his closest friends met for a *ritual sweat lodge.* Christina and the women met for a special blessing of the bride.

Tantra Tutorial

A **sweat** is a Native American ritual gathering in which groups of men or women (or both) gather in a teepeelike structure where stones are set on a fire and participants incant prayers.

The wedding took place at a friend's home in California. Everyone was in festive costume, with the couple in sensual and colorful Gypsylike costumes. The groom, William, wore no shirt.

Many elements of the event reflected typical tantric rituals, such as dancing, invoking spirits, chanting, a sensual feast, and doing the yab yum position. At the end of the ceremony, the couple received a blessing from the deep vibrational tones of the didgeridoo, an Australian Aboriginal flutelike instrument.)

The festivities started at 6 P.M. Men congregated at the pool, and women gathered in the living room, holding flowers and chanting a Sanskrit mantra (*Om Mani Padme Hum*). In keeping with the tantric theme as the union of male and female divine energies, the men and women met in a circle, dancing and chanting, with the men singing, "I am the god, I am the father, all acts of love and pleasure are my ritual," as the women chanted, "I am the goddess, I am the mother, all acts of love and pleasure are my ritual." Every so often they all chanted, "Pleasure sacred, sacred pleasure." They also reversed the chants of the opposite sex with the women singing, "I am the god …" and men singing, "I am the goddess …."

Christina and William celebrate their tantric union.

In another demonstration of the embrace of opposites, the group gathered in a circle chant, with the men starting on the outside and the women forming an inside circle. The men danced counterclockwise as the women circled clockwise. But then the women passed through the raised arms of the men, moving to the outer circle and allowing the men to enter and create an inner circle. After a few minutes they paused and bowed to one another and then came into one big circle, completing the union.

William and Christina entered the room carrying flowers and crystals as a friend recited a poem. They placed gifts for each other on the altar as guests hummed in chorus.

Ecstasy Essentials

Following ancient tradition, both a priest and priestess are often chosen as masters of ceremony (to facilitate the activities), further maintaining the balance of male and female energies.

To synchronize the group energy, everyone was invited to face his or her beloved or someone near them, eye gaze and breathe together, recite a blessing, and affirm being a "circle of family." The couple introduced the guests with a few words about who each is to them and their appreciation to them for being family. There was much drumming and chanting; everyone proceeded into the couple's ceremony area, chanting, "I am god/goddess, the mother/father, all acts of love and pleasure are my ritual."

In true tantric style, the couple took time just being there, present in the moment, moving slowly, taking time to breathe deeply. They even did exercises I have described in this book, moving energy into each other's heart.

Christina sending love energy into William's heart at the wedding.

Ecstasy Essentials _____

As is traditional in ceremonies of indigenous peoples, a tantric union may include invoking and inviting the spirits, energy or influence of ancestors, family members not present, everyone from the couple's past, and even their previous lives (for those who believe in reincarnation). Those present bow in *namaste*, the Hindu greeting acknowledging that the "god/goddess in me greets and celebrates god/goddess in you."

Dancing is an integral part of the ceremony—many tantric couples are well versed in this art (Christina and William teach it together). Their dance included blessing of each of the energy centers (chakras) in the body.

The couple made dedications and vows, ringing a crystal bowl after each one. William's dedication was, "Part of our relationship is that we each have our individual goals, intentions, and aspirations, which we work toward and put energy into. We want to share these with you." His other statements to everyone included the following:

- We believe in service and extending our love and relationship into the world through our work together. We recognize that we are on a journey of growth and healing as individuals and together, and it is our desire to become increasingly conscious and aware of ourselves on every level.

- We have chosen tantra as part of our spiritual practice because we believe the path to god/goddess realization, and conscious evolution must include the body and all that we are.

- We also recognize that we have shadow sides and we are committed to have, be with, and love all parts of ourselves. We believe in the spiritual path of relationship and see all our experiences as opportunities for growth and healing.

- It is okay to be imperfect, to not know, to be open to possibility. We believe in learning through joy, fun, and pleasure.

- We revel in our many dimensions and saying yes to being partners with god/goddess in creating heaven here on earth.

- We experience profoundly in our bodies the love that we feel and generate together, and when we fall into a fixation that is not of this loving space, the affinity that is in every cell of our bodies and permeating our beings always brings us back to this simple truth.

- Support our love.

These are William and Christina's vows to each other:

♦ I love you and I love myself without conditions or reservations.

♦ I vow to continue with you on our path of growth and service to myself, each other, our family, and our community.

♦ I know that I shall love you forever and beyond forever, and that my highest good is served by acting in alignment with this great love.

After the vows the couple sat in yab yum, kissing and breathing together, as the didgeridoo sounds blessed them.

Christina and William connecting at their wedding.

As I have mentioned many times throughout this book, setting intention is a fundamental part of tantric lovemaking. Christina and William's intentions included the following:

♦ I am devoted to my spiritual path, bringing forth all the talent, artistry, knowledge, wisdom, and love that is my birthright for the evolution of my being and all others. I ask for your support of this intention.

♦ Most of all I wish to grow and deepen the love for myself and you in this sacred union, and our capacity to work together, cooperatively and tantrically. I ask for your support of this intention.

◆ I intend to be of service to both men and women and to help bring about a more loving, peaceful world. I ask for your support of this intention.

Christina added, "I am a mother and will always love my children. I intend to be there for them as much as I am able. I ask for your support of this intention." William's similar intention was, "I am a brother, son, friend, and family member to many. I intend to be there for them as well as your children and the new family I am entering into as much as I am able." And he added, "It is my intention to allow for the free flow of abundance, travel, creativity, music, enjoyable work, health, playfulness, and bodily pleasures. I ask for your support of this intention."

Acknowledging truths and each other is another intrinsic part of the tantric love tradition. Christina and William's acknowledgments included these:

◆ We acknowledge that we are multidimensional beings, different yet equal. We acknowledge that there are infinite possibilities, and we seek to know exactly what we want so we can delight in the joy of creating it.

◆ We embrace tantra as a way of life that gives us the key to healing, knowing, and opening our hearts and bodies to truth, and celebrating all of life and the divine essence within all things and all beings.

◆ We honor, celebrate, and bring together in harmonic vibration and expression the sacred union of our inner male and female energies.

◆ We are committed to nourishing ourselves—body, mind, and spirit—and keeping our bodies healthy and vibrant. Let any division between body and soul be healed completely in this loving relationship.

◆ Our love does not forsake others; it embraces all others.

Rundy and Lisa's Four-Day Wedding Ritual

The pretty and fit mother of an adolescent daughter, Lisa writes greetings cards for a living but performs her own exquisite poetry. Rundy is a tall, dark, and handsome actor, yoga teacher, and professional athlete, who also is a tantra teacher. They met at a yoga class, and she knew he was her prince. Lisa joined the training classes that Rundy was teaching, giving them added time to be together, as she was living in Cleveland while he was in California.

These meetings gave them an opportunity to have many magical settings for their vows to each other. One night, particularly auspicious because of the placement of the moon in the sky, they traveled to the top of a mountain, despite the cold, to be closer to the sky and slept outdoors to be connected to the elements.

Consistent with the tantric tradition of taking turns, as described in Chapters 11 and 12, Rundy and Lisa each had a turn to be giver and also to receive the other's nurturing, service, honoring, and loving. Their marriage ceremony lasted 4 days and included many ritualistic and beautifully choreographed steps:

- **Day 1: Honoring the goddess.** Lisa's day started with Rundy nurturing her with massages and baths scented with candles, oils, and hibiscus and rose petals. All day long he fed her exotic fruits, surprised her with love letters and small presents, sang to her, read poetry, brushed her hair, and kissed every part of her to make her feel honored and cherished.

- **Day 2: Honoring the god.** The following day was Rundy's turn to receive. During those 24 hours they made love without coming to climax, breathing in each other's desire, allowing the energy to build inside their bodies.

- **Day 3: *Rebirthing*.** This day was dedicated to the advanced tantric ritual of rebirthing, followed by a feast. The foods represent colors of the energy centers (for example, red tomatoes or green artichokes) to symbolize total connection. Lovemaking continued without coming to orgasm, to continue to build energy and desire.

> **Tantra Tutorial**
>
> **Rebirthing,** summarized in Chapter 17, is a sacred process in which a person's birth is re-enacted, but ensuring that it is a positive experience. The process is attended and assisted by those who greatly honor and respect it and treat it with great reverence.

- **Day 4: Taking the vows.** At sunrise, the couple went naked to the top of a cliff overlooking the ocean, near their home, with a *shamaness* minister (enlightened being) as a witness. As the sun came up, they exchanged their vows in a maithuna-style ceremony (described in Chapter 17). They sat in yab yum with lingam inside yoni to create a total connection, looking into each other's eyes, honoring the 108 gods and goddesses in each other. They spoke their heartfelt promises for their life together, written by them especially for the occasion.

Other rituals in Rundy and Lisa's ceremony:

- The shamaness brought in the energies of the four directions, earth and sky, and all the ancients so that their bodies would become one with each other's and all the cosmos.

- Rundy and Lisa did extended breathing together, connecting all their chakras (sex, heart, third eyes kissing), their bodies vibrating (not having orgasm), melting deeper and deeper into each other.

- The couple lay back to back with their sacrums touching to allow their powerful kundalini energy to rise, as the sun rose.

Mark and Patricia's Hindu Fire Ceremony

Mark Michaels and Patricia Johnson are a tantra-teacher team. They got married in a tantric ceremony, at which their dear friend and teacher Bhagavan Das performed a *Hindu fire ceremony*, assisted by his wife, Mira. Guests included their parents, who participated in the ritual. Later, a small group of tantrikas gathered to invoke ancient traditions and bless their union.

"It was a beautiful and profound experience," says Mark (whose initiated name is Swami Umeshanand Saraswati). "We feel it is only one of many marriage ceremonies we will have." This is consistent with the tradition of the Hindu wedding ceremony, in which you make a commitment for seven lifetimes.

"Perhaps more important," Mark adds, "we view marriage not as a state of being or something brought into being by a ceremony. Rather it is a process, an ongoing unfolding. Thus, we are constantly in the process of marrying each other. *Conjugal* comes from the same Sanskrit root as the word *yoga*. The root, *yug*, means 'yoking' or 'union.' Dr. Jonn Mumford (their teacher) tells us that it is the most difficult yoga of all. As in other forms of yoga, the process of marriage is not about achieving a goal; it is all about what happens along the way."

Tantra teachers Mark and Patricia doing eye gazing at their wedding.

Tantra Tales _____

Tantra teachers Sasha and Janet Lessin were at a conference at a California retreat center, attended by many tantric friends, when they decided one evening to get married and created a ceremony on the spot. The bride and groom were lifted in the air in chairs as friends (and anyone else at the conference!) danced around them in celebration.

Kutira and Raphael's Wedding and Ten-Year Anniversary

Hawaii-based Kutira and Raphael have been in loving union for more than 10 years. Their wedding ceremony was held on the beach with elaborate rituals and ceremony. Both were carried by attendants (friends) and recited personalized vows. Everyone wore goddess and god wear. For their anniversary 10 years later, they performed a four-part musical concert, invoking the four elements (earth, sky, water, and fire), with guest performances from a holy Hawaiian and other friends.

Raphael being carried out for the ceremony.

Raphael's fiftieth birthday was marked with another dramatic ceremony. Held at a friend's California mansion, a virgin and then Raphael were sent off a rock cliff into the pool below, whereupon Raphael swam underwater to the opposite end where he was transferred by friends (representing the "mother") into a hot tub where he was symbolically "birthed." Friends then entered a tent and some performed (sang, danced, recited poetry) for him and the assembled crowd.

Kutira and Raphael's wedding vows.

Kutira and Raphael's tenth anniversary concert, with them wearing their original wedding crowns.

Keeping the Fires Burning

Following tantric practices can help couples stay together long term in bliss. Some tantra teaching couples are good examples of this.

Antoinette and Richard Asimus, a Cincinnati-based, loving, tantra-teaching couple, have maintained their monogamous commitment to each other in a marriage that has lasted more than 30 years. "Our love is stronger because of our tantric practice," says Antoinette. How do they do it? Antoinette shares two of their secrets. "We honor our commitment to each other every day by making love and including some yogic and spiritual practices in our lovemaking. And every 2 or 3 months, we make a date for a tantra day where we experience the timelessness of tantric lovemaking for a whole day, celebrating at the end of the day with dinner at a five-star restaurant." "Yummy!" she adds.

Lexi and Kip are tantra-teaching partners who have been together for 10 years. Although they choose not to be formally married, they recommit to their evolving relationship every 6 months—on Valentine's Day and then again in August. One week after they met, Kip requested that they each write what they wanted in a relationship. Out of Lexi's 14 things, and Kip's 9, they had 8 that were the same. They synergized the rest and continue to update this process.

Paul Ramana Das and Marilena Silbey called their 10-year tantric partnership an *alignment and aloinment*, meaning they are lined up spiritually and sexually, no matter what their individual paths. On a trip to Hawaii to celebrate Marilena's birthday, they made a promise to have "a honeymoon every day." They also wrote a partnership constitution, in which they pledged to continually practice the following:

◆ Love in their hearts for each other

◆ Good intentions

◆ Clear communication

◆ Positive language

◆ Celebration of their male and female aspects in the healthy dance of sacred sexuality

◆ A deep commitment to an ongoing intimate relationship

"We encourage everyone to come up with their own list of decrees for their love," says Ramana Das. "This gives you a sense of joint willingness to weave a strong relationship and build love forever."

Group Ceremonies

Celebrations can be in groups, besides just for couples. These can be devoted to an individual person, as in a ritual for a pregnancy—or book release! Such rituals (also called a *puja*) can involve the group lighting candles, stating prayers or intentions, putting written statements of what they want to release into a fire, and presenting small gifts.

The group assists by becoming witnesses to the event, supporting each other. New York–based minister Barbara Biziou, author of *The Joys of Everyday Ritual*, explains, "The group blessing empowers each participant to hold their intention, and to be open to receive what they say they want." (See Appendix B for contact information.)

Tantra Tutorial

A **puja** is a sacred circle of worship performed by a group of people. The group can form inner and outer circles and rotate around the circle, as in a wheel, moving around the circle to the next person, sharing experiences that might include eye gazing, breathing, sounding, or expressing feelings. In one variation, men can create "temples" with cushions and sacred objects, set up side by side, for the women in the group to visit.

Parting Tantrically

Separation, divorce, or the death of a loved one can be exceedingly painful. But by using tantric principles, you can part with less pain and free yourself up for more joy. Partings can use any of the practices and rituals described earlier for commitments, including prayers and blessings for each other's happiness.

Dr. Judy's TantrAdvice

When you have lost a love, remember that the love is still inside you; say to yourself, "I am love."

Untying the Knot: Separations and Divorce

Some tantric teaching couples have parted ways but continue to speak highly of each other; and a few, like Charles and Caroline Muir, continue to teach together and incorporate lessons about the transformation in their relationship as part of the tantric path.

Transitions into Deterioration, Death, and Dying

Tantric rituals can also be useful to connect with the soul when ready for another transition. In one example of this, business executive David Hollies and close friends pulled together a "Celebration of Life" service for himself, friends, and family. Calling it a "living memorial," David wanted to say good-bye to the many aspects of his life that dementia was bringing to a close. But just as important, he wanted to share his deepening appreciation of the daily joys of life.

Held in a church, loved ones sang songs, recited poetry, and recalled experiences of David over the years. There was much laughing and crying. "I wanted to share this crossroads with you and show you that while there is much in my life that is ending," David said from the podium at his turn to talk, "there are new joys and delights showing up each day, and I'm finding my way."

The celebration continued at a nearby retreat center, with a sharing circle and a puja. The women retreated to dress in goddess wear as the men gathered in a bonding ritual and drumming circle to welcome back the women, who then performed a goddess dance. That led to dancing, conversation, food, and hot tubbing.

When news rocked the tantra community of the sudden death of a beloved "brother," Robert Frey, many memorials were immediately arranged. Frey, a tantra and Sufi master whose work has been quoted in this book, had written many songs used at tantra events, like "Opening to Love." Shockingly, Robert fell in the bathtub, subsequently developed pneumonia, and died. The purpose of the gatherings was announced: "to share our grief about Robert's passing, to continue our own healing process, to connect even more fully with others present, to expand even further our capacity to love, to connect even more fully with Spirit, and to celebrate Robert's unique and gracious contributions to our community and to the world." Robert's songs and Sufi dances were performed. He is sorely missed but his legacy lives on!

The Least You Need to Know

- Tantric ceremonies can be performed to sanctify a union at any time and in any stage, including an engagement, marriage, re-commitment, or even separation.

- Tantric ceremonies include many rituals of song, dance, and dedications to honor spirits, gods and goddesses, all guests, and each other.

- Tantric marriage ceremonies are not always legal but are sacred and include personal statements from the couple and sometimes from guests, to set intentions, make acknowledgments, and state lifetime pledges.

- Ongoing tantric practice can help solidify a couple's long-term commitment.

- Tantric rituals performed for separation help the couple make this transition with a loving spirit.

22

When He Resists or She Strays

In This Chapter

- ◆ When you're sure about tantric sex but your partner isn't
- ◆ Making it work despite different points of view
- ◆ Can tantric love survive an affair?
- ◆ Energy boosters: what you can do to re-ignite the spark

Surely by now you are excited about your tantric journey. You've shifted your perspective about sex and love and are becoming intrigued with the possibilities for the deepest connection you have ever known. But wait—there's a rock in the road. What if your partner is not as intrigued as you, even after you've shown him or her this book? Can you ever convince someone to share your new vision? This chapter will help you with that dilemma.

Worse yet, what if you've already convinced your partner to enjoy tantalizing tantra, but then he or she took it farther than the boundaries of your relationship and let the sexual energy lead him or her into bed with someone else? Or perhaps it's you who is tempted to taste the treasures of another tantric lover and fear the havoc it will wreak on your present relationship. What to do now? This chapter addresses those issues, too.

What If You Aren't on the Same Page?

If you're in a relationship and you both agree to find out what tantric sex is all about, it's easy to begin practicing immediately. Check Appendix B for workshops and recommended teachers, and sign up for a seminar to learn more.

But what if you really want to pursue the exciting things you're reading about in this book, but your current partner is unsure? It is not uncommon that one person in a relationship is intrigued and ready for a new path whereas the other has reservations. Don't despair; all is not lost. I can offer you some hope. I've seen it happen: a partner can come around. Here are some suggestions to approach a resistant beloved with your desire to travel this path together:

- ◆ Be prepared for excuses. Your partner might say there's not enough time for practice or money for courses. Instead of protesting, listen and accept his or her point of view. Resistance only gets stronger if you argue or insist your partner is wrong.

- ◆ Understand and accept the fears. The practices in tantric sex can make you feel vulnerable, as feelings come up that might have been suppressed for years. Instead of getting angry, empathize that your partner might not have the strength at this time to be so open and vulnerable.

- ◆ Explain your point of view and your interest in the practices clearly and without defensiveness.

Talking through your differences about tantra.

- ◆ Point out the benefits that your partner can relate to. If he values physical fitness, emphasize the health benefits. If she is more psychologically oriented, describe possible growth from an emotional point of view.

- ◆ Supply your partner with videos, books, audiotapes, flyers, and website links (check those listed in Appendixes B and C) to illustrate that this is a sacred practice. Explain the mood, energy, spirit, and philosophy of tantra. Sometimes a picture is worth a thousand words, so videos can offer clear pictures of what tantra is about; they're especially helpful for beginners on any spiritual path.

- ◆ Be honest about what you think and feel. Offer to show your partner what you have discovered and why you feel tantric sex is a wonderful lifestyle choice. Speak openly about your desire to study tantra, and give your partner a chance to be supportive.

- ◆ Don't nag. Attitudes can change, so bring the subject up every now and then, but not with persistence or annoyance.

- ◆ Avoid climbing on a pulpit. It's difficult to convert someone to what you think and believe. Honor your partner's path. Allow your partner to be himself or herself—and allow you to be you. Like philosophy or religion, deep thoughts regarding spirituality and sexuality are unique to each individual and are very personal choices.

- ◆ Ultimately support your partner's position, as that is the spirit of tantra. Continue your lovingness, despite differences, as that is the best example of the beauty of the path.

Hell No, I Won't Go!

The dread, of course, is that you are really gung ho about taking this high road to bliss, but your partner is dead set against it. It can happen. But don't be so quick to throw in the towel on the relationship. Partnerships have survived when one person studies tantra but the other doesn't. Of course it would be better if you both spoke the same language. It's more serious than if one of you likes sushi and the other cringes at the thought of raw fish, or if one of you likes romance movies and the other prefers classic comedies, or if one of you wants to climb the Himalayas and the other can think of nothing better than vegging out on a beach. It's more serious than that, because tantra is a commitment to a lifestyle. But when your love is working on other levels, you can still be a team, raising kids, sharing your dreams, and even making love.

Know What's Best for You

Stay on your personal path. Recognize your own fears of being alone or disagreeing with a partner whose opinion or approval you value. When you maintain your integrity, you might suffer some consequences, but you'll never lose yourself; in the last analysis, you have to decide what's best for you. If your partner just won't share this path with you, you might have to go on the journey alone. But you can still stay together—if you bring home the love you learn to generate and make it benefit this relationship.

Dr. Judy's TantrAdvice

It is possible that pursuing tantric sex can draw you toward like-minded people with whom you share more time and intimacy, which can lead you to decide that your primary relationship is not so satisfying. That's the time to talk seriously with your partner about your future together and consider seeking professional counseling.

A partner's reaction is a test of his or her character. Karin's husband told her, "If you feel you'll be happy finding out what this is all about, go for it. I'm not interested, but I support you doing what you need to do." That shows true love! On the other hand, Donna was so dismayed at Frank's desire to go to a tantra introductory class that she threatened to date other men and hid mail that he received from the tantra organization. Her intolerance revealed her true character, which had not been as evident before. Eventually Frank knew it had to be over.

Honor Your Agreements

Tantra teaches honor. Respect your agreements with a partner, especially regarding the most sensitive issue of commitment and exclusivity about sexuality. Be honest about what your intentions are. Offer reassurance—if you can do so honestly—that you will not engage in any activities that are not in alignment with your relationship agreement. Your partner deserves your love and respect. Be sure you are studying tantra with a practitioner who will honor, respect, and support your relationship agreement; ask the teacher any questions that you have about your situation to get some advice and support.

Don't Sneak Off to a Tantra Talk

Be honest if you decide to attend an evening event or class, or see a practitioner or healer without your partner. Explain that your intention in gaining this knowledge, experience, or healing is to grow and transform your ability to deepen your love in this relationship and in all your life.

Share Your Growth

After your tantra class, private healing session, or tantra seminar, share what you experienced with your partner, even if he or she doesn't have a deep appreciation or understanding of what you are going through. As you learn, show your partner the immediate effects of your training and your newfound sensitivity, loving ways, caring attitudes, and spiritual depth. Keep making low-key invitations to join you at some entry-level event that would be especially safe and nonthreatening. Be patient. Remember to allow your partner to keep sharing his or her concerns over time.

When the Going Gets Tough

Be prepared that a partner's differing experience, feelings, or judgments about tantra can precipitate a confrontation in your relationship. I know this could be traumatic, but welcome it! Don't blame it directly on tantra. A blowup just means that you were headed toward some pivotal moment anyway; this just happened to be the catalyst—it could have been something else!

The topic of tantra presses people's hot buttons, because it's associated with sex (an already threatening subject) and promises transformation (which is worrisome if you fear the unknown). Reread and share with your partner the sections about the corrections of myths about sex and tantra in Chapter 1.

> **Blocks to Bliss**
>
> If you attend tantra functions, don't keep it a secret from your beloved. This kind of deception is contrary to tantric practice and erodes the energy that you are trying to purify. In fact, your practices might make you more vulnerable to being caught in any deceit, because they make you more transparent in the course of being open and loving.

> **Tantra Tutorial**
>
> A partner's resistance to tantra might be based on past abuse that has been repressed. Unconscious conflicts and fears might be triggered at the thought of being open to feelings and love.

When a Relationship Has to End

Sometimes you can thank your lucky stars that things came to a head and that you and your partner broke up because of your separate paths. Be grateful you found out now that you were incompatible. Don't second-guess what could have happened. Face the sadness, and use the experience as a real-life experience of tantric principles: the love you have never leaves you, even though particular people might.

> **Tantra Tales** _____
>
> Cassie dragged Steve to three tantra weekend workshops around the country, desperate to break through his controlling nature and get him to be more intimate. "I love making love with him," she said, "but when he's deep inside me he gets to thrusting fast and I try to get him to feel the love we have, but it's too late." Steve enjoyed some of the exercises during the workshops, but back home he complained that he had no time or interest to do them; eventually he told her, "I can't do this anymore," and asked her to move out. Cassie came to see the value of being set free from this unfulfilling relationship and honor her own desire for a more intimate connection instead of being obsessed with changing Steve.

Tantric Tolerance

In these modern times, many relationship paradigms are acceptable. More and more people are choosing to define their own rules. Couplings that were once seen as alternative are now more mainstream, and people are becoming more open about their choices and living what's real for them instead of leading double lives in fear of what others think of them.

This new era is seeing a re-emergence of the open relationships that bloomed but bombed in the 1970s. Couples choosing more love for all, called *polyamorous*, accept and invite third, fourth, or more parties to join their intimate circle, including sexual activity. Polyamorous men and women face challenges with commitment and jealousy like traditional monogamous pairs, but feel this way of relating is more satisfying for them. There are communities and conventions for couples in this lifestyle.

What to Do About Tantric Sex Affairs

Most affairs are painful, and they can be even more so when tantric sex practices are involved, because of the association to higher levels of eroticism and therefore deeper connections. One partner's sexual relations or liaisons that the other does not sanction are inevitably hurtful. Before betrayal sends you off the deep end, evaluate the situation, including the reasons it happened, your choices about what to do, and what new level you can reach in your relationship as a result.

Considerations About Tantric Affairs

If one of you has an affair, it's time to ask some hard questions of yourself and your partner. Use these questions as a guide to clarify some issues and start a confronting conversation:

- ◆ Are you or your partner involved romantically in a relationship with someone else but not having sex with that person?

Tantra Tutorial

An affair always involves some breakdown in communication in a relationship. Learn to effectively communicate your wants and desires to each other. When you open up, you might be surprised at what you each have longed to share. From that place of openness, all things are possible.

- ◆ If sex is involved, what type of sexual activity is it? Is protection being used, and what types of diseases could you be exposed to?

- ◆ What are your agreements about fidelity, and has either of you violated those agreements?

- ◆ What is the nature of the "other" relationship? Is the "third person" an ongoing lover or a fleeting relationship?

- ◆ Are you both being honest now, or are you telling lies?

- ◆ Do you both really want to know what's going on?

- ◆ What are the motivations behind the affair?

- ◆ How have you each contributed to this situation and to any behavior you find upsetting?

- ◆ What steps can you take to improve or change the situation?

- ◆ Do you want the relationship to end?

- ◆ Is the relationship already dead and you just haven't buried the corpse?

- ◆ Do you want to try to fix the relationship?

It's not easy to have a confrontation, but when it's necessary, have the courage to do it. In the course of a lifetime, everyone experiences disappointments in love, rejecting and being rejected, abandoning or being abandoned. Neither position feels good. Always keep in mind that denial only postpones pain; discussing difficult issues leads to some relief—and resolve.

There's much more about how to affair-proof your relationship, and how to handle infidelity, in my book, *The Complete Idiot's Guide to a Healthy Relationship*, but the bottom line is this: as a relationship therapist for many years, I know that any relationship can work if both people want it to. You can heal from tantric love affairs if you work at staying together. Doing the practices in this book will help by increasing your intimacy.

> ### Tantra Tales
>
> Expert tantra teacher Richard Asimus explains a powerful and impressive view of passionate monogamy possible through tantra practice that he calls the "Any woman/ Everywoman, Any man/Everyman." He and his wife Antoinette have been together more than 30 years, inspired that Shiva and Shakti have been together for more than a thousand years. Says Richard, "In our practices, I can be any man and Antoinette can be any woman." Because we experience being so many facets of ourselves, we are infinitely changing and growing, individually and together."

An Affair Used as Energy Booster

The reasons people cheat are diverse, including intimacy and commitment fears, situations that separate partners or put two people together under intense circumstances, anger toward the partner, or even different philosophies of life. Some people don't want to be monogamous, and their cheating doesn't necessarily point to any underlying problem in the relationship. In many relationships, however, an affair is a wake-up call to a situation that desperately needs to be addressed.

> ### Ecstasy Essentials
>
> We often are attracted to, and attract, lovers who reflect unresolved issues we had with our primary caregivers while growing up, and then want to hurt, cheat, or leave them. Identify how present partners resemble past important people in your life in some physical, emotional, psychological, or energetic way so you don't repeat the same patterns.

In tantric terms, seeing relationships as energy, there is another reason for affairs. It's called a search for an *energy booster*. Because everything in tantra can be seen as energy, an affair is not necessary; all that is necessary is a new and equally exciting way to boost energy.

A related theory postulates that people seek what is called *New Relationship Energy* (*NRE*), a phrase used by *Loving More* magazine to describe that high-energy spark and rush of chemicals felt when you meet someone new and get a surge of excitement from the attraction. *Extra Relationship Energy* or

External Relationship Energy has the same effect but comes about between people who have known each other a while or had infrequent contact.

Affairs arise from an illusion that someone outside the relationship appears more sexy, exciting, and desirable because they're not the one handling bills, taking the cat to the vet, or messing up the bathroom. This is a good way to affair-proof your relationship: when you're tempted to stray, always imagine what it would be like in daily life with a new lover.

Dr. Judy's TantrAdvice

As a therapist, I am constantly struck by how much couples take each other for granted so soon in a relationship. Instead of looking for sparks with someone else, create that desirable energy by tapping into new parts of yourself with your partner.

A common area that breaks down in long-term relationships is sexuality. Either the sex itself isn't good, or other problems arise and lovemaking goes from infrequent to never. Anger or guilt shows up in impotence or withdrawal from sex. Couples build up resentments and disappointments that, if left unresolved, could erode a couple's ability to open up in sex. If the problem is never addressed, the entire relationship erodes and can lead to a breakup over something that seems unrelated. Have courage to talk about what your sexual needs and problems are, and get help.

Tantric partners are tuned in to energies within themselves and the people around them, so they are more likely to sense when something is awry. If you sense a problem brewing in your relationship, address it now with your partner before it gets bigger and more difficult to solve. Trust your tantric intuition!

The Energy Booster Checklist

You can recapture your attraction to each other, recover from an affair, and even prevent infidelity—I know, because I have helped many couples do these things. I've written a lot about how to do this in *The Complete Idiot's Guide to a Healthy Relationship*. The bottom line is this: any problem in your relationship is an opportunity for healing and boosting the energy between you. Remember my principle: any relationship can work if you want it to! Reflect on what you and your partner can do to give your relationship an energy booster so you continue to be fascinated with each other. Can you learn not to interrupt while he is talking? Take a class or find other interests to become more well rounded? Lose weight to feel more attractive and confident about yourself? Make your list here. Ask your partner to make a list, too.

Your Relationship Energy Boosters

How Can I Infuse More Energy
in My Relationship   **What Can My Partner Do**

1. _____   _____

2. _____   _____

3. _____   _____

4. _____   _____

5. _____   _____

Look over your lists and talk about which energy boosters you can both put into practice. How do you feel about each other's suggestions? Decide to implement at least one of these each week.

The Least You Need to Know

- It is possible to pursue tantric sex whether or not your partner is committed to the same path.

- When one partner wants to pursue tantric sexuality but the other doesn't, the relationship is put to a test. Some survive if communication and love keeps growing.

- Temptation for liaisons with others on the same path is possible and can lead to affairs that threaten an existing relationship. However, staying together is possible if the couple really wants to.

- The tantric lifestyle demands honesty, so eventually if one of you has an affair, the truth about your level of commitment has to be faced and new agreements made about your future together.

- Brainstorm ways to put more energy into your relationship to keep your commitment strong.

Part 6

The Tantric Path to Wellness and Peace for All

Now that you've learned how powerfully these practices can manifest sexual energy, empowering you to have more joy, passion, and love, you'll wonder whether they can apply to you and people you know. The answer is "yes": no matter what relationship you are in, no matter what your age, tantric principles can make your life a thousand times richer.

Tantra is about honor, respect, and healing. So in this part, you'll learn how to extend that respect and healing to yourself, to be ready to adjust to life changes with new life force. And you'll see how you can apply tantric principles to every aspect of your relationships—and every living thing around you. This will take you beyond sex to a more intense force that can actually reach out and help heal the planet.

Chapter

23

Tantric Love at All Ages and Stages

In This Chapter

♦ The new anti-aging: how tantric sex keeps you young

♦ Easing midlife transitions

♦ The seven keys to healthier life transitions

♦ Adapting tantric sex practices for kids

♦ Teaching tantra in schools

In this chapter, you'll learn the benefits of practicing tantra at all ages and stages of life. Whether young or old, the secrets revealed can bring more health and happiness. I know this is true because I have trained many groups in different types of tantra, including people of all ages. Of course, I'm not referring to specific sexual practices here, because I'm including young people, but to the nonsexual tantra practices that still build and harness amazing energy.

Perhaps best of all, you'll see how tantra is a genuine fountain of youth! That's right, you can feel, look, and be young forever.

Want to Feel and Look Young Again?

Anti-aging! It's always been a desire to stay young, but our current society seems obsessed with it. Anti-aging creams, supplements, exercise, and eating programs are billion-dollar business. Tantra is the new secret to staying young After tantric love-making, you can look at least 10 years younger—and other people notice. I've heard men say to 40-year-old women after tantric sex, "You look like a kid again!" Participants' faces dramatically change, their skin glistens, and lines disappear! Eyes sparkle and open wide, and smiles spread from ear to ear.

Tantra Tales _____

The benefits of tantra happened for Nancy. After her husband died, Nancy panicked, fearing, "There will never be another man who knew me as a young lover, who saw my face at 20. No one will remember how pretty I was as a young woman." However, practicing tantric sex provided a solution. Much to her delight, new lovers remarked to her anyway, "You look 20."

Tantra Tales _____

Carla is more than 50 years old but looks much younger, something she has been told by lovers. "I'm convinced it is my tantric sex practices," says Carla. "I know that bringing my sexual energy into my heart and living from love every moment of my life is what makes me look so much younger."

Rejuvenation happens on several levels. Psychologically, you feel young! And physiologically, there are real changes. The physical activities in tantric sex practices—cycling energy, breathing deeply, exercising muscles through white tantra (yoga) practices—keep organs vital by feeding them with blood and nutrients and keep the body supple and toned. The neurons in the brain are activated, and the immune system is stimulated—contributing to all-around health and maintenance of youthfulness.

The Real Fountain of Youth in Amrita Flow

Some very experienced tantra teachers and tantrikas, such as Caroline Muir in Maui, credit the flow of amrita (the liquid emitted during female ejaculation) for rejuvenation. (The techniques for bringing about the flow have been described in earlier chapters) "Amrita is considered the 'nectar of the goddess,' the key to her immortality and youthfulness. It is a woman's gift to herself and her lover," says Caroline, "and definitely keeps me young." Another expert disagrees, claiming that the amrita flow ages women. Although this point of view seems consistent with Taoist belief that a man's ejaculation drains his energy, most women I know who have this experience (myself included) agree with Caroline and treasure the experience and its positive effects. As one woman said, "When my love liquid flows, my whole face and being is so full of joy and so relaxed that of course I look young again!"

Tantra in Older Years

As the percentage of the population over 65 has tripled during the past century, understanding, accepting, and enjoying sexuality throughout the entire life span has become essential. Forget any notions you might have about cutting back on sex as you age. Studies show that although sexual activity does decline with age, this is partly due to illness and unavailability of partners. Sexuality is normal and natural in older years! And it also insures better general health. In any case, remember that tantric sex as the transmission of energy goes way beyond any specific sexual activity or intercourse; therefore, pleasure is possible for your entire life.

Facing the Changes

As we age, hormones can wreak havoc on our physical, emotional, and sexual life. Emotional challenges escalate at critical ages, such as the classic midlife crisis. Some experts claim that midlife crises are even starting now as early as age 35. Even younger men and women in their mid-20s are going through what I call the "quarter-life crisis," stressing out that they are no longer "young" and now have to bear huge responsibilities as adults in a fast-paced, competitive, and money-obsessed society. Baby boomers bemoan passing years, as their parents become ill, children grow up and leave the nest, friends suffer heart attacks at younger ages, and they face the ever-dreaded life review with regrets or broken dreams. But if you keep your energy surging, as you can through tantric practices, biological slowdowns and emotional lows don't have to ruin your life. In fact, you can have more courage to heal wounds and can become more balanced and more energized.

"She may not look like a cover girl … but there's pleasure and treasure beyond all measure," sings one songwriter about "A Woman in Her Prime" touting a women's sex appeal through the years (find more about Marcie Boyd's music at www.marcieboyd.com).

Tantra Tutorial

Several research studies show that continued sexual activity keeps you healthy, and that general satisfaction with life, love, and sex helps you live longer. Both men and women who continued satisfying relationships had fewer physical ailments and lower mortality rates.

Easing Her Time Through Menopause

During a woman's fertile years, energy flows through the body for reproduction (among other things); even when this is no longer possible after menopause, the good news is that energy is still there!

No need, either, to suffer during this time. Moving your energy in a tantric way can ease the symptoms of menopause, including body aches and pains, night sweats, headaches, and even depression. While the change of life can lead to thinning and shortening of the vaginal canal and dryness that causes pain, tantric sex practices limber the body, help the mind focus on other pleasures, and can even create more lubrication naturally. Instead of "drying up," the menopausal woman can experience a higher sex drive and more sexual freedom than ever before.

Tantra Tales _____

For Kathryn, sex got better after menopause. "My husband and I lie quietly in bed without the intention to have sex," she told me, "but when he strokes my inner thighs and rubs my stomach and mound, tapping on the top of my pubic bone, my energy and desire awakens. Then he puts his hand on my mound and shakes it and I have intense feelings like orgasm."

As tantric lover Pam says, "I sailed through menopause without even noticing except that I stopped having my period." Menopausal women like Pam who practice tantric sex also accept their change of life, seeing it as a blessing—a "reunion with the ancient mother." Even though fertility is revered in the tantra tradition, the goddess in older age (in the form of the wise woman) is revered and respected as well.

Tantra Tales _____

During the change of life, one of the major problems is lack of lubrication. However, tantra practices can make you moist again. Says Nancy, "Now over 50, I don't get as excited instantly as I did before, but the tantric practices have taught me how to move my pelvis and loosen up the energy flow in my body. When I add the movements to my breathing, within 10 minutes I get very lubricated. Sometimes I don't even need to reach orgasm because the practices and pleasure are enough. I love this new stage of life and love."

Spiritual counselor Barbara Bizou runs workshops for people in life transition. An expert on rituals, as documented in her book *The Joys of Everyday Rituals*, Barbara recommends this ritual that a menopausal woman can do to celebrate her life stage and acknowledge her transition into a new—and rich—stage of life. Invite your friends over, including those who are also going through menopause, and ask each to write down a memory about some painful time at another stage of life. This helps people release the energy of that old memory and make room for the new stage that they are entering. Then burn the pieces of paper in a big pot in the middle of the room, and as they burn, each woman should light a candle and say a prayer for healing the past and opening up to the start of a new life.

When He Has a Midlife Crisis

Similarly, tantric sex practices can ease the symptoms of what has become known as male menopause (or *andropause*)—men's gradual lowering of testosterone levels as they age and go through slumps and depressions similar to women. Lowered hormone levels can lead to a man's reduced sex drive, along with less interest in relationships and career. As with midlife women, the midlife man can get tired, anxious, irritable, sweaty, and achy, and feel helpless and hopeless. Sexually, he worries about being less potent, having less ejaculate, and even whether his penis is shrinking.

Tantric sex helps these men by reviving their energy and teaching them to direct energy through their body (instead of just out their penis!). They learn to generate more energy in their sex center; more blood there leads to stronger erections and a seemingly bigger penis. And they learn to enjoy new levels of love and creativity, energizing them in every aspect of their family, relationships, and business life.

By learning techniques to prolong sexual stimulation, as I outlined in Chapter 13, men gain more control over their ejaculation. The result is more pleasure in their sexual relationship, which escalates in a positive cycle of better sex, more love, more happiness, and feeling more potent. What a good deal!

Ecstasy Essentials

There are many benefits of tantric orgasm to the body and brain. Cycling sexual and orgasmic energy throughout the body vitalizes major organs and body systems (including the circulatory, cardiovascular, nervous, immune, and endocrine systems). Stimulating the pituitary and pineal glands is especially positive, as the pathway to bliss is through the brain.

Seven Keys to Happier Life Transitions Through Tantric Love

Practicing tantric sex offers many ways to keep you fit through all of life's changes:

1. Tantra unleashes feelings, emotions, and attitudes that you've always wanted to express in a relationship. It focuses you on intimacy, closeness, affection, and

tenderness toward a partner, which sustains sexuality, and also provides self-esteem and inspiration—all of which are essential with passing years.

2. Tantric sex takes you beyond sex as just intercourse to realms of intimate expression so that just looking in each other's eyes or breathing together can set off orgasmic waves. Romance, kissing, hand holding, and oral sex are all honored to create closeness when intercourse is not possible.

3. In tantric sex, limp lingams are just as loveable as erect ones. Energy can be generated from the lingam no matter what its state.

4. Tantric sex creates more lubrication for the yoni and relaxes, heals, and revitalizes the woman at any age.

5. Because synchronizing the partners' energies is fundamental in tantric sex, some physiological changes (such as a man taking longer to achieve an erection or ejaculation) can benefit the couple's lovemaking.

6. Tantric sex emphasizes loving touch, which triggers chemicals from the body that are proven to strengthen the immune system, and therefore ensure longer life—besides making you feel loved and good all over.

7. Tantra encourages expression and leads to higher states of sexual and emotional satisfaction, which result in higher self-esteem, intensifying overall well-being.

Filling the Empty Nest

Parents often suffer distress from what's called "the empty nest syndrome," when kids leave home for school or marriage. Depression can result from being separated from children as well as from being faced with a spouse whom they hardly know anymore because the marriage took a backseat to child rearing or careers. Yet this can be a terrific time for starting tantric practice, when the couple needs to get to know each other again and when they now have more time to spend together.

When a Partner Dies

The largest obstacle for older couples is illness or the death of a partner. When this tragedy happens, your tantric love life doesn't have to end. Go back to being your own beloved, and pleasure yourself. After you've mourned, seek a new love and relive days of happiness—believe that you won't be betraying your partner and that you deserve pleasure.

Tantra for College Students

When Meghan and Ryan were college students and training in Kriya Tantra yoga through Tantrika International, they ran tantra groups for other coeds. Ryan considered their age group "indigo children" or "children of the golden age," meaning that their spiritual consciousness has naturally evolved into an awareness of heart connections and subtle energies. "This allows us as teachers to do a lot more with the group," said Meghan, "since they bring with them a creative passion for this material, which amplifies the group energy."

"Young people are ready to discover who they are as a creative and sexual being, and to channel that to get to a deeper place of intimacy within themselves and within all forms of relationship," explained Meghan, who authored a self-published book called *Free Like a Dolphin*. "Because college kids are so open to experience, our groups get very juicy," she explains, "which means everyone is excited and having fun."

"Having knowledge of tantra at this age, when you're having a lot of insecurity about yourself and in your relationships can eliminate a lot of stumbling and experiences that end up being unfulfilling," says Ryan. "If you receive the teachings as a young adult about how to evolve spiritually and heal yourself, imagine what kind of marriage you can create, and imagine how rich and powerful your relationships will be at 30, 40, or older."

I've run many tantric-type groups for college- as well as high-school-age students, without any sexual element, and the results are powerful for both the male and female students. They make comments like, "I feel more alive than ever," "I feel stoned without taking any drug," "I feel closer to people than ever," "I wish my boy-friend would breathe like this with me," and "This is the best experience I ever had."

When tantra teacher Laurie Handlers facilitated a group of African American college fraternity brothers at the University of Maryland in tantric techniques, she was amazed at how the energy shifted from initial rowdiness to attentiveness. "There is real potential for young men today to shift their stereotype, drop some machismo image, and open to a mature and connected being. The guys particularly liked the technique of building a sexual charge and then being able to transmute the sexual energy up to the rest of the body for use in fueling intentions."

Tantra for Teens

Teens even younger than college students can also relate to tantra, although formal workshops for this age group are still in their infancy. This work is not about teens being sexual; to the contrary, in my own experience running tantra-type workshops for young people, they learn powerful ways to use their energy and channel their feelings in ways other than sex. The changes they report are moving and impressive.

In a particularly valuable example of this, I conducted a tantra training with a group of inner-city teens who were Planned Parenthood sexuality peer group educators. In the 3-hour seminar, the teens learned breathing techniques, how to control their energy, and how to share deeper feelings without fear. The boys reported liking the meditation techniques, and the girls liked the sharing exercises (particularly when relating to a favorite object). Ironically, there was a drive-by shooting in the violence-ridden town at the same time the youngsters in the group were learning peace and love.

Setting boundaries—saying "yes" or "no" to others, whether about sex or anything else, was another powerful exercise, consistent with the importance of this process in adolescent development.

In another group for teens that integrated energy work with safer sex practices that I facilitated at Planned Parenthood of Nassau County with the help of my Columbia Teachers College students, the kids learned increased openness and trust of one another and personal power in making decisions. "I'm glad I came here instead of just hanging out tonight," one teen said. "I feel great about me, and really close to everybody here like I never felt before."

Tantric Parents Raise Healthier Kids

Following a tantric lifestyle can help you raise healthy children. Here are several ways to do that:

♦ Be a model of a loving relationship. Kids learn from what they see at home; if you are loving, they are more likely to be loving, too.

♦ Work out your own problems. The happier you are as a person, the better mood you will be in when you relate to your kids. If you harbor anger toward men or women, they will pick up on it.

♦ Show affection. When I'm asked, as I so often am, "When should I teach my kids about sex?" I always respond, "You're already teaching them about sex from the moment they are born, like by how you hold them." Hold them often to give them comfort and security.

♦ Give them positive attitudes. Too many men and women I have counseled suffer from fears, embarrassment, and shame about their bodies or about sex; teach your kids to say nice things about themselves, and encourage them to feel good about how they look, think, and act.

◆ Teach youngsters stress-reducing techniques such as meditation.

◆ Play with kids in ways that heighten their sensitivity to relationships and to their bodies, and let them have fun! One mother told me that on rainy days she did veil dancing with her children. "This was a wonderful game that taught my kids to feel comfortable with their bodies. Even though people think of veils as 'sissy,' it was a great activity for my son, to help him get past the macho ways his father was always teaching him."

Tantra Tales

The adolescent daughter of one of my best friends was getting depressed about all the normal problems of her age group (school, friends, body changes). Then she decided to redecorate her room as a meditation sanctuary, asking her mom to paint stars on the ceiling, draping gold cloth over a dresser as an altar on which to set a statue of Buddha, and collecting other objects that felt spiritual to her (crystals, painted boxes). Doing this helped her relax and feel more connected to strong spirits.

How the School System Can Be Tantric

Certain schooling practices might actually be tantric in nature, even though they are not identified as such. Certainly they are not meant to be sexual, but they *are* meant to increase a child's sensory perception. That skill prepares children for more self-awareness and greater capability to be totally present in each experience and moment.

One certified educator, who is also a tantra teacher and my good friend, recognizes the astounding similarities between adult tantra training and teaching young children. "Of course the exercises for the children are not intended for sexual purposes," she told me, "But the value in terms of sensory perception and encouraging spirit, self-awareness, and presence in the moment are equivalent—and wonderful."

Examples of these exercises include one that stimulates sensitivity to the environment by having kids truly smell the air when they go outside. Another encourages the capability to truly experience and distinguish different sensations. For example, in a fabric game, kids pick pieces of fabric from a box that match the texture of fabric rubbed on their palms. Or they hold cotton, jersey knit, or velvet and answer the question, "Are these the same or different?"

In a fruit play game, strawberries are put on the kids' tongues and they answer the question, "What does that feel like?" In another exercise, the kids are given 12 containers with substances inside that represent different scents (like peppermint, vanilla, or coffee) and are challenged to arrange the containers by similar scents.

Sensory ("tantric") exercises also encourage kids to fully experience each moment—the same goal of adult tantra training. "The kids' eyes would sparkle the more they tuned in to their senses," the teacher said, "because they felt pride over mastering their environment."

Florida education consultant Liliana Gonzalez Cunningham developed a program using principles of directing energy to revitalize schools with a positive environment to nurture joyous and intellectually stimulated students and teachers. In her book, *Schools Are Depressed* (xLibris Press, 2004), Liliana describes the three practices, which include the following:

Tantra Tutorial

Women enjoy soft, sensuous touch in lovemaking, yet fewer men than women have the natural knack for sensuous massage. For this reason, it is especially helpful to teach young boys how to develop keen sensory perception.

- Focusing sessions for Centering, Expanding, Connecting, Releasing Anger, and Developing Concentration, and Confidence guided by music and confidence-building words. The CD tracks range from 3 to 11 minutes for easy, practical use in the classroom.

- Classroom practices. Teacher activity cards and Eye Cue Cards with words (like Support, Gratitude, Joy, Trust, Self-Esteem) help cue the brain in a disciplined way, with a positive approach.

- Energy exchanges. Youngsters learn ways to work with their own energy and help each other exchange energy in positive ways.

The Payoff of Sensory Training at All Ages

"Children more fully experienced in tactile sense approach each other with hugs more than aggressiveness that is more common in children not trained in this way," the teacher also told me, calling the phenomenon, "gentle hands for gentle creatures." Such sensory training helps develop respect, an honoring attitude toward each other, and more expressiveness in communication. Sensory awareness similarly improves adult communication and self-esteem. For example, the more adults are sensitive to touch, the more nurtured the cells in their body feel, and the more softly they approach and touch others.

The Least You Need to Know

- Tantric sex practices are rejuvenating and help you look and feel younger.

- Tantra can help men and women deal with the emotional, psychological, physiological, and hormonal changes that come with menopause, midlife crises, and any life transition.

- The principles of tantra help teens develop healthier attitudes toward sex, higher self-esteem, and wiser decision-making in their relationships.

- Raising children with tantric sex principles in mind does not encourage irresponsible sexuality; rather, it helps them grow up to be loving people.

- Teaching the principles of tantra to people of all ages makes them more sensitive toward the world around them and kinder to other people.

Chapter 24

Tantric Love for All Relationships

In This Chapter

- ◆ Tantra in the world of cyberspace
- ◆ Seeing beyond the physical to the soul
- ◆ Tantric sex for gay men and women
- ◆ The value of tantra in disability
- ◆ Tantra in new models of relating
- ◆ How tantric loving energy benefits everything around you

In Chapter 23, I talked about how tantra teaches valuable lessons and love for people of all ages and stages in life, but what about all persuasions? Yes, the practices can apply to every relationship or situation you're in, because tantra is based on the union of energies, not specific entities or even specific genitalia. This makes the practices applicable to everyone regardless of sexual orientation, physical form, or even presence in the flesh—because tantra, like every other topic, is taking on a cyberform!

Cybertantra

With the increasing presence of the Internet and advances in technology, some people are becoming technological tantric partners, including practicing *cybertantra*. Just as in other aspects of relationships, the practices of tantra are being exchanged over the Internet with tantra enthusiasts communicating with each other or even clients seeking sessions over cyberspace.

Tantra e-groups include postings of discussions, announcements, and reflections. California tantrika Francesca Gentile refers to her active communication on the net and e-exchanges as a "virtual temple" for tantra, with the temple's purpose to "empower, heal, and educate."

In the latest edition of my book *The Complete Idiot's Guide to a Healthy Relationship*, I devote an entire chapter to the upsides and downsides of new technology on relationships and how to use it to your advantage. Get a copy and read "Digital Duos in Cyberlove: The Eighth Dimension of a Healthy Relationship" to get a full picture of how this new world is changing and how you can keep your love alive in the midst of it all! All the valuable advice given there serves as a good foundation and addition to what I am sharing with you here about practicing tantra.

The Pros of Cybertantra

Tantra is about opening one's heart to love. For many people who are too shy or afraid to be open in personal relationships, the anonymity of the Internet allows them to be more open in an apparent shield of safety. Connecting through technology rather than in person can help those who are insecure about setting their boundaries learn to do so.

Blocks to Bliss

Be very cautious in opening to love to strangers over the Internet, keeping in mind the possibility of predators. Deal with known tantric groups on the web; check them out first or get a reference.

Cyberconnecters can also practice getting close to others and test their intimacy limits. They can allow hidden aspects of their selves to emerge without as much fear as those who meet face to face, because they can pretend to be someone other than who they really are and escape easily. The Internet has allowed people to achieve "instant intimacy" by writing e-mails, pouring out their most intimate feelings and needs to strangers, or developing "deep" sharing with people whom they hardly know and have not met in person.

Technological advances beyond even cell phones and beepers allow ever-increasing connections between people, so that long-distance love is even more possible and physical separations less painful. Advances such as sound cards, video streaming, and camera attachments in cell phones and on computers now allow both voice and visual contact between people, increasing the potential for closer connections. Computer technology is making contact easily possible between peoples around the world, facilitating the worldview that is consistent with tantra.

Tantra and sacred sexuality are best studied in person because they are about human connection. Yet energies can also be felt without being face to face—even electronically. Tantric lovers can stay in touch by typing out instant messages or sending e-mails describing exactly what they are doing; for example, writing messages such as "I am exhaling now, sending my love energy out my heart and into your heart."

The Cons of Cybertantra

There is a downside to cybertantra connections. Tantra is about honesty, authenticity, and being who you really are; in contrast, the Internet allows dishonesty in relating. People do pretend to be something they are not, and they do lie about their looks, age, or sex. Great disappointment and deception are possible.

The depersonalization of some technological mediums can facilitate emotional distance and offer escapes from true intimacy and commitment and is the bane of relationships today! The method of interaction through words and writing on the Internet itself can provide an easy escape for those who have deep fears of intimacy or commitment, letting them pretend to be close but actually keeping them away from person-to-person contact. People can withdraw from interactions easily, logging off and disappearing into the safety net and ether of cyberspace.

Dr. Judy's TantrAdvice

An increasing number of tantra coaching and courses are being offered on the Internet. Explore their value to you, but don't use them as replacements for face-to-face meetings. Attend gatherings or take courses in person whenever you can; these are available in cities across the country.

Tantra Tutorial

The web's depersonalization has created an even greater need for methods that facilitate people meeting and connecting in a face-to-face way. Tantra offers this through its workshops and coaching sessions.

Love at Any Weight

Millions of people in this country are unhappy with their weight. Over the years of being a sex therapist, it has been painfully clear to me that such unhappiness has also wrecked millions of men's and women's sex lives, making them feel unattractive and withdrawn from sex. Tantra teaches love for your body that helps heal body hate and self-hate. It also teaches us to see beyond the physical, to stop judging others by how they look.

Lasting Love for Seemingly Odd Couples

Because tantra demands seeing beyond the physical into the soul of the other being, love is possible where it once might never have flourished. Seemingly odd couples become attracted and deeply committed.

Couples who practice tantra might have larger age differences than even the average couple, as well as differences in race, background, economic status, and other characteristics you can think of. Increasingly common are the pairings between older women and younger men, and people of different races.

Elsbeth Meuth is a German-born tantra teacher. Her beloved and teaching partner is descended from one grandfather who was Cherokee Indian and another from an African tribe. Elsbeth feels this is a positive for their love and their students. "We are truly a successful example of opposites attracting where we complement each other more than clash, partly because of our personal style and partly because of our cultural differences," she explains. "I bring to our relationship—and to our work—a more structured approach, because I am Germanic. That makes me more serious, setting goals and going for it, saying 'we have to get this done,' while Freddy is a free bird who plays music in our workshops, and in general is more spontaneous. He learned that from his dad, who brought him up in the tantric tradition of freer expression. He parties and makes music because he is alive in the here and now and knows how to have fun. Our relationship works because we learn and grow from each other: I loosen up following him, and he learns more structure from me.

"People who come to work with us have seen our picture, so they are ready to be accepting of an interracial couple," she explains. "In fact, it's part of our ticket—the fact that we bring opposites together is attractive, and appropriate, too, because it is the outward expression of the yin/yang tantric joining of opposites."

TantraNova teaching couple who share a special love despite differences in ethnicity.

Facing Society's Opinions

Seemingly odd couples often have to deal with the criticisms or discomfort of others who are not used to unusual pairings. Parents can have a particularly hard time accepting their children's choices. Don't be dissuaded by others when you know what's right for you. Discuss your differences to help others understand and accept your choice of partner.

The New World of Sexuality

Having a space to express intimacy, as is created in tantra, gives people a chance to explore a broad range of feelings in whatever way fits their boundaries and is mutually agreeable. This allows for relationships between people that go beyond sexual roles or orientation. Even though I've explained how tantra emphasizes the union of male and female, you'll recall I keep emphasizing that these are meant as *energies;* not genitalia.

Learning to integrate and be open to energy can lead to more openness in any type of relationship in which you see beyond the physical into the soul. Heterosexual people could be surprised by falling in love with someone of the same sex or find themselves bi-curious (attracted to both sexes). Following this principle, tantra is equally applicable to any relationship, regardless of the sex of the partners.

Tantric Sex for Men Who Love Men

Bruce Anderson is a pioneer in applying tantric principles for gay men. Trained by noted tantra teacher Sunyata, Anderson leads classes and workshops for gay male singles and partners and notes a difference between heterosexual tantric sex seminars and those for gay men: "Gay men are far more eager to interact with everyone in the group, compared to heterosexual groups, in which women put many more limits on intimate interactions."

Anderson's groups do not include emotional clearing exercises (as others do), concentrating instead on learning the cobra breath and yoga postures. Here's one of his favorite exercises (after reminding partners to always practice safe, protected sex). He instructs, "As part of your erotic play, move into a position in which you sit facing each other in a spider legs position [a modified yab yum in which one leg is crossed over and the other leg crossed under, instead of one partner's legs inside the other's]. Have your lingams touching. With one hand on your beloved's sacrum [at the base of his spine], use the other hand to create erotic delights for yourself and for him. As you feel the sparks rising, take deep breaths, concentrating on the inhalation, feeling a warm current rising up your spine. Stimulate with the intention of surfing on the edges of orgasm!

Foreheads touch in the tantric kiss.

"Keep gazing in each other's eyes. As you are moved to ejaculate, allow your love to rise up and ride the crests, pouring it through your eyes, your heart, and all of your being into your partner. Stay connected as you enjoy and follow the infinite blissful delight as the divine courses through you and your lover."

Anderson became motivated to teach tantra for gay men because, as a gay male himself, he discovered that intensifying his own erotic play led to his most profound experiences of the divine. "Tantra speaks to men who love men," says Anderson, "because it starts from the same premise and impulse upon which we know that we are gay: deep listening and understanding from the core of our bodies."

Anderson explains that the basic tantric sex concept, which is built on the union of polar opposites (male and female) has to be interpreted as an *alchemical marriage* of male and female within oneself, not between the partners. "According to physics, opposite poles ground each other in tantra," he explains, "but in gay tantra, like poles—of two men—create a tantric spark. It's just a different flavor."

Tantric Sex for Goddesses

There are an increasing number of workshops for women to get in touch with the divine feminine, together in groups. As in any education environment, women can feel safe when with only other women, particularly when it comes to sexuality. Even in the consciousness-raising groups started during the 1970s sexual revolution, women met together and shared with, as well as showed, each other ways to be more responsive sexually. Weekend introductory tantra trainings include women-only (and men-only) sessions to talk about the needs of their own, and the other, sex; more advanced sessions can include demonstrations and practices.

"I found myself really understanding the meaning of the word 'sisterhood,'" one female workshop participant told me, "but even more, I found myself appreciating being with other women in ways I never did before."

 Tantra Tales _____

Betsy Kalin and her partner, Candace, are both spiritual people and wanted to deepen their intimacy by studying tantra, but like other lesbian and bisexual women, they were reluctant to go to a heterosexual workshop with its emphasis on "male" and "female." Then they discovered a tantra teacher, Marcia Singer, was offering a lesbian tantra class at the Los Angeles Gay and Lesbian Center. It worked! "The eye gazing was transformative," Betsy told me. "You can see a person every day, but when you really look into their eyes deeply, you see new things. Everyone bursts into tears." The practices helped ease Betsy's chronic pain and depression from fibromyalgia. A filmmaker, Betsy was inspired to make a film about the experience, called *Hearts Cracked Open*, to let other women know the magic and heal from homophobia, sexism, lesbian invisibility, "bed death" (no sex), and negative images of lesbian coupling in our society.

"Women are ideal healers for each other," one tantra teacher told me. "They are naturally warm, loving, and sensitive." In one exercise in which women break into small groups and practice dancing sensuously for each other, some women end up really enjoying watching and holding each other. They can feel safer with other women than with men, even in doing healing work in the most sensitive internal places within the vagina (called the sacred sector or G space). This is especially true if they've been hurt by men in the past.

Tantra groups for lesbians are just beginning to become popular. As famed sexologist and performer/artist Annie Sprinkle says, "A tantric lesbian is a happy lesbian."

Tantra Tutorial

Hearts Cracked Open—the first film about women loving women in tantra—shows experts talking about the techniques and experiences in a real workshop meant to crack open the heart, such as eye gazing, hand on heart holding, the fire breath, feasting, and G-spot massage. It was premiered at the San Francisco Gay and Lesbian Film Festival to great reviews (www.heartscrackedopen.com).

Love Devoted to God

Tantrically trained Dr. Pat Sheehan, a counselor and speaker on sexuality, trauma, and addictions, is so convinced of the value of tantra for all populations, she incorporated tantric principles into a sermon on St. Francis of Assisi at a Catholic Mass and also teaches tantra techniques to nuns. Fearing that nuns have a risk of certain types of cancer, Sheehan is working to help nuns learn to embrace and move their sexual energy.

Tantric Love for Those with Disabilities

Mitch Tepper had already had his accident—diving into a shallow lake when he was just 20 years old, which snapped his spinal cord and confined him to a wheelchair—when he met Cheryl. She says she never noticed the chair. When she met Mitch in college, she fell in love with his charm, humor, and intelligence. Nineteen years later, Mitch can give a woman a good whirl around on his lap at a dance party, and the limited movement in his legs and hands hasn't stopped him from enjoying sex or running a popular pioneer website all about the subject (www.Sexualhealth.com).

"Tantric sex practices are a perfect fit if you're not the perfectly fit specimen," says Mitch, as he describes the unique perspective that tantric sex takes. Tantra shifts the attention away from intercourse or any particular sex act and onto slowing down, focusing on sensations, connecting with your partner, and exchanging energy.

Here are some exercises that Mitch recommends:

- Look at your right hand for a few moments and pay attention to what you feel, then focus your attention on your left hand. Pay close attention to the changes you feel from one hand to the other. If you are able, slowly move your hands closer together until you can feel the energy between them. Then you can practice moving that energy around by changing the distance between your hands or the positions of your hands.

- Control the pace of your breathing to a slow, relaxed pace with equal time on the inhale and exhale. If you can sense your heartbeat, use that as a clock to time the breaths.

- Learn to connect with a partner by matching the pace of your breathing while gazing into his or her eyes. Place your hand near your partner's heart while doing this.

- Develop sensitivity to touch by paying attention to tiny sensations. Become aware of the feelings and sensations, subtle as they might seem at first.

Healing Relationships with Your Parents

Some people who experience a growth experience want to share it with important others in their life, to bring them closer or to heal their relationship. Tantra teacher Laurie Handlers finally convinced her father to come to a tantra weekend she was teaching. "I had stored up so much anger toward him over the years," she explained. "He never listened to me and always made promises he never kept, even as minor as saying he would call and then not calling for weeks." But after her father attended the weekend, their relationship took a major turn for the better. "I finally told him how I felt all those years and for the first time I felt he really heard me—and he apologized. That did wonders for me. Now he's the father I always wanted."

One man reported similar success when his mother came to a tantra weekend. "She was always angry with men because my father left her and she had such bad relationships with men, that I think she took it out on me," he told me. "But afterwards, she felt so much better about herself that she became less angry and controlling of me."

Tantra with Your Pets

Hold on, before you have any visions about what I mean here! Being tantric with your pets means being loving, and every pet owner knows the value of that. Being loving and open in your heart space will transmit to all living beings around you—including your pets—helping them to better health and well-being. There's no doubt that pets pick up on human emotions. The happier and more joyous you are (from tantric practices for more love and better sex), the better you will treat your pets and the more similar to that vibration your pet's disposition will be. Expand the circle of acceptance and love. Research has shown that pet owners often feel closer to their pets than to other humans, letting out deep emotions and trusting the animal. Use this as a rehearsal for deep sharing with another human being.

Tantra with Your Plants

If you're convinced you about the value of sending love energy to your pets, would you also accept that you can extend the same loving energy to plants? Stay with me on this one! Research has suggested that plants, like other living things, also respond to people's emotions, growing healthier in a happier environment. Plant lovers know that. The happier you are, the more attuned you will be to the needs of your plants, from watering to sunshine to extra nutrients. In summary, love and positive feelings become a cycle. The more tantrically satisfied you are, the more you will give to people, pets, and plants around you, and the more they will reciprocate.

The Least You Need to Know

- Today's advances in technology can help you stay in touch with other tantric partners but should not take the place of in-person contact.

- The theories and practices of tantra as the exchange of energy and honoring of self and others are appropriate for every relationship, regardless of its nature, and allows people to explore all parts of themselves without fear.

- Although tantra technically represents the union of male and female opposites, this refers to energies rather than gender; therefore, tantric practices are equally applicable—and proving valuable—for same-sex partners.

- The road to higher consciousness and bliss is possible no matter what your particular circumstances or health status.

- Every relationship, whether with people, pets, or plants, can be positively affected by your tantric sex pursuits by generating more love.

Chapter 25

Which Path Is Right for You?

In This Chapter

- ◆ Why guidance is so important on the tantric path
- ◆ Making sense of different traditions and schools of tantra
- ◆ Various types and costs of tantra workshops
- ◆ Understanding the orientation of different teachers
- ◆ Choosing the path that's best for you

As in every spiritual practice, philosophy, journey, religion, and school of thought, tantric sex practices have been passed down through the ages, and different disciplines have evolved. As such, there are practitioners of different styles of tantric sex, many schools of tantra, and different teachers to whom different lineages have been passed down. Some paths are more focused on sexuality and others on using sexual energy to attain higher states. This chapter will help you sort out those differences so you can choose which path might be best for you.

The Importance of Guidance

The use of the breath to move sexual energy through the body is a process that should not be taken lightly. It can be dangerous to engage in some advanced breathing practices, healings, and other rituals before one is fully both psychologically and physically prepared. Thrill seekers and overenthusiastic students can be left in serious emotional trauma or even develop physical disorders by rushing too quickly down the path to expected bliss. For example, one expert in tantra says that when he was a novice at the practices, sending strong rushes of breath up and down his spine released powerful emotions that caused such violent shaking of his head that his spinal cord was injured, leaving him with serious disabilities.

Tantra Tutorial

In his book *Introduction to Tantra: A Vision of Totality* (Wisdom Publications, 1987), Lama Yeshe has likened the need for proper guidance in a teacher/student relationship to the confusion that would arise if instead of getting a Rolls Royce you got a pile of unassembled parts and an instruction manual. Unless you already were a skilled mechanic, you would likely be completely lost.

Contrary to myth, great sex does not always happen intuitively. Even ancient wisdom maintained that sexual arts had to be taught. Teachers help by …

- Giving you feedback on how practices should be done for maximum benefit and safety.

- Showing how all the practices fit together until you actually feel it for yourself.

- Supporting you in your pursuit and answering any questions you have.

- Helping you derive benefits from association with a lineage, as enlightened experience is often passed down to chosen students. In addition, some teachings might not be recorded anywhere and are meant only for oral communication from teacher to student.

Blocks to Bliss

In the ideal world, all teachers and types of tantra would peaceably coexist, allowing you to freely sample from all types. However, as with so many other areas of specialty, competition and schisms have arisen between different schools of tantra. Fallouts happen over many issues, such as violating the rules of certain practices, forcing some students to choose between teachers. One advanced student of tantra had a falling out with her teacher and felt excommunicated from the entire tantra community. Be careful not to fall into the approval trap, thinking that anyone holds the key to your enlightenment or acceptance.

- Giving you individual tutoring in complex individual practices (such as whether the breath in a practice goes up and down the spine, or central body). I remember being so worried about whether certain experiences, such as flashes of light or colors, were "right."

◆ Inspiring you, because they have achieved the goals you seek: of sacred love union or of specific practices such as delaying ejaculation or prolonging orgasm.

> **Blocks to Bliss**
>
> The spirit of tantra is to unleash your own individuality, your own specialness—to find your own special path. Don't blindly follow someone else's path because you are insecure about your own choices or fearful of trusting your own experiences. Also, be very wary of wounded healers who want to use you to validate or heal themselves—or worse yet, sex addicts or energy vampires (people who suck energy out of others for their own selfish use).

Finding the Right Guide

It can be difficult to sort out the best direction for your tantric practice. Ideally, a teacher would be a model of developing beyond selfishness and transcending petty concerns, while still living in the world and being dedicated to wisdom and the welfare of others. Some are better examples of this than others.

As the field grows, there is an increasing number of practitioners from all backgrounds. These can include men and women who call themselves "tantra educators," "tantra teachers," "sacred healers," "tantrikas," "dakinis," or "dakas." They could be spiritual counselors and bodyworkers, sex workers, or professionals licensed in a field of study such as massage or dance therapy or with some experience in yoga, meditation, shadow/soul work, and various methods of counseling (intuitive, transpersonal, bio-energetic). Others might have specific tantric training or be certified by a tantra master (one general progression of levels of expertise goes from educator to teacher to healer). Only a few are medical doctors with M.D.s or psychologists who have a Ph.D. (there are very few of the latter like myself who are licensed in their health discipline and also well trained in tantra, but this type of practitioner can be particularly helpful when emotional or relationship issues are triggered and need to be processed, as I've done for many participants at tantra workshops). The maze can be as complicated as sorting out any counselor who is right for you, for any problem, from depression or anxiety to a marital problem.

Teachers' orientations and techniques also vary widely. Most combine Hindu and Buddhist meditations, yoga practices, and breathwork, and others like myself add Western teachings in psychology and communication. Some focus on techniques to open the heart for more love, while others focus on spirituality, and still others on sexual healing or enhancing orgasm.

Here are some guidelines to help you choose a teacher or practitioner who is right for you:

♦ Check what is written in this book about what tantra involves and about specific teachers and schools. Refer to Appendix B or get in touch with me directly about your needs.

♦ Surf the web for sites about tantra, and follow all links. Send an e-mail, but then follow up on the phone. Ask what is offered, and match that to what you want.

♦ Mention your interest to friends and other people you know. You never know who might have similar interests, experience, or contacts.

♦ Contact potential teachers for their materials and get references from other students.

♦ Check the teacher's background training. Interview the person thoroughly, as you would in picking any health professional. What is his specialty? What degrees does she have? With whom did he train? Assess qualifications in yogic practices, spiritual journeys, counseling, and other health professions. Ask for—and talk with—references. Inquire if they have an organized program to follow.

♦ Follow your intuition. Let yourself be guided about whether this teacher is the right person for you to learn from. Does that person reflect your goals, understand you, seem to know what she is talking about?

Ecstasy Essentials

There is no uniform certification system or licensure to ensure a teacher's credentials, although established teachers are increasingly offering certification in their methods.

It has been said that a true master does not want to be called a "guru" or a "master," because being enlightened involves a state of detachment to a title, ego needs, or having followers. (One teacher suggests the term *fellow journeyer*.) True gurus, it is said, want you to find the guru inside you. In truth, everyone and every experience is our teacher—but tantra teachers have much to share with us.

Tantra teachers can give sessions or run workshops individually or work in teams. Learning from a committed couple can present an example of a loving relationship, which can be inspiring to students, and give you a male and female point of view. Some of these couples are listed in Appendix B.

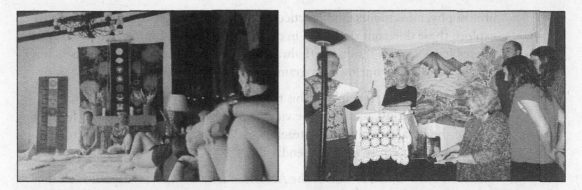

(Left) Charles and Caroline Muir teaching a class. (Right) Bohdi Avinasha playing music at a tantra teacher training in a lesson about the power of voice.

The Different Traditions of Sacred Sexuality

Adding to its complexity, tantra has filtered through and intertwined with many other spiritual paths. Indian tantra of Hindu heritage varies from Tibetan tantra of Buddhist heritage, which differs from tantra of Japanese Zen or Chinese Taoist heritage. There is also sacred sexuality from a more ancient Middle Eastern and ancient European (Roman) context. Within each of these flavors of tantra are many splintered paths, each more liberal or conservative than the root path they sprang from. Yet they also have dramatic similarities, as does tantra practiced in Eastern cultures and that of Native Americans. Here are some of the traditions or terms that describe these practices.

- ◆ **Hindu.** The Hindus can be credited with the origins of this sacred path because tantra studies flourished in the temples of India centuries ago. Its practices are most commonly known by the texts of the Kama Sutra, the ancient bible of lovemaking that describes not just sexual positions but the value and practices of love.

- ◆ **Buddhist.** Tantric sex practices spread from India through Nepal and into China, where the Taoist traditions incorporated sacred rites and added their own specific

Tantra Tutorial

Seattle tantra teacher Kirby Jacobson has deeply connected to the tantric teachings of many different lineages. He says that because his teachers have been very generous with him, he's happy to share the knowledge. You can contact him with questions at earth2kirby@yahoo. com or 206-579-4421.

philosophy, movements, and practices. There are many books you can read to explore these different traditions in detail; in this book, I introduce you to techniques from various traditions (I always teach and treat clients in a holistic way), so you can design your own program that works for you.

♦ **Taoist.** The major principle of this tradition is unswerving adherence to ejaculatory control, consistent with the view that not to do so ruins a man's health. One of the best-known of these teachers is Mantak Chia, who has written extensively on the Tao of sex (see Appendix B).

♦ **Western Neo-Tantra.** This is the American and European adaptation of the earlier traditions, based on sexual and spiritual practices made accessible for Western lifestyles and understanding. It blends ancient tantric practices and Eastern teachings of yoga, tantra, and Kama Sutra with more familiar Western psychological techniques of various psychological disciplines (transpersonal, cognitive-behavioral, neurolinguistic, gestalt), emotional release processes, massage, somatic therapies (music and dance therapy), and sexual enhancement skills. The specifics depend on the interests, skills, and background of the teacher.

♦ **Ipsalu Tantra.** This is an adapted system for the Western world that focuses on realizing the true self by attention to emotional flow and skillfully designed techniques for safely activating kundalini (powerful and creative) energy. The word *Ipsalu* is Sanskrit for "transcending illusions of desire," meaning to free ego desires to reach bliss through union with the self, the beloved, and the universe. Tantrika International has developed a complete system with effective practices following a five-step formula of activation, meditation, awakening sexual energy, transmuting it into love energy, and play.

♦ **Quodoushka.** Originally practices of sacred sexuality from ancient Mayan and Toltec schools of learning, this once-secret Native American system is now being revived. Similar to some forms of tantric sex based on breathing techniques and chakras, Quodoushka teaches the fire breath as a means to full-body orgasm. Unique to this tradition is the concept of the *medicine wheel* (sacred hoop) that connects all peoples and elements. As such, a sexual encounter is meant to align the four directions: south (representing water, heart, plants), west (representing earth, body, rocks), north (representing wind, mind, animals), and east (representing human beings). Sexuality is in the center, representing the soul, the life force that and connects the body and mind, all beings, and all that exists.

Trained teachers introduce this knowledge to others, including five different levels and types of orgasm for men and women.

In its original form, adolescent males and females would spend 3 days and nights with no food and water to purify themselves in preparation for initiation into sexual knowledge by a Spiritual Fire Woman (also called the Phoenix Fire Woman).

Osho: The Spiritually Incorrect Mystic

Osho is an Indian mystic who transcended all religions and traditions. Formerly known as Bhagwan Shree Rajneesh and referred to as the "spiritually incorrect mystic" in a biography, Osho spoke extensively about tantric practices as a vehicle for transformation and achieving personal, interpersonal, and universal freedom, ecstasy, and enlightenment. Unlike other meditation gurus who demand celibacy, Osho celebrated physical pleasures, becoming embroiled in scandals in the 1970s and 1980s that resulted in his deportation from the United States. Osho came to be called (to his displeasure!) the "Sex Guru." Although he died years ago, his spirit lives on at his popular ashram in Pune, India, and devoted followers teach his techniques throughout the world. Many current tantric masters, such as Margot Anand and Bodhi Avinasha, were early students of Osho and credit him for the origins of many of their teachings as well as for their personal transformations.

An example of Osho's teaching on love: "Become loving. When you are in the embrace, become the embrace. Become the kiss. Forget yourself so totally that you can say, 'I am no more. Only love exists.'"

Different Trainings

Teachers of tantric sex usually offer a varied menu of services, including individual sessions, evening seminars, weekend or week-long workshops, or teacher trainings. Some teachers will even travel to your area and tailor events to your needs. For example, I have done 3-hour presentations and weekend or week-long workshops of varied types of trainings integrating tantra, depending on what people need, across our country and from Hong Kong and Singapore to India and Prague. Some trainings are more geared toward sexual practices (such as learning ejaculation control or helping women free their expression); others include practices like meditation, yoga postures, and emotional clearing. You might find different trainings helpful at different points in your journey. I recommend that you get a balanced experience, so that you don't just experience sexual energy in sexual activities. The goal should be to achieve higher states of consciousness that unite body, mind, and soul for spiritual enlightenment.

Dr. Judy instructing a couple in tantra practices.

Types of Healers and Other Practitioners

As with tantra teachers, there are various kinds of healers. Some are devoted to tantric healing as their central job; others have a career in other fields.

Some of these healers might interact with their students to demonstrate how specific practices are done, supervise couples' practices, or engage in hands-on educational sessions or more intense healings as described in Chapter 18. They might describe their "sultry voice" or "clear blue eyes" and advertise on the Internet as "sacred space healer" or "priestess of sexual arts" offering services—for men, women, or couples— such as temple dances, sacred spot work (described in Chapter 18), bodywork and massage, bathing and lovemaking rituals, and goddess celebrations.

Blocks to Bliss _____

Concerned about people following fads, craving instant gratification, and New Age consumerism, tantra teacher Reverend Keith Hall warns against following any teacher or practices that go too quickly. "I have seen people physically and emotionally harmed by doing Cobra Breath and other tantric and Kundalini energy practices when they are not prepared," he says. "This can lead to falls, somatic and psychic symptoms, and even development of autoimmune disorders. Students should be grounded and do practices daily under the guidance of a teacher with many years of experience."

Tantric priests and healers offer similar services but are far fewer in numbers than females (partly because women are more nurturing by nature). Male healers often use their given Western name, as opposed to female healers, who often assume names of goddesses (as in Chapter 5).

Starting—and Keeping Up—Your Practice

When you are considering a path, go to introductory tantric evenings to experience whether it's a good fit for you. After workshops and weekends, you can continue your study with booster sessions that some teachers offer to keep your individual practices growing and the community cohesive.

Continuing Your Tantra Education

Most established tantra teachers offer workshops on various themes as well as different levels of training. These usually start with an introductory weekend workshop and progress to a week-long course. Many students want to participate more because they enjoy it so much and it gives them support in their practices; you can repeat courses you like (usually for a reduced rate) or take a teacher training course even if you don't plan to teach. Some men and women who train as sexual healers don't practice as such, but do so for their own learning. As one said, "In real life I have a day job."

Related training in other areas (such as meditation, dance, or making relationships work) can help your tantric practice. For example, shaman training greatly deepened my appreciation for spirituality and even the role of spirits in healing. As a result, I spent considerable time at temples in Nepal and studied with a Tibetan shaman as part of a training program given by an American expert in shamanism, Larry Peters.

Dr. Judy's TantrAdvice

Treat levels of tantra expertise with the same respect as you would getting a black belt in karate. It is unwise to dabble in tantric sex, read a book, or take a course and then proclaim, "I am a tantrika," to announce this to potential partners, or use this to entice lovers.

*Being blessed at the shrine of
Kali outside Kathmandu,
Nepal.*

*Training in Tamang
Buddhism in Nepal with
Aama in an intensive course.*

Virtual Tantra Training

Consistent with distance learning over the Internet now being available for many
subjects and degrees, tantric sex classes and exchanges with interested others is also
increasingly possible over the Internet. Some e-groups are open to anyone, while
others are for graduates of particular trainings, to exchange ideas and even get further
teachings.

Correspondence courses or distance learning in tantra have advantages—access to
teachers who are far away, one-on-one tutoring—and also downsides—danger of
too-soon exposure to practices or misunderstanding of instructions that might be
corrected only if visually observed.

A Few Things to Be Aware Of

If you go to a tantra gathering, be aware of some things that might cause discomfort for you. Ask ahead of time about the following concerns:

♦ **Can I stay with my partner?** If you come as a couple, ask whether you will be allowed to stay together for all the exercises, or if you will be required to interact with the group and choose people you don't know as a partner for some exercises. Some participants are insecure about a partner's commitment and get jealous seeing him or her working with—and perhaps deeply connecting with—another person, even if nothing comes of it.

♦ **How will I be paired up if I come alone?** If you come as a single, be prepared to be asked to pair up for some exercises with someone you don't know, or someone of the opposite sex. Many tantric sex workshops are designed for singles as well as couples and make efforts to achieve gender balance—an equal number of males and females. Various games create these pairings (picking matching cards, wandering the room to whomever your energy draws you). Where numbers are not balanced, you might be asked to play the role of the opposite sex. In any case, your choices and boundaries should always be respected.

♦ **How much time is required?** Everyone is busy, but it is recommended that you do not be distracted by phone calls, e-mail, cell phones and other business in a tantra workshop or retreat, to devote full attention to the experience.

♦ **Will there be nudity?** Although exhibitionism (displays of nudity) is generally frowned upon, some workshops create a safe space for you to take off your clothes during exercises if you choose. In others, various states of disrobing occur, especially for certain massage experiences (although nudity is not intended to be sexual). Couples might do exercises together unclothed but have no interaction with others in the group, or there might be massages or other exercises in groups of varying numbers. More advanced classes are more relaxed about such things. Ask beforehand what's in store so you are not caught unaware or disturb others by unpredicted distress.

Dr. Judy's TantrAdvice

Check the experience level (beginner or advanced) of events. For example, one tantra event was advertised as "We strip down and are covered in oil by multiple attentive hands." Know whether you are prepared for this.

◆ **Is there sexual activity?** Actual sex is not what responsible workshops are about, but some places and teachers are more permissive, and activities can go on after class if people so choose. There is controversy within the tantra community over physical contact. Be clear about your boundaries and the teacher's or healer's orientation. If private coaching by specific types of healers includes some intimate activity at your request, this will usually be obvious from their website or an initial conversation. More conservative practitioners—certainly those who belong to professional organizations and are state licensed—will not engage in such interaction; instead, they will instruct couples in exercises to do at home in private.

Don't look to tantric sex workshops to solve serious emotional or relationship problems. Seek professional advice. At one of her week-long workshops, Margot Anand offered a unique service: counseling sessions with qualified therapists—myself, a licensed clinical psychologist, and a medical doctor. This proved highly successful and useful for participants, because the exercises in the workshop, while pleasurable, also stimulated some deeper emotional issues. For example, one woman remembered for the first time after 20 years having been abused as a child. Another woman became intensely jealous about her husband appearing to flirt with another woman. And a man became distraught over rejection when he was not chosen to do an exercise by the woman he eyed. Ask about the availability of such assistance, or referrals, as they can be essential when you are processing deeper feelings aroused by practices.

Costs

Costs of individual evenings average about $20, or are based on contributions or ability to pay. Weekend workshops can cost from $180 to $395 and up. Retreats can run more than a thousand dollars. Discounts are available for couples, or if you sign up several people, work as an assistant, or repeat the course. Because many trainings like to have an equal number of men and women present, they might offer discounts if they need an extra Shiva or Shakti. If you sponsor or organize the weekend and invite a qualified teacher, you can come free or even earn money for your work.

Ecstasy Essentials

Budget your money for courses. Consider it an expense for continuing education that is valuable for your growth.

Does Tantra Training Work?

Many men and women can give testimonials after just an evening introduction or one weekend of tantra, citing peak experiences, major breakthroughs, or impressive transformations. The gratitude and positive experiences are inspiring! I've heard so many participants tell of more love and better sex than ever before. Statements like these are common: "I never believed I could feel this good," "I'm changed forever," "Why didn't I know this years ago?"

As a research scientist as well as a clinician, I am always interested in proof. As a result, I have conducted some of the first research ever done on the impact of tantra experiences, from how people feel after just an introductory lecture, to the deeper effects of learning sacred loving and healing. All these—with varied groups and in various countries—have shown that participants' ratings showed many positive changes, in self-esteem, confidence, awareness about energy, and experience of higher states of love and connection.

The findings of one project—done with a group attending a weekend workshop led by master yoga and tantra teacher Sasha Lessin with me as co-teacher—are particularly important. Before the workshop, many of the female participants described themselves as shy, embarrassed, and even shameful about sex—feelings that were often linked to dissatisfaction about their body (mostly feeling overweight), fears of intimacy and rejection, and past sexual abuses. After the workshop, participants reported useful lessons in improved communication, honoring themselves and their relationships, and feeling more open and trusting. The results indicated an improvement in the quality of intimacy and communication, and in the amount of pleasure the women—and the men—felt in their sexual and everyday lives.

Tantra Tutorial

In the tantric sex community, **playshops** refer to gatherings that focus on the pursuit of pleasure; these give permission for people to play together as couples or in groups. Be aware of the kind of openness this could involve.

New Trends in Tantric Experiences

Gatherings is a recent term referring to a playful social that provides some organized activities and ice breakers (games, pujas, massage round-robins, potluck meals) to facilitate connecting with like-minded people in a sacred, sensual, loving, and safe environment. These gatherings are consistent with tantric principles and lifestyle but are more free-form than workshops. Although there is some structure, you might never know exactly what's going to happen, because each gathering is co-created by the group and its unique combination of people. The events often include dance, singing, drumming, feasts, and, depending on the facilities, outdoor activities such as hiking or spending time on a beach. Often people bring favorite foods and musical instruments. Come dressed casually.

Some tantra teachers now offer exotic escapes that are like vacations, but consistent with tantric lifestyle and practices. These are held at elaborate homes (sometimes their own) or other locations with sensual environments (complete with hot tubs, saunas, lakes, and indoor pools). These might be the same places where they hold workshops, seminars, and private coaching. Tantric mini-vacations offer a less structured and more fun atmosphere with built-in playtime such as sightseeing, hikes, outings to waterfalls, and even shopping (for tantric items, of course!).

Tantric retreat centers feature nature and sensuous environments.

Dolphin and whale trips run by tantra teachers are also increasingly popular. Dolphin consciousness is part of the tantric wave (the undulation that is characteristic of ecstasy). Certainly, awareness and preservation of these amazing beings is consistent with tantric appreciation of preservation of the environment, nature, and all beings. Tantra teacher Kutira is an expert in dolphin and whale consciousness and leads groups on mind-expanding trips known as Oceanic Tantra. Participants can stay overnight at the Hawaiian retreat center she runs with composer and tantra teacher partner, Raphael, in spirit-infused temple housing nestled in nature with jungle, waterfalls, and ocean.

Various retreat centers are known as locales for seminars and workshops about tantric sex and workshops on related topics, often taught by noted teachers and experts. Some are bed and breakfasts, and others are large-scale centers. Some offer private and exotic accommodations and on-site services like massages and yoga lessons. The surroundings and facilities are particularly conducive to heart-centered events and opening to love.

Integrating Tantric Sex with Other Techniques

Many of the tantric sex techniques described in this book and used by noted tantric masters are adapted from emotional processes used in other therapeutic modalities or spiritual practices. For example, the emotional release processes are adapted from techniques used by other Western therapists, and many meditation and breathing practices as well as yoga postures are taken from various Eastern traditions.

The practices of tantric sex can often be smoothly integrated into spiritual growth routines with many other disciplines. Western practitioners of tantra are increasingly following this trend, as more collaborate on developing workshops and as the techniques of tantric sex become more popular. And tantric practices are increasingly used by more traditional therapists who follow different Western disciplines. Therapists like myself, with extensive training in clinical psychology and backgrounds in psychoanalytic theory, use tantra in a mixture of many other therapeutic tools and techniques to coach people and professionals. This holistic approach includes disciplines such as cognitive-behavioral therapy, neurolinguistic programming, and Gestalt therapy. I call it being an "eclectic" therapist—custom designing the approach for whatever the person needs. I find this approach highly effective, and all my patients have gained from it.

The Least You Need to Know

♦ Tantra is a growing discipline, with an increasing number of options available for seminars, workshops, and evening events you can attend.

♦ Because there are no uniform guidelines for the certification of tantra teachers, it can be difficult to choose one; do considerable research and get recommendations before making your choice.

♦ Research tantric teachers and events, but also follow your heart about what's right for you. Attending an introductory evening is a good idea.

♦ Engaging in some advanced breathing practices, healings, and other rituals before you are fully prepared can be dangerous; find a qualified teacher to guide you.

♦ Budget your money and time to allow for continued education to keep you focused on your practice and to advance your growth. Take ongoing courses at advancing levels, repeat courses, or get individual coaching.

Chapter

26

Chapter 26

Better Health and Peace Through Tantra

In This Chapter

◆ Tantra as a global community

◆ How tantra can stop the terrible cycle of abuse

◆ Turning away from artificial highs

◆ Tantra as a healing force in the face of illness

◆ More tolerance is possible the tantra way

As we move forward in this new millennium, life becomes more complicated and challenging and world conflicts become more threatening. Tantric love and tantric sex can help in adjusting to the fast-paced, stressful, and technologically digitized world we live in. In this chapter, you'll learn how the tantric lifestyle can help you survive—and thrive—in this new age and make a better future for you, your loved ones, and the world.

You Are Not Alone

People on certain paths or with similar interests tend to travel in similar circles and pursue similar interests. This is especially true when it comes to tantra. One of the most touching aspects of studying tantra is that you become connected to a group of people referred to as the "tantra community." Serious students even refer to the "tantra family." Of course this can lead to all the typical conflicts that might arise in any family (from petty complaints to big fallouts). However, in general the participants feel a sense of belonging and mutual caring that is especially valuable in these trying, isolating times.

The Internet has made it possible for everyone to communicate more freely all around the world. It's easy to join the online global tantra community to feel more connected to the world, ask questions, and share your experiences.

Sending Energy, Especially in the Face of Tragedy

With a growing spiritual community and more people committed to healing, there is an increasing number of global events intended to heal the planet. The annual World AIDS Day is a model for this paradigm, in which people all over the world are invited to focus their attention on a particular subject; in this case, AIDS. As another example, the We Are Family Foundation, started a healing effort after the September 11 attacks on America by re-recording famous music producer Nile Rodgers's hit song of the same name with more than 200 celebrities. It continues to promote a global family of multiculturalism and tolerance. The tantra community has also promoted such healing events, consistent with tantric principles of spreading energy of tolerance and love.

When the devastating tragedy of the terrorist attacks on America took place in September 2001, e-mails of love and support instantly flooded the Internet. Members of the tantra community were particularly active in sending out messages of support and healing. I posted many such messages on my website, in-cluding "mini" therapy sessions with people on the street who wanted my advice about troubling issues. One man wanted to know if it was okay to want more sex; he was ashamed to feel this way in the face of others losing their lives and loved ones. I reassured him that was normal. Another woman asked me if she should divorce her husband, as she was consumed with anger that she needed to talk about the tragedy but he refused to discuss it.

Any threat to life can lead to depression and withdrawal from relationships and sex, or the opposite—a desire for deeper connection in love and even more sex, out of a desire to reaffirm life. For example, one San Francisco hospital reported more babies born 9 months after a devastating earthquake. And think of the number of marriages and babies conceived before men went off to World War II. When life is threatened, people need love and seek intimacy (my research has shown this is true). It's the time for the spirit, energy, and practice of tantra, with its emphasis on love.

Tantra Tales

People need to be told how much they are loved, but they often fear that they won't get the love they need. Saying "I love you" is a basic teaching in tantra. After the World Trade Center attacks, one Arab college student asked me whether girls would not date him now out of distrust for people of his ethnicity. A young woman asked my help to get her boyfriend to commit to her. She had asked him what he would do if she were in danger, a question I told him really meant that she needed him to tell her how much he cares. He finally understood her needs and agreed to her requests to spend more time together.

At one session of our advanced teacher training with Tantrika International, Bodhi Avinasha invited students to spiritually join a similar advanced group in Germany, to put our energies together to send healing energy to the planet. The practice started with a process called *Yoga Nidra*, leading to deep relaxation. This was followed by guided imagery, in which Bodhi described exactly what the hill in Germany where the group lived looked like, and the route of light energy that we would ride to get there. Several of the participants successfully had the experience.

A Tibetan tradition to help someone who is ill is to dedicate any act of love or giving to the ill person. The bliss, peace, and joy of giving expands a thousand-fold and builds the receiving person's "spiritual bank account."

The next time you are with your beloved, send love energy you have charged through your chakras and cycled together out to the world— for love and healing for all.

Tantra Tutorial

Yoga Nidra, known as "sleep of the yogi," is a technique to progressively relax body parts and still the mind, to reach that moment when you feel about to fall asleep but are still awake. This is a magical time to direct your consciousness and empower your intentions. Being in that state is also useful to help people stop smoking and beat other addictions.

Sending out healing love energy to the world.

Collective prayer is another method of healing. When one member of the tantric community was diagnosed with cancer, others all over the world communicated through e-mail to devote a specific time at a particular hour once a week for everyone to send a prayer of life force energy, power, courage, and love. After this group healing, the woman said she experienced a real shift and woke up the next day deciding that she "wants to stick around in this world." Others gained from the experience, as one woman said, "As many of us are going through our own dark nights, this is inspiring. It is time to cry out, to know that we are one body and to join together, to see that cries for help are being heard and we are loved and cared for."

Tantra Tutorial

Increasingly, research focuses on energy transmission for healing. Deepak Chopra's Center for Well Being is collaborating with the Institute of Noetic Sciences and Bastyr University, along with federal monies from the National Institutes of Health, on "The Neural-Energy Transfer Project" to scientifically explain the power of prayer.

Healing the Cycles of Abuse

The number of women and men of all ages who have been abused—emotionally, physically, or sexually—is shocking. I have heard so many of these sad tales from people calling my radio show to share their stories. Fortunately, people are paying more attention to these traumas, facilitating healing and preventing further victimization. But more needs to be done! Tantric practices can actually create a future with less prevalence of such violations in several ways:

♦ Tantric practices encourage men and women to set their boundaries, respect the rights of others, and communicate with more loving intention. In this way, there will be less possibility of misunderstanding or power struggles that lead to sexual harassment or more serious issues.

♦ By fostering self-esteem in youngsters and teaching them to expect respect, they will be more capable of resisting peer pressures that get them in trouble, and instead make wise decisions and develop healthy relationships.

♦ Tantric practices can actually reduce the possibility of becoming a victim of abuse. This is partly due to the fact that becoming sensitive to energies can help you detect potential dangers and deflect attacks.

♦ Such awareness about energy can help youngsters resist potentially predatory behaviors. By learning that their body is a sacred area, they can understand the lesson that no one has a right to see or touch their sacred areas without their permission. And if anything bad happens, they will be more likely to tell an adult immediately and express their feelings.

♦ Practicing tantra can help heal women and men who have been abused to regain self-respect and trust, because the philosophy puts such emphasis on respect, equality of partners, maintaining control over your own body, and self-expression. Having a partner who honors these principles and generates loving energy can also help these women and men trust new beloveds to allow healthy physical contact and closeness.

♦ Tantric practices can help stop the victim/victimizer cycle by focusing on feeling loved and sending out love, asking permission before you touch, transmuting sexual urges into other energies, and healing past pains.

Fortunately, people now feel less stigmatized when seeking help when faced with problems such as abuse. Following a tantric lifestyle that fosters kindness toward oneself continues this healthy attitude that problems are not shameful defects or disasters, but opportunities for personal growth. Couples and even extended family groups can seek help together, consistent with the tantric spirit of empathy, caring, and extended community.

A Healthy Way to Get High

Now that you know about tantric practices, you might be willing to see how the type of exercises, including breathing and generating energy, can pale the pursuit of artificial highs through drugs and alcohol. Why take drugs and risk those dangers when you can get the same—and *better*—effects the natural, tantric way? Here are just a few examples:

♦ The Shakti shake, fire breath, Osho meditation, lama breaths, freestyle dancing, and sexercises get adrenaline going just like dangerous drugs like speed but without negative side effects.

♦ Meditative practices, such as chanting "om" and alternate nostril breathing, can make you as calm as taking a downer. Best of all, you get to control it all!

♦ Breathing and sending energy through your body can make your brain explode in the same way as mind-altering drugs. Try doing the bandhas (muscle holds described in Chapter 6) and hold your breath before you shoot it through your chakras. You'll get a better, more natural blast than any drug can give you, with no complication, addiction, or side effects. Pleasure is at your fingertips. Take it in through the nose (your breath that is), and blow your mind!

Dr. Pat Sheehan, trained in tantra and former coordinator of the family program at an alcohol and drug treatment program at a Midwest veterans' hospital, found the tantra techniques notably useful as an adjunct to treatment for addicts in these ways:

♦ It quiets the mind. Recovering people have difficulty managing thoughts ("stinking thinking"), and meditation assists in directing the mind to more positive thinking.

♦ It heals the split between the sexual and spiritual. Addicts often feel intense guilt and shame about their sexual experiences; tantra helps them unite sexual energy with love to reclaim innocence.

♦ Much of addiction treatment involves confronting denial; tantra opens the "third eye" energy center to allow seeing the truth about one's self, relationships, and life, therefore, diminishing denial.

♦ Because the energy of tantra is more gentle and internal than other techniques such as confrontation, it's harder to make excuses or blame others, and resistance is minimized.

◆ The Witness Consciousness learned in Ipsalu Tantra helps one to observe thoughts and sensations without judgment—an important relief for addicts.

◆ The combined process of awakening the body, quieting the mind, arousing sexual energy, and transmuting it to love energy creates the state of bliss addicts seek in chemicals, but without all the downsides!

Dr. Sheehan applies these techniques to recovering addicts at halfway houses and is training counselors and addiction program managers in the techniques.

Tantra as a Healing Force in the Face of Illness

Tantric sex utilizes energy to heal pains stored in the body. These apply to sexual hurts from past sexual experiences, to emotional wounds that are associated with hurts and rejections, and even to real physical illnesses. The techniques work because they give a person control over his or her energy and also help a person build powerful pools of energy through the sexual charge and direct this energy.

Directing energy through tantra practice is consistent with techniques used to heal serious illnesses, by helping patients use imagery to identify where bad cells are and to direct their good cells to overcome the bad ones. This can be used in many disorders, even life-threatening illnesses such as cancer. Tantric breathing, meditation, building energy, and emotional release can help strengthen the immune system, develop inner peace, and foster more loving interpersonal relationships—all of which are helpful for people who are ill.

California tantra teacher Diane Greenberg specializes in working with women and includes helping women with cancer by teaching them tantric sex techniques. "My major approach, and the belief that I teach women, is that being turned on—and especially receiving sensation in your body however you value the experience—is

> **Ecstasy Essentials**
>
> Imagery techniques give patients control over their illnesses. Famed medical doctor and cancer specialist Bernie Siegel has been recommending these techniques and successfully using them with his patients for years.

> **Tantra Tutorial**
>
> A study of a 3-year cancer support program at Stanford University School of Medicine showed that more than 9 out of 10 patients experienced increased well-being and reduced pain and stress after practicing yoga and other energy routines (such as QiGong).

a major healing force," says Greenberg. She notes that this life-threatening disease often insults a woman's sense of femininity, and that drugs often cause what she labels a "libido-ectomy" or an excising of sex drive.

Tantra Tales

Former entrepreneur, TV consumer expert, and economics lecturer David Hollies practices tantra in his present journey as a 45-year-old dealing with dementia. "Tantra has helped me to stay focused on the present and squeezing every drop of joy out of the moment even as I feel my mind slipping away," says David.

In a letter to his friends, David writes: "Suffice it say that the doctors are clueless and my symptoms get slowly worse. Dementia is a mystery about which little is known. I now use a walking stick and a wheelchair to help me get around and my life is a continuing process of letting go. I get lost in the simplest of activities, like holding a plate of food in my hands and not being able to figure out why or what do with it. The other day I got confused pumping gas and ended up spraying gasoline all over myself.

"But it has not all been bad, by any means. I have found more depth and joy in the connection to others than at any previous point in my life. In that, there have been many miracles. I am loving and I am loved. My life that way is richer than ever. Last year I had three wonderful girlfriends: Beth, Gail, and Radiance. Everything was above board and they all knew and honored one another. It seemed somehow right despite all the predictable challenges. And then with grace and ease, things began to shift and Gail and I eventually decided to marry. The others remain dear friends."

Writing poetry also helps David. Some of his writings have appeared in Alzheimer's newsletters. From a recent poem:

> I am David. Yes.
> Yes, I'm quite sure.
> Should I get ready for work?
> No, not that David
> Oh.
> Realities shredded
> Filed, misfiled, or not
> Things gone
> I ams that aren't

Greenberg invites women to consider that even during a cancer crisis, a woman can still receive attention and enjoy her sexuality and sense of womanhood. She helps women acknowledge—and then release—their blocks and encourages them to be present to their feelings, to give attention to their yoni and breast areas, and to use breathing and mudras to send love, energy, and "juice" to their own body and to their partner. Greenberg insists that women should not ignore their anatomy and genitalia, as many do when their libido is low and embarrassment about their body is high. She helps them reframe what they define as attractive (such as accepting mastectomy scars) and encourages them to let love help them heal. "Magic happens," says Greenberg, "when women with cancer practice tantra and receive more pleasure and love."

The tantric tradition teaches to allow all feelings. Many people run from grief, yet it is helpful and healthy to reframe grief as opening your heart to experience the depth of emotion (experience in motion) and the possibility of love, loss, and then opening up to something new.

Tantra for Those in Trouble

The elements of tantra can be applied to many diverse populations for personal growth work, with the focus not on sex but on going into the heart. Rich Menges, managing director of Sharing Inside Time Inc., notes improvements in prison inmates taught breathing techniques, emotional processing, and drumming. Menges, who has trained in tantra himself, recognizes the importance of staff providing a positive role model.

Helping the Helpers

People often ask me if helping others so much is draining; to the contrary, open sharing—even of pain—has always created more love and inner peace in my experience, for myself and those I counseled over so many years. But I know other helpers feel depleted; tantra provides techniques to keep energy—and hopes—high.

How Tantra Promotes Tolerance and Diversity

We cannot avoid news stories about tragedies that evolve from racial, ethnic, and lifestyle diversity. Cultural groups with different religious orientations are still killing each other. Prejudice persists against people who choose different lifestyles, such as homosexuals and transgendered people. History is full of wars that create an "us against them" mentality.

Yet we are becoming a global community, with all races, cultures, and creeds blending to create a new breed of human. Groups with so-called

Dr. Judy's TantrAdvice

Encourage children to open their hearts more readily to others of different backgrounds. Do the same, and you might be surprised at the love that comes your way!

alternative lifestyles have formed communities and action organizations. Organizations bring peoples of differing cultures together to work for peace in their region. The tantric lifestyle fosters cooperation and trust rather than distrust and aggression. A generation of humans embracing tantra is capable of breaking the cycle of dysfunction and destruction by fostering a desire to support rather than destroy others.

Ecstasy Essentials

Diversity expert and tantra teacher John Hill travels around the country teaching organizations how to become more tolerant of differences in race, age, and sexual orientation. He says, "When we realize that we are all the same, we can approach people with the respect they deserve, which will not only benefit the individual but the entire organization, with ripples felt in the larger community."

How Tantric Sex Can Help Heal the World

Tantra communities often network to come together at times of *harmonic convergence* to anchor in peace and love for the planet. It happened after the September 11 attacks, when members of the tantra community sent out e-mail messages requesting people to all pray for peace at exactly the same time. Other tantra practitioners practiced sex magic, as described in Chapter 16, which means that at the height of sexual energy arousal, they sent out healing love energy to the world.

Over the past years, I have incorporated tantric techniques in innumerable workshops for various groups of people around the world, from a conference in Dubai on Arab psychology with peoples from the Arab world and 20 other countries, to Arab and Israeli students after the bombing at Hebrew University in Jerusalem, and in workshops and presentations in other cities from Singapore to Sagar, India. The techniques are particularly geared toward establishing trust, honoring others, controlling one's energy, and feeling inner peace. Many of these have been with diverse cultural groups and in war-torn regions. The positive impact reported by participants has been significant and rewarding, and offers hope for contributing, at least in this small way, toward peace.

A lofty goal, indeed—tantric sex saving the world! Yet practicing tantric sex can actually help bring about more peace in the world. The fact is, the happier you are with yourself, the more tolerant you are of others. The more satisfied you are with your relationships, the more willing you are to treat others well and see to it that they are as happy as you are.

A seminar I led in Dubai, United Arab Emirates, of a process using yarn to symbolize uniting peoples of differing cultures.

Israeli and Arab students holding hands in a tantra for peace workshop I ran after a bombing.

Several efforts are being made to apply tantra toward healing world tensions and facilitating peace. For example, The SpiritWorks Church for Spiritual Partnerships is a northern California–based organization whose mission is to promote global transformation through ecstatic living and cultivating sacred relationships based on power "with" one another, not power "over" another and, thereby, to encourage universal worship of the divine without respect to cultural origins, gender, or previous condition. The church is developed by Margot Anand, founder of SkyDancing Tantra Institutes, who has also presented panels addressing this theme in which I have participated titled "Sex, Power, and Politics" at State of the World Forum conferences.

Tantric practices help you go beyond a patriarchal world of dominator consciousness in which one feels superior over the other, and enter a world of balance, harmony, and peace. Through tantra, you realize that nothing in the human condition is alien to yourself; you begin to feel your sisters and brothers and other creatures who share this world with you. When you feel others, you can no longer wish them ill or harm them. With this new paradigm, you change individually, and the planet as a whole changes to create a true partnership in society with equality for all.

The Least You Need to Know

- Studying tantra connects you to a global tantric community that can provide you with a sense of belonging and mutual caring.

- The practices of tantra can heal the wounds of abuse and put an end to the victim/victimizer cycle of abuse.

- Tantric practices hold the power to help heal many physical and emotional illnesses, even those that are life-threatening.

- The tolerance and understanding necessary to heal racial and international tensions are facilitated by tantric practices that teach people to come from love.

- Love, honor, and respect for oneself and partners consistent with a tantric lifestyle can extend to the larger community and the world, creating the potential for peace.

Appendix A

Glossary

amrita   Female ejaculate, also called the nectar of the goddess, is considered a blessing for the partner and the fountain of youth.

bandha   Muscular lock, used to direct and intensify sacred energy.

beloved   A person with whom you share loving energy at the most committed level and with the highest of intentions toward your mutual good.

bindi   A decoration that tantric women place on the third eye to dazzle but also to aid the woman and her partner in focusing during meditation. The word formally means "seed" or "dot," which symbolizes the union of male and female.

bliss   An extremely ecstatic and expansive feeling often characterized by clear light that fills the mind and body.

chakra   A center of energy, shaped like a wheel, that emanates from body areas and is the focus of concentration in tantric sex practices. The seven centers are located at the base of spine, genitals, belly, heart, throat, forehead, and top of the head.

daka   The Sanskrit name for a highly trained male who helps arouse blissful sexual energy in someone who wants to learn tantric practices. This male healer embodies Shiva energy, serves Shakti unconditionally, and is considered a priest versed in many disciplines, including healing, yoga, sexuality, philosophy, psychology, and metaphysics.

dakini   The female equivalent of the daka. The Sanskrit name for a highly trained female who helps arouse blissful sexual energy in another person who is learning tantric practices. Also a goddess or priestess who is a healer and, like the daka, can have varied expertise in a number of disciplines.

deity yoga   The practice of aligning oneself with a deity in meditation for the specific purpose of attaining the qualities embodied by that deity.

deva/devi   Another term to refer to gods and goddesses, respectively, a deity, cosmic power, or holy creative force.

energy   The life force from within that can be pooled internally and then channeled to create magnificent results in the inner and outer worlds.

goddess/god deities   Spiritually enlightened, powerful, erotic, or fertility-related energies worshipped in ritualistic ways. Refers to ancient beings as well as every contemporary woman and man deserving of being treated with respect and honor.

grounding   Connecting solidly to the earth; feeling secure and centered within one's body, as through the energy of the first (base) chakra.

healer   A person who facilitates the growth of another.

holding the space   Contributing your positive energy to whatever is happening to make the environment or people feel safe.

initiation   A process by which an authorized teacher trains you in and deems that you are ready for specific practices.

inner flute   A clear breathing pathway through the energy centers of the body, so that the air traveling through the body makes a flutelike sound.

kundalini   Blissful energy dormant within the spine until activated by tantric practices. Often depicted as a coiled serpent that moves up the spine.

lingam   The phallus. A man's "wand of light," derived from the word *linga*, meaning "pillar of adoration and worship."

maithuna   Elaborate tantric ritual with many ceremonial steps, usually culminating in some form of sacred sexual union.

mandala   A diagram symbolic of a message about life, death, and the nature of being that is used as a tool for meditation. The design often depicts animal forms, nature scenes, and particular deities and evokes their properties or aspects.

mantra   Recitations (of words, phrases, or sacred Sanskrit syllables) used in practicing meditations, the repeating of which focuses attention and invokes spiritual powers.

meditation   Concentration that stills the mind to allow pure energy to exist without the interference of thoughts or emotions.

mudra   Sacred hand gestures to focus the body's energy with intention.

nadis   Subtle nerve channels related to physical body and energy healing.

nirvana   The highest state of bliss and enlightenment, which is liberated from attachment to worldly possessions. Considered the ultimate spiritual peace that transcends birth and death, it results in the soul no longer needing to incarnate on the earth plane.

prana   Energy, air, breath, and life force that is generated in the body by nurturing, healing, physical and mental practices, healthy eating, and devotion to self-transformation and enlightenment.

puja   A specific ritual, or sacred circle of worship, performed by a group of people.

rituals   Actions that are special or ceremonial in nature. Those done during tantric lovemaking include bathing, making dedications of love, and setting intentions.

safe space   The experience of being protected from danger, in a physical location or by the ambiance created by the people present, which facilitates free expression.

Sanskrit   The ancient sacred Hindu language in which most religious texts are written that expresses a total philosophical, scientific, and religious body of knowledge about spiritual and sacred practices to reach higher states of consciousness. *Sanskrit* means "perfect" or "complete."

separation   The sensation of being apart from others, created by our thinking that we are different or by withholding emotions or thoughts from others.

sexual healing   An experience in which a healer facilitates someone in a session where sexual energy is aroused and expressed for the person's highest good.

Shakti   A name used to refer to the ultimate energy created by the force of the feminine and any woman as a goddess. Also the name of a Hindu deity who represents the divine mother and lover who unites with Lord Shiva for blissful consciousness.

Shiva   A name used to refer to any man as the ultimate representation of male energy. Also, the cosmic masculine force capable of creation or destruction, the divine male, worshipped in tantric practices and manifested in many forms, who unites with Shakti for blissful consciousness.

Shiva/Shakti mudra   An exercise of bringing energy up from the earth (the source of feminine Shakti energy) into the heart area and bringing it down from the sky (the source of male Shiva energy) into the heart area.

shushumma   The central energy channel visualized as a tube of light down the spine.

spooning position   A position where one partner lies with the chest pressed against the other's back to create connection or provide safety and protection.

tanghka   Sacred paintings, usually of deities and other life forms, that represent universal themes and forces. Focusing on the images assists in the attainment of various states of consciousness and awareness of the nature of life and death.

tantra   Sanskrit word for sacred teachings and practices that lead to high states of bliss and enlightenment. A mystical and spiritual system that combines philosophy, psychology, and cosmology and transmutes energy to achieve a balance between opposites and the integration and evolution of mind, body, and spirit. Characterized by an honoring of the goddess uniting with god energy.

tantric sex master   A person trained in tantric sex practices who can teach others on the path.

tantric temple   Your body, in the sacred act of giving and receiving pleasure for yourself and your partner; also, any place in which you engage in tantric lovemaking rituals (bedroom, another room in the house, hotel room that you specify as a sacred place for lovemaking for even one night).

tantrika   From ancient times, any woman practiced in the art of moving sexual energy to reach higher states of consciousness and bliss for herself and a partner.

third eye   The symbolic eye on the forehead between our two eyes that is a focal point for concentration toward higher states of consciousness.

transmuting energy   Moving energy from one energy center to another, such as using the breath to pull up energy from the sexual center into the heart area.

vajra   A Sanskrit term for the male genital organ, or lingam (also called a jewel, or *dorje* in Tibetan), symbolic of power, indestructibility, and great worth. As an object considered a magical weapon or thunderbolt, it is forged with two crown-like shapes connected with a ball in the center. This male symbol is combined with a bell, symbolizing the female, to unite both energies.

visualization   Using creative imagination in meditation to influence states of being.

yab yum   A pose used in many tantric sex practices in which woman sits astride her partner, facing him so that their chakras are aligned to facilitate their connection. Their feet can meet behind each other's backs to further encircle the pair.

yang   Energy that manifests as masculine energy, symbolic of qualities that are active, analytic, and associated with the heaven and father. Meant to unite with yin (feminine) energy to achieve balance necessary for enlightenment.

yantra   Mystic geometrical diagram used for healing meditation.

yin   Energy that manifests as feminine, considered symbolic of receptivity, nurturance, earth, and all that is opposite to yang energy. Meant to unite with yang to achieve balance and wholeness, necessary for enlightenment.

yoga   A physical discipline that conditions the body as a vehicle through which the mind can attain higher states of consciousness.

yogi/yogini   Sanskrit names to refer to devas and devis or spiritual beings, as well as those males and females who engage in yoga practices.

yoni   Sanskrit word for the vagina, a woman's sacred temple, the symbol of Shakti or female power.

B

Workshops, Websites, Teachers, and Tantra Communities

Listed here are some helpful resources for starting—and continuing—your practice. I've listed the type of information each source provides. After you get started, you'll inevitably jump from one site to another to find what you need. Get in touch with me (see the ad page at the back of this book) with any questions.

Teachers and Workshops

This section contains contact information about various tantra teachers, practices, and training experiences. The list includes resources referred to in this book and others to help guide your choice of what's best for you. Many of these resources offer a variety of services, including events, workshops for individuals and couples, various levels of advanced work, private coaching, retreats, and teacher training. Most have a unique blend of contemporary Western tantra with traditional Eastern practices. (Some use this book in their courses, so bring your copy with you.) Although the headquarters or home base of each is noted, many will travel to you. Some sites also offer various products, books, videos, CDs, clothing, and other items for tantric practice.

Certainly, you can call me for the presentations, workshops, and unique blend of individual and couple counseling that I do, tailored to your needs and based on my many years of experience using Eastern and Western therapy techniques, with my background as a Ph.D. in clinical psychology and extensive experience in all types of therapy techniques from psychoanalytic to person-centered as well as advanced training in tantra traditions (which is rare in the field). You can come in person, or if it is better for you, given time and distance, arrange coaching by phone or through e-mail. For expertise and support, reach me at …

718-761-6910
DrJudyKuri@aol.com
www.DrJudy.net
www.DrJudy.org
www.DrJudy.biz

Or I can direct you to other places in your area or for your needs. If you contact any of these people, to ensure special attention, be *sure* to tell them that you found them in Dr. Judy's tantric sex book:

Tantrika International (TI)
Executive Director: Mary Manera
PO Box 516
Loveland, OH 45140
1-888-TANTRIKA (1-888-826-8745)
info@tantrabliss.com
www.tantrabliss.com

TI offers weekend workshops and week-long trainings at introductory and more advanced levels for mainstream or intensive groups, held in cities around the country and facilitated by teachers trained in the Kriya Yoga tradition as founded by Bodhi Avinasha, author of *Jewel in the Lotus*. This comprehensive approach unifies mind, body, and spirit to harness sexual energy to higher states of consciousness and ecstasy. Also offered are extensive training and teacher certification, books, videos, and other items, including a 12-lesson home practice course with reading, writing, daily practice, and energy exercises. TI is a federally recognized nonprofit corporation dedicated to tantra education. It also runs a biannual Festival Multiversity, where practitioners come to share techniques.

Charles and Caroline Muir
Source School of Tantra
PO Box 368
Kahului, HI 96733
1-888-6-TANTRA or 1-888-682-6872
Fax: 808-573-6864
school@sourcetantra.com
www.sourcetantra.com

Hawaii-based yoga master and sexual healer for more than 20 years, Charles Muir, along with his teaching partner Caroline, is a pioneer in the field of tantra in America and offers a popular weekend workshop for beginning or advanced singles and couples, sexual healings, vacation retreats, and certification for teachers. Thousands of men and women have taken the weekend workshops with special emphasis on freeing—and healing—sexual energy and honoring the goddess. Books and videos on "conscious loving" and secrets of female sexual ecstasy as well as other items are also available. Ask for a free audiotape that describes the practices.

Butterfly Workshops
Laurie Handlers
3701 Reno Road, NW
Washington, DC 20008
202-686-7440
info@butterflyworkshops.com
www.butterflyworkshops.com

Butterflies transform, and this "place where people fly" is a Washington, D.C.–headquartered community based on the vision of "women and men dancing in eternal ecstasy on earth now." Workshops and retreats on bliss and personal empowerment are offered, as well as courses in creative techniques like Yogaboxing. Butterfly Workshops also sells clothing, jewelry, videos, books, music, and artwork.

Carla Tara
917-513-2500
carla@1tantra.com
www.1tantra.com

Carla Tara offers private tantric energy sessions with communication skills and counseling support for men, women, and couples, and tantra seminars and workshops for small and large groups in Maui, New York, and around the country. Highly talented, spiritual and caring, Carla has more than 20 years of experience as a yoga instructor and relationship counselor.

Celebrations of Love
Founder: Lori Star
c/o Sunrise Center
45 San Clemente Drive, Suite C-200
Corte Madera, CA 94925
415-924-LIVE (415-924-5483)
info@celebrationsoflove.com
www.celebrationsoflove.com

Celebrations of Love offers comprehensive and ever-expanding programs of tantric study with noted tantric teachers, and special events on particular topics with experts, as well as weekend and other vacation retreats in Big Sur and the San Francisco area. Popular courses are offered in "Tantra, Healing, and Sacred Sexuality" and "Breath, Love, and Passion," as well as seminars on compassionate communication. Related Hale Akua Shangri-LA retreat center in Maui, Hawaii, offers comprehensive health programs and various tantric trainings in an exotic setting.

Sky Dancing Tantra
Founder: Margot Anand
PO Box 2967
San Rafael, CA 94912-2967
415-454-6030
skyoffice@infoasis.com
www.margotanand.com

A pioneer of tantra and student of Osho, Margot Anand does special weeklong workshops and trainings. Anand's brand of tantra, Skydancing, is taught by her trainees in the United States. Author of many books on tantric sex, including *The Art of Sexual Magic*, she is currently pursuing a life-long dream to set up a spiritual church.

The Art of Being, LLC
Founder: Alan Lowen
PO Box 790269
Paia, HI 96770
808-572-1435
jan@artofbeing.com
www.artofbeing.com

Alan Lowen, Hawaii-based experienced workshop leader, runs workshops including "Body, Heart and Soul" tantra trainings and "The Universal Experience."

Teachers in a Committed Male/Female Team

Richard and Antoinette Asimus
6611 Edwood Avenue
Cincinnati, OH 45224
1-877-931-3030 or 513-931-3030
richardasimus@fuse.net or aa@fuse.net
www.tantraheart.com

This expert, loving, and supportive tantric couple, married in loving and passionate union for more than 30 years, "guide discovery of the union of sex and spirit, using Ipsalu tantra techniques." They lead well-choreographed evening events, ceremonies, workshops, and retreats in their local area (an active tantra community in Cincinnati) and around the country, from the tradition of Tantrika International's tantric Kriya yoga.

Lexi Fisher and Kip Moore
Tantra Transformation
Palm Springs, CA
760-327-4041 or 760-329-2718
Tantricsky@aol.com or goddeslexi@aol.com
www.TantraT.com

This southern California–based committed tantric couple offer weekly mediations, private sessions, and varied workshops including the Ipsalu Tantra Cobra Breath Level 1 intensives and co-teaching Level 2 with Bodhi Avinasha. Lexi and Kip also lead the advanced tantric retreat called "Sexual Wholeness." Fisher also teaches the special Vajrayogini practices for women at the Palm Springs Serenity Retreat.

Kutira and Raphael
Kahua Hawaiian Institute
PO Box 1747
Makawao, Maui, HI 96768
1-877-KAHUA-50 or 808-572-6006
kahua@OceanicTantra.com
www.OceanicTantra.com

This Hawaii-based committed couple leads tantra and shamanic experiences, workshops, and sacred retreats centered around planetary awareness and dolphin and whale consciousness, including resources for meditation, healing, and outdoor adventures as well as musical concerts. Their Kahua O'Mali'O Maui retreat center (the name of a mythical woman known for entertaining with music and love magic ability) offers temple housing in sensual nature settings of jungles, waterfalls, and ocean views.

Francesca Gentille and John Mariotti
The LifeDance Center
San Francisco, CA, and Reno, NV
510-759-3839
sacreddancer@mindspring.com
www.lifedancecenter.com

Co-directors of The LifeDance Center, based in San Francisco, these "passionate living coaches" teach Sacred Sensual Dance and offer varied workshops including Conscious Flirting, The Sensual Secrets of the Martial Arts (includes John's QiGong training), and relationship skills they've learned, such as Viva Romanza: Lifelong Intimacy, Passion and Romance for Couples. They also run an active ongoing tantra community at www.ishtartemple.org that shares information, offers support, and raises awareness about sacred positive sexuality and learning opportunities.

Steve and Lokita Carter
Institute for Ecstatic Living
1-877-982-6872 or 707-928-6964
office@ecstaticliving.com
www.ecstaticliving.com

This northern California–based committed couple and trained tantra teachers, also experts in techniques of bodywork, breathwork, and watsu (healing in warm water), offer workshops such as Timeless Loving dedicated to living more ecstatically, with an open heart, vibrant body, and radiant spirit. They also coordinate Skydancing tantra workshops, which were originated and developed by pioneer tantra teacher Margot Anand.

Elsbeth Meuth and Freddy Weaver
Directors, TantraNova
Transitions Learning Center
1750 North Kingsbury Street
Chicago, IL 60614
1-800-963-TANTRA or 312-787-7642
tantranova@tantranova.com
www.tantranova.com

This committed couple offers seminars, workshops, programs, bodywork, home study CDs, and private sessions to bring back joy, humor, and passion in relationships. German-born Elsbeth uses coaching methodology based on the philosophy of language, emphasizing that we generate our reality based on language. Her partner and co-teacher Freddy, son of a psychiatrist and author, is a corporate comedy sales trainer, percussionist, and certified massage trainer who has been featured in many videotapes about tantra.

Mark Michaels (Swami Umeshanand Saraswati) and Patricia Johnson (Veenanand)
Kailash Center for Personal Development, Inc.
1992 Commerce Street, #301
Yorktown Heights, NY 10598
914-962-7328
info@tantrapm.com
www.tantrapm.com

This devoted married couple and senior students of Dr. Jonn Mumford (Swami Anandakapila Saraswati) are named as lineage holders of the OM Kara Kriya™ system and authorized to initiate students into all four levels of Naga Pranayama (Cobra Breath). Mark also holds degrees from NYU law school and Yale. They offer workshops in the United States and distance learning programs with Mumford, a leading figure in contemporary tantra who now lives in Australia.

Tantric Services and Workshops for Special Populations

Gay Men

Bruce Anderson
Somananda@gaytantra.com
www.gaytantra.com

Here you can find information on classes on tantra for gay men given by the California-based tantra teacher, using Kriya Jyoti Cobra Breath, massage, and other tantra techniques.

Lesbians

Evalena Rose
LoveJourney: The Healing Path of Tantra for Women
707-528-1980 or 415-457-1904
contactus@tantraforwomen.com
www.tantraforwomen.com

Workshops on intimacy and Sacred Sexuality and a community of women developing sex-positive lifestyles. Spiritual work includes MetaTherapy, multidimensional healing, soul retrieval, channeled readings, and abuse and addiction recovery.

Marcia Singer
Foundation for Intimacy
818-623-6434
lovearts@worldnet.att.net

A clinical social worker trained in body-centered hypnotherapy, tantric Shamanism and a pioneer in Touch Awareness, sexual-sensual wholeness for all solos/partners, Marcia is a heterosexual woman who has adapted her tantra teachings for lesbians. She was featured in the first film about tantra for women who love women, *Hearts Cracked Open.*

Disability

Mitch Tepper, Ph.D.
www.sexualhealth.com

This website has extensive information about all aspects of sexuality, including sexuality for those with disabilities.

Bodywork

Marci Javril
13428 Maxella Avenue #136
Marina del Rey, CA 90292
866-551-0062 or 310-306-9838
mjavril@vitalenergycenter.com or ezine@yogaoftouch.com
vitalenergycenter.com/classes.html

Based in southern California, highly experienced and certified body worker and massage therapist Marci Javril is knowledgeable on all issues of bodywork for health; she is also a talented intuitive healer and tantric sex teacher who runs various tantra events and courses, offers coaching for men and women, and publishes an active e-newsletter.

Men's Groups

Rundy Duphiney
rundyduphiney@yahoo.com
www.BodyImmortal.com

Duphiney is California-based and offers workshops for men to open to deeper intimacy in their life, working with issues around fathers, but also including mothers, relationships, sexuality, and health.

Women Retreats

www.divine-feminine.com
Awakening the essence of the feminine, this retreat is run by women with long traditions in teaching tantra.

Singles

Joan and Tomas Heartfield
joan-tomas@talkinghearts.com
www.talkinghearts.com

Ceremonies and workshops on relationship counseling, intimacy issues, and "Conversations That Matter" especially for singles are facilitated by a committed couple in a Maui setting.

Bonding Technique

Juliana Dahl (Shakti Joy)
Paradise at Harmony, LLC
1455 Gillaspie Drive
Boulder, CO 80305
303-593-2995
info@sacredsexyes.com
www.sacredsexyes.com

Juliana Dahl offers workshops at a lake retreat center in Colorado as well as in other cities. She specializes in combining tantra with bonding techniques, lying in embrace, and sharing love and was trained by Muir and others in sexual healing.

QiGong-Related Practices

Keith Hall
301-924-2245
jadegardentantra@aol.com
groups.yahoo.com/group/jadegardentantra/

This Maryland-based teacher has 30 years of experience in tantra and Taoist disciplines, with special classes adapting Eastern meditations and movement exercises for Western students.

Dance

Christina Sophia and William Florian
962 Dorthel Street
Sebastopol, CA 95472
707-524-7898
williamflorian@aol.com or christinasophia@aol.com
www.TantraDance.com

Sacred dance workshops for couples are offered that include training in belly dancing as well as varied workshops on yoga and massage and other tantric topics and events, with original music designed for peace.

Native American Tradition

Quodoushka
Deer Tribe Metis Medicine Society (DTMMS)
408-443-3851
www.Spiritualsexuality.com or www.dtmms.org

This Native American tantric tradition uses breathwork and other rituals of special sexual skills to achieve overall well-being.

Cancer

Diane Greenberg
415-898-7510
keener58@hotmail.com

This San Francisco–based tantra educator is certified by the Muirs' Source School of Tantra. Greenberg is also a sexual healer and advocate for women and specializes in helping women with cancer heal.

Sustainable Environment

The Spirit Church for Spiritual Partnerships
Margot Anand
1-877-982-6872 or 707-987-3456
info@margotanand.com
www.spiritworkschurch.net or www.margotanand.com

Margot Anand is a pioneer of tantric sex training. She studied with several spiritual masters, including Osho; she's an author, the developer of the "Love and Ecstasy Training," and the founder of SkyDancing Tantra Institutes (conducting trainings abroad—for example, in her native France). She also developed the SpiritWorks church, whose mission is to promote global transformation through ecstatic living and to encourage universal worship of the divine without respect to cultural origins, gender, or previous condition.

Outside the United States

Australia

Jonn Mumford (Swami Anandakapila Saraswati)
tantrapm@aol.com
www.jonnmumfordconsult.com/Contact

Jonn Mumford offers distance learning online courses in the practice of Tantric Kriya Yoga ($60 for a consultation). The Om Kara Kriya course (originally published as *Dr. Jonn Mumford's Yoga Magik International Correspondence Course*) is a distillation of Swamijii's life-time study and practice (more than 50 years), offering direct personal guidance from a traditionally trained Western Tantric Master, for beginners and advanced students.

Thailand

Universal Tao Center Co. Ltd.
Founder: Mantak Chia
274/1 Moo 7, Luang Nua, Doi
Saket, Chiang Mai 50220, Thailand
1-66-53-495-596
Fax: 1-66-53-495-852
universaltao@universal-tao.com or info@tao-garden.com
www.universal-tao.com

Expert in Eastern Taoist techniques in sexuality for men and women, Mantak Chia has been teaching for three decades. He has written many books on these techniques and offers trainings at his retreat center in Thailand.

Vienna

Greg Emhka
GregEhmka@aol.com
www.etceterra.at

Greg Emhka specializes in "Joyful Empowerment" using emotional release techniques, lathihan and sexyhan, that he developed independently and in workshops with Bodhi Avinasha. The name of his community living center, Etceterra, stands for *e*cstasy, *t*ruth, and *c*larity, *e*ternally on *e*arth.

Related Trainings and Services

Wedding Ceremonies

Reverend Laurie Sue Brockway and Reverend Vic Fuhrman
212-631-3520
RevLaurieSue@aol.com
www.weddinggoddess.com

These ordained interfaith ministers and spiritually creative wedding officiates work with couples to design personalized ceremonies using varied cultural rituals and prayers, tantric sacred love principles, ancient love stories, and traditions of divine consorts.

Other Rituals

Barbara Biziou
britual@aol.com
www.joyofritual.com

Biziou is a minister who performs personalized rituals for individuals, couples, or groups, based on her book, *The Joy of Everyday Ritual*. These can be for any occasion, from births to separations, and to resolve couples' problems as well as enrich relationships.

Tantra Sound Toning

Ohana of Joy
Founder: Karin Schelde
PO Box 1173
Haiku, HI 96708
1-800-841-7457 or 808-249-6434
Karin@soundandvoice.com

This talented healer gives workshops and private coaching in using voice, sounds, chanting, and other breathwork exercises for transformation, expansion of ability to communicate, healing, and empowerment. She also offers videos, audiotapes, and CDs.

Compassionate Communication

Center for Nonviolent Communication
2428 Foothill Boulevard, Suite E
La Crescenta, CA 91214
818-957-9393 or 1-800-255-7696 (in the USA)
www.cnvc.org

Training in Marshall Rosenberg's Nonviolent Communication technique, also called Compassionate Communication, complements tantra trainings by teaching non-threatening skills in communication. It is promoted and taught internationally by trainers and at Lori Star's *Celebrations of Love* center.

Spinal Alignment

Lexi Fisher D.C.
Abundant Health Associates
Palm Springs, CA
760-327-4041 or 760-329-2718
Lexi@DrLexi.com
www.DrLexi.com

Lexi Fisher is a tantra teacher who is also trained in nutritional counseling and special techniques to keep the spine healthy.

Polyamory

Sasha and Janet Lessin
1371 Malaihi
Wailuku, HI 96793
1-877-244-4103 or 808-244-4103
planetsexy@aol.com
www.schooloftantra.com

This committed couple runs evening events, parties, and workshops in their home in Maui and in other parts of the country. Experienced in tantra, as well as in yoga and breathing techniques, they specialize in creating polyamorous tantric communities.

New Relationship Choices
Deborah Anapol
415-507-1739
www.lovewithoutlimits.com

Deborah Anapol runs events, workshops, and intensive trainings for individuals and couples interested in new lovestyle choices, based on her book, *Polymory, the New Love Without Limits*. Also offered on the website is the video, *Erotic Spirituality*, based on the first Celebration of Sacred Sexuality Conference she organized.

Related Centers for Personal Growth

Osho International
210 East 68 Street
New York, NY 10021
212-585-3666
Fax: 212-879-8680
osho-international@osho.com
www.osho.org
Also contact: Karuna Kress, Ed.D., Director, Center for Consciousness
PO Box 186
Easthampton, MA 01027
413-527-2697
NEITC@earthlink

This extensive organization is dedicated to the teachings of the "spiritually incorrect mystic," Osho, and includes a meditation resort, books, tapes, and a magazine and hosts teachers from all over the world who offer classes.

Harbin Hot Springs
PO Box 782
Middletown, CA 95461
1-800-622-2477
reception@harbin.org
www.harbin.org or www.harbinhotsprings.com

The retreat center north of San Francisco known for its hot spring pools hosts conferences and workshops of various healing topics, led by noted experts in various healing arts fields. This clothing-optional vacation spot also offers evening events such as dances and prayer circles.

Omega Institute
150 Lake Drive
Rhinebeck, NY 12572
1-800-933-1001
registration@eomega.org
www.eomega.org

This healing center headquartered in upstate New York also organizes journeys to other parts of the country and abroad. More than 250 workshops related to health and wellness and conducted by noted experts are hosted throughout the year. The Omega Institute also sponsors wellness vacations and a wide variety of healing services.

New Life Expo
218 West 72nd Street
New York, NY 10024
212-787-1600
www.newlifeexpo.com

New Life Expo hosts occasional weekend-long health fairs where a wide variety of health providers exhibit their services and experts lead panels and classes.

The Prophets Conference
1-888-777-5981
prophets@greatmystery.org

Travel programs and weekend conferences with renowned experts and avant thinkers are presented in a wide spectrum of worldviews, from philosophy to spirituality.

We Are Family Foundation
310 W. 52nd Street
New York, NY 10019
212-397-4333
webmaster@wearefamilyfoundation.org

Started as a healing effort in response to the events of September 11 by famous music producer Nile Rodgers and Tommy Boy Music president, Tom Silverman, the We Are Family Project is built around the theme of Rodgers's hit song, "We Are Family." It promotes tolerance.

Dr. Larry Peters
Shamanic Counseling and Training
1212 Old Topanga Canyon Road
Topanga, CA 90290
310-455-2713
lpshaman@aol.com
www.tibetanshaman.com

Dr. Peters offers counseling and treks to sacred sites with training with Tibetan shamans, especially in Nepal, and has authored several books on the subject.

Related Courses (Not Necessarily Tantra)

Institute for Advanced Study of Human Sexuality
415-928-1133
iashs@ihot.com

This is a training institute in all aspects of sexuality. It offers the first certificate course in Sexological Bodywork that incorporates tantric techniques, taught by Joseph Kramer, noted for his many DVDs about tantric practices.

Human Awareness Institute (HAI)
1-800-800-4117
office@hai.org
www.hai.org

Workshops on all aspects of sexuality and intimate relationships are offered, including topics such as "Love, Sex, and Intimacy."

Woman Within, Inc.
1-800-732-0890
WWithin@aol.com
www.womanwithin.org

Check out the many workshops and support groups available for women's empowerment and healing on this website.

Mankind Project

1-800-870-4611

www.mkp.org

Mankind Project offers "The New Warrior" training for men—originally called "The Wildman Weekend"—for initiation processes and empowerment for men.

Dennis Mead-Shikaly

541-488-7800

Fax: 541-488-2730

info@sacredrelationships.com

www.sacredrelationships.com

Workshops by two male facilitators on "Healing Relationships with Father: Leaving My Father's House" help women face and transform unresolved issues related to their father that impede their relationships with men. Meditation, music, visualization, guided imagery, journaling, group discussion, and individual process work are all explored.

Websites

www.tantra.com

Founder: Suzie Heumann

707-823-3063

This pioneer website extensively covers the products and services in the tantra community, including a wide range of videos, books, audiotapes, and CDs. This site also produced a video, *The Ancient Secrets of Sexual Ecstasy*, featuring many tantra experts and techniques. It is a good source to get an idea of the breadth of products in the field of tantra.

www.sexuality.com

contact@sexuality.com

This site offers information about a wide range of sexuality issues from sexual harassment to bondage and is a clearinghouse for information on the field of sex in general.

1-800-870-1611

Tantric Tools

Books

I recommend these books on tantra and related topics.

Tantric Sex

The Ipsalu Formula—A Method for TantraBliss by Bodhi Avinasha (Ipsalu Publishing, 2003).

Jewel in the Lotus: The Tantric Path to Higher Consciousness by Bodhi Avinasha (Ipsalu Publishing, 1987).

The Art of Conscious Loving by Charles and Caroline Muir (Mercury House, 1990).

The Art of Sexual Magic: Cultivating Sexual Energy to Transform Your Life by Margot Anand (Putnam Publishing Group, 1996).

The Complete Idiot's Guide to the Kama Sutra by Johanina Wikoff and Deborah Romaine (Alpha Books, 2000).

Ecstasy Through Tantra by Jonn Mumford (Llewellyn Publications, 1988).

The Encyclopedia of Sacred Sexuality: From Aphrodisiacs and Ecstasy to Yoni Worship and Zap-Lam Yoga by Rufus Camphausen (Inner Traditions, 1999).

The Essential Tantra: A Modern Guide to Sacred Sexuality by Kenneth Ray Stubbs (JP Tarcher, 1989).

Healing Love Through the Tao: Cultivating Female Sex Energy and Taoist Secrets of Love and *Cultivating Male Sexual Energy* by Mantak Chia (Healing Tao Books, 1991 and 1984).

Sexual Energy Ecstasy: A Practical Guide to Lovemaking by David and Ellen Ramsdale (Bantam Doubleday Dell Publications, 1993).

Spiritual Sex: Secrets of Tantra from the Ice Age to the New Millennium by Nik Douglas (Pocket Books, 1997).

The Tao of Love and Sex: The Ancient Chinese Way to Ecstasy by Jolan Chang (Viking Press, 1993).

The Yin-Yang Butterfly: Ancient Chinese Sexual Secrets for Western Lovers by Valentin Chu (Putnam, 1993).

Related Books on Tantra and Healing

A Goddess Is a Girls' Best Friend: A Divine Guide to Finding Love, Success and Happiness by Laurie Sue Brockway (Perigee Books/Penguin, 2002).

The Complete Idiot's Guide to Sensual Massage by Patti Britton and Helen Hodgson (Alpha Books, 2003).

Conversations with the Goddess: Revealing the Divine Power Within You by Agapi Stassinopolous (Stewart, Tabori and Chang, 1999).

Introduction to Tantra: A Vision of Totality by Lama Yeshe (Wisdom Publications, 1987).

The Joys of Everyday Ritual by Barbara Bizou (St. Martin's Griffin, 1999).

Legends and Prophecies of the Quero Apache by Maria Yraceburu (Inner Traditions International/Bear Books, 2002).

Prostate Health in 90 Days by Dr. Larry Clapp (Hay House, 1997).

Schools Are Depressed: Positive Energy Practices for Transformation by Liliana Gonzalez Cunningham (xLibris, 2004).

Secrets of Western Tantra: The Sexuality of the Middle Path by Christopher S. Hyatte, Ph.D. (New Falcon Publications, 1989).

Tamang Shamans: An Ethnopsychiatric Study of Ecstasy and Healing in Nepal by Larry Peters (Nivala, 1998).

The Tantra Experience: Discourse on the Royal Song of Saraha and *Tantric Transformation: Further Discourses on the Royal Song of Saraha* by Osho (Rebel Publishing House Pvt. Ltd., 1978).

The Tao and *The Tree of Life: Alchemical and Sexual Mysteries of the East and West* by Eric Steven Yudelov (Llewellyn Publications, 1996).

Tools for Tantra by Harish Johari (Density Books, 1986).

Wedding Goddess: A Bride's Guide to Radiating Beauty, Grace, and Confidence by Laurie Sue Brockway (Perigee Books/Penguin, 2005).

Sex

Generation Sex by Dr. Judy Kuriansky (Harper, 1996).

The Clitoral Truth: The Secret World at Your Fingertips by Rebecca Chalker (Seven Stories Press, 2000).

Forbidden Art: The World of Erotica and *Visions of Erotica* by Miss Naomi (Schiffer Books, 1998, 2000).

Sex for One by Betty Dodsen (Harmony Books, 1987).

The Art of Arousal by Dr. Ruth Westheimer (Artabras, 1997).

Relationships

The Complete Idiot's Guide to Dating, Third Edition, by Dr. Judy Kuriansky (Alpha Books, 2003).

The Complete Idiot's Guide to a Healthy Relationship, Second Edition, by Dr. Judy Kuriansky (Alpha Books, 2002).

How to Love a Nice Guy by Dr. Judy Kuriansky (Doubleday 1990, www.drjudy.net).

The New Physics of Love: The Power of Mind and Spirit in Relationships (audiocassette program) by Henry Grayson (Sounds True Inc., 2000).

Getting Together and Staying Together: Solving the Mystery of Marriage by William Glasser, M.D., and Carleen Glasser (HarperCollins Inc., 2000).

Release the Seductress Within: How to Seduce a Man ... and Thrill You Both by Laurie Sue Brockway (Gramercy Books/Random House, 2004).

The Unimaginable Life by Kenny and Julia Loggins (Morrow, William and Co., 1998).

Love-Centered Marriage in a Self-Centered World by Irving Sarnoff and Suzanne Sarnoff (Hemisphere, 1989).

Music

Here are some CDs that are excellent for meditation, massage, and lovemaking and are personal favorites that are regularly in my CD changer.

Sex 'n' Violets and *Songs of the Earthschild*
Jaiia Earthschild
808-573-4284
jaiia@Earthschild.com
www.Earthschild.com
Beautiful songs about learning how to love oneself, be honored by a beloved, and care for the planet.

Music to Disappear In II, *The Tantric Wave*, *The Calling*, and *The Essence of Oceanic Tantra (4-Volume Set)*
Raphael and Kutira
Kahua Hawaiian Institute, LLC
1-877-524-8250 or 808-572-6006
info@KahuaInstitute.com
www.KahuaInstitute.com
Ritualistic music and pulsating chants that put you in spiritual love mood, or relaxed or undulatory oceanic trance states. Instrumental or voice tracks guide you to an ecstatic experience.

Trance, Bones, Endless Wave
Gabrielle Roth
The Moving Center and Raven Recording
1-800-76-RAVEN (1-800-767-2836) or 212-760-1381
ravenrec@Panix.com
www.gabrielleroth.com
An extensive library of selections of trance dance and urban primitive music for dancing and inspiring the soul, moving spirit, and activating ecstasy. Universal rhythms free the body and the mind, and are also used in Roth's popular workshops.

Journey into Love, Return, and *Hidden Waters/Sacred Ground Sophia*
Ivory Moon Recordings
1-800-515-8515
www.songhealer.com
Profound yet simple songs that lead to deep tantric embrace.

Spirit of Love
Awakening Heart Productions
409-835-7327
Collection of inspiring songs that will touch your heart.

Sounds True
www.soundstruc.com
Music to put you in the mood for love.

Opening to Love
Robert Frey
310-636-1644
info@sacredtantra.com
www.sacredtantra.com
Chants that inspire loving feelings.

Ecstatica 1: A Sound Track for Lovers, Love's Healing Touch, River of Romance
Paul Ramana Das
U-Music, Inc.
415-499-1769
Primal, playful; passionate, or percussive sound track for love experience that goes through seven different sensual soundscapes to a blissful completion.

Bruch Violin Concert No. 1 and *Brahms Violin Concerto Op. 77*
Hideko Udagawa
London Symphony Orchestra
www.hidekoudagawa.com
Classical music that facilitates romance.

The Essence
Deva Premal
White Swan Music
303-494-9060
swan@netone.com
www.mitendevapremal.com
A definitive chant album.

A Gift of Love: Deepak and Friends with the Love Poems of Rumi
raSa Music
aum@rasamusic.com
www.rasamusic.com
Recitations set to music to create the spirit of ecstatic love.

Inner Journey
Metamusic
Interstate Industries, Inc.
804-263-8692
Interstate@Hemi-Sync.com
www.Hemi-Sync.com
Ethereal sounds use a special method of synchronizing brain spheres to relax and give free reign to the imagination.

Spiritual Environment Tantra
Anugama
Meistersinger Music USA Inc. Nightingale Records
520-733-9382
Fax: 520-722-8293
meistersinger-us@TheRiver.com
www.meistersinger.com
The first half is energizing and sexually stimulating; the second half stimulates the feminine and meditative side of sexual energy.

Songs to Shiva
Vyaas Houston and Mark Kelso
The American Sanskrit Institute
845-986-8652
Collection of ancient Sanskrit songs to Shiva, the great god.

ORFF—Carmina Burana
Saint Louis Symphony Orchestra and Chorus
BMG Music
Classic operatic piece evoking dynamic moods.

Graceful Passages: A Companion for Living and Dying
Michael Stillwater
415-492-0123
music@innerharmony.com
www.innerharmony.com

Enhancing Sensual Pleasure and many other selections
Steven Halpern
Sound Wave Rx/ESP Productions
1-800-909-0707
www.stevenhalpern.com
Stimulates passion with subliminal affirmations.

Chakra Chants
Jonathan Goldman Etherean Music
1-888-384-3732
www.Etherean.com

Spirit in Sound Chant the Best of World Chant
Robert Gass
Spring Hill Music
303-938-1188
Traditional and contemporary chant from the world's greatest chant artists.
Companion to Gass's book, *Chanting: Discovering Spirit in Sound*

Tantric Sexuality
The Mind Body and Soul series
New World Music Inc.
1-800-771-0987
Facilitates and enhances tantric practice, especially ecstatic breathing.

Videos and DVDs

Many of these videos are geared toward tantric sex; others are geared toward sexuality in general.

Kama Sutra, Tantra and Tao, Hot Sex in Erotic Art, The Ecstasy of Exotic Sex, The Amazing G Spot and Female Ejaculation, and many others
Access Instructional Media (AIM)
16311 Ventura Boulevard, Suite 780
Encino, CA 91436
818-784-0420
www.sexualintimacy.com
A wide variety of expertly produced videos, some specifically geared toward tantric sex practices, with detailed instructions and demonstrations that are excellent how-to guides by sexologist Michael Perry.

Secrets of Female Sexual Ecstasy
Charles and Caroline Muir
Source School of Tantra
PO Box 69
Paia, HI 96779
808-572-8364
tantra@mauigateway.com
www.sourcetantra.com
Depicts sexual loving with exquisite art and original music, showing secrets of erotic kissing and touch, and facts about male ejaculatory control, female sacred spot (G spot) massage, and female ejaculation.

Intimate Secrets of Sex and Spirit
Marilina and Paul Silbey
415-499-9163
yaluie@pacbell.net
www.3mmagic.com
Sexually explicit and entertaining video shows a variety of ways to enhance experiencing your body as a vibrant temple of divine energy.

Kama Sutra, The Art of Making Love and *Kama Sutra II*
Penthouse
A Vision
75 Rockefeller Plaza
New York, NY 10019
Beautifully shot videos with explicit demonstrations of positions and ancient love arts by modern-day couples.

Tantric Massage for Lovers with Steve and Lokita Carter
Institute for Ecstatic Living
877-982-6872
www.ecstaticliving.com
Instructional program on tantric massage for lovers to enhance intimacy and connection. Beautifully filmed and expertly guided massage for man and woman, introduction to tantra and ideas for further tantra practice.

Bliss, a Video Documentary of the Workshop
202-686-7440
info@butterflyworkshops.com
www.butterflyworkshops.com
A documentary of the workshop given by Butterfly Workshops, showing what happens over the weekend transformation process.

Sluts and Goddesses: Video Workshop: How to Be a Sex Goddess in 101 Easy Steps
Annie Sprinkle
Beatty/Sprinkle, 1992
Gates of Heck
1-800-213-8170
www.gatesofheck.com
A workshop for women on tape, showing tantric and Taoist principles along with very advanced activities such as group masturbation, shaving, and gender play.

Video Portrait of a Woman's Sexuality Seminar and *Viva La Vulva*
Betty Dodson Productions
PO Box 1933
Murray Hill
New York, NY 10156
212-679-4240
www.bettydodson.com
Sexuality pioneer shows women how to reclaim their erotic bodies and eliminate body shame. Teaches self-loving in a group seminar, combined with breathwork and heightened awareness of body sensations to increase pleasure.

Better Sex video series
The Sinclair Institute
PO Box 8865
Chapel Hill, NC 27515
1-800-955-0888
www.intimacyinstitute.com or www.sexedvideo.com
An extensive library of videos on sexual topics, from fantasy and aids to advanced lovemaking techniques.

Hearts Cracked Open
Betsy Kalin
323-650-0370
betsy@heartscrackedopen.com
www.heartscrackedopen.com
A documentary presenting an inside look into the world of lesbian tantra, including commentary from tantra teachers and film of real-life group of women who love women doing tantric practices.

The Secrets of Sacred Sex
Healing Arts
1-800-2-LIVING (1-800-254-8464)
Video that shows tantric lovemaking with commentary by experts.

Sensual Escape, Urban Heat, and other titles
Femme Productions
302 Meadowland Drive
Hillsborough, NC 27278
1-800-456-LOVE (orders, catalogs); 1-888-416-6130 (wholesale orders)
www.royalle.com
A library of erotic videos from a woman's perspective that has erotic as well as romantic themes.

Caballero videos
Especially selections of Andrew Blake.

Movies

The Best Ever produced by Paul Williams, Richard Hillman Sr., and Charles Muir
Golden Light Productions and Innovation Film Group
310-314-6444
Feature film that covers what happens in one of Muir's tantric workshops in Hawaii, particularly following the story of a woman and her HIV-positive young man who participate.

Bliss, produced by Allyn Stewart. A 1997 film about newlyweds having trouble with their sex life, when the wife who admits faking it and never having had orgasm, secretly goes for treatment by a "mysterious" doctor (played by Terence Stamp) who also works as a sex therapist "on the edge of the law" who says his customers must understand that the highest point in a sexual relationship is not an orgasm, but "emotional bliss."

Spoken Word Audio, Tantric Meditations, and Practice Guides

Love Making Secrets
Richard and Antoinette Asimus
1-877-931-3030 or 513-931-3030 in Cincinnati
richardasimus@fuse.net or aa@fuse.net
www.tantraheart.com
A committed couple share their discoveries, opening "rooms in the mansion" of love "most people do not imagine."

The Breath of Love (CD)
Steve and Lokita Carter
Institute for Ecstatic Living
1-877-982-6872
www.ecstaticliving.com
An ancient tantric practice guided by Steve and Lokita Carter about connecting with
your partner in bliss, timelessness, and arousal through breath and sharing energy.
Includes booklet with photos.

Chakra Wisdom (CD)
Steve and Lokita Carter
Institute for Ecstatic Living
1-877-982-6872
www.ecstaticliving.com
Tap into the wisdom of your seven energy centers in this guided musical journey
through the chakras. Can be done alone or with a partner.

The Art of Sexual Magic, Sexual Magic Meditations, and *The Art of Sexual Ecstasy* (CDs)
Margot Anand
This 6-tape set or 2-tape set includes meditations with music by Steve Halpern.

Catalogs and Gifts

Most tantra sites and teachers also offer various items for sale, many of which are
listed in Appendix B. Here are some examples of special sites for items related to
tantra.

Eve's Garden
119 West 57th Street
New York, NY 10019
1-800-848-3837
huntress@evesgarden.com
www.evesgarden.com
An extensive catalog of videos, books, oils, vibrators, clothing, and other aids, all
meant to empower women and celebrate female sexuality; the boutique in New York
offers a discreet place for men and women to shop.

www.DoctorG.com
65 Flicker Drive
Novato, CA 94949
415-459-2801

DoctorG@DoctorG.com
www.DoctorG.com
Dr. Gary Schubach offers educational articles, some from professional journals and his own research, and the latest reliable sexual enhancement products for a better sex life, including videos, books, toys, videos, and lubricants.

Cynthia Taylor Lamborne

LoveNectar Products (Gifts for Sacred, Loving Intimacy)
622 Seabright Lane
Solana Beach, CA 92075
858-794-4001
nectarproducts@lovenectar.com
www.LoveNectar.com
Boutique of tantric aids, gifts, and sexual healing tools for women and men. Also gives lectures, counseling, and instruction to individuals and couples, including information on using these tools for self-healing and pleasure.

E-sensuals

1-800-9-TANTRA (1-800-982-6872)
e-sensuals@tantra.com
www.tantra.com
Probably the most extensive clearinghouse and selection of all items relevant to tantra and tantric practice.

House O'Chicks

2215 R Market Street
San Francisco, CA 94144
415-861-9849
Fax: 415-626-5049
Dorrie@houseochicks.com
www.houseochicks.com
Vulva puppets of silk, velvet, and gems, made to order ($200).

Tantra Goddess/God Wear

Gorgeous Goddess Wear

310-455-1603
goddessWear4us@aol.com
www.gorgeousgoddesswear.com
Cut silk, velvet, beaded and crocheted outfits, dresses, shawls, scarves, and other wear for freeing your divine femininity.

Silk Angel Productions
808-573-1124
Special-order hand-painted silk sarongs ($90 to $150) with designs featuring mermaids inside a unicorn, lavender hibiscus flowers, or ocean scene with dolphins; silk chiffon jackets; velvet dresses.

Sacred and Erotic Art

Hrana Janto
PO Box 18
Tilson, NY 12486
hj@hranajanto.com
www.hranajanto.com
Illustrations, graphics, and paintings; posters of sacred art and myth; folk and fairy tales in historical, cultural, or fantasy style; goddesses; historical scenes; lovers. Also, goddess oracle card set.

Paul Heussenstamm
949-497-2708
heartcenter@mandalas.com
www.mandalas.com
Custom paintings of mandalas and commissioned art of male and female unions surrounded by geometric figures and nature forms with ruby and crystal stones. Also runs workshops in California and around the world on "Discovering Your Soul Mandala" to connect with your "inner artist" and explore the soul.

Meadow
108 Sheldon Road
Pine Bush, NY 12566-5518
845-744-4847
Fax: 845-744-4852
Illustrations, paintings, and sculptures on many subjects including eroticism (including in this book). Developing "Woodrock Sanctuary" art park, a healing center and wildlife sanctuary.

Al Hughes
212-330-9070
New York–based illustrator specializing in fashion, children's books, celebrity caricatures, and art on request (he did some of the illustrations in this book).

Rampal
714-968-8614
info@jeweledlotus.com
www.jeweledlotus.com
Creates tantric meditative fine art for healing and higher consciousness, also done in silk pillows, which reinterpret for the Western world the ancient symbol of sacred union between masculine and feminine principles.

Sex Museums with Tantric Art Exhibits

Shanghai: The Chinese Sex Museum
1133 Wu Ding Road
Shanghai China
011 86 21 623 1243
hu-h@163.com

Prague: SEX MACHINE MUSEUM
Melantrichova 18,
Prague 1-Old Town Czech Republic

London: The London Museum of Sexuality
29 Harley Street
London W1G 9QR
020 7016 2590
director@tlmos.com
www.tlmos.com

Amsterdam: Erotic Museum
OZ. Achterburgwal 54
Amsterdam
www.channels.nl/amsterdam/eroticmu

Index

CONTACT DR. JUDY

Dr. Judy is an expert on relationships, sex, dating, and love, as well as other topics like creativity, brain styles, the psychology of current events, and trends. Call her for personal coaching or addressing your group. You can get your copy of her books at your local bookstore or amazon.com (English and foreign language versions) for yourself, to give as gifts, or to use at your own events:

The Complete Idiot's Guide to Dating, Third Edition (Alpha, 2003). Everything you need to know about how to meet your mate.

The Idiot's Guide to a Healthy Relationship, Second Edition (Alpha, 2003). Everything you need to know about making a love relationship last.

Generation Sex (Harper, 1996). A collection of touching questions on a very broad range of topics about sex—with advice you won't find anywhere else—and good humor! Culled from questions from the radio show *LovePhones*, including comments from rock stars. Contact Dr. Judy for copies.

How to Love a Nice Guy. A helpful and effective 10-step program to learn to be attracted to nice guys instead of bad boys. Also appropriate for guys who keep going for the "wrong" girls. Contact Dr. Judy for copies.

Contact Dr. Judy at DrJudyKuri@aol.com, or call Alissa at 718-761-6910, or beep 917-354-3029, to inquire about the following:

❏ Private coaching or counseling with Dr. Judy, in person or by phone or e-mail. For individuals or couples, using a unique approach unifying mind, body, and spirit, combining a variety of techniques.

❏ Dr. Judy giving a lecture, seminar, workshop, keynote speech to your group.

❏ Dr. Judy hosting your event. (Has done "The Dating Game" for *Details* magazine, Calvin Klein Menswear and Bloomingdales stores; Volunteer Recognition Programs for New York Cares; JC Penney's community drug awareness.)

❏ Dr. Judy consulting for your products, business, marketing, or public relations campaign (on trends, women, men, youth).

❏ Dr. Judy helping you plan and judge your contest (e.g., Revlon's Most Unforgettable Woman, Lane Bryant's Real Woman, Close-Up Rap 'n Roll Contest.)

❏ Dr. Judy being your spokesperson (as for Universal Studios Florida "Theme Park Therapy," Durex's World Survey, Virginia Slims Opinion Poll, Holiday Depression, Church & Dwight, "First Impressions" campaign, Organon's blues in the bedroom and women's health campaigns).

❏ Dr. Judy consulting on your advertising or public service campaign (from perfumes and plays to phone services, vacation romance packages, and Herpes Awareness).

❏ Dr. Judy serving on your advisory committee/board (with experience at *Brides* magazine, Environmental Visionary Efforts, Planned Parenthood, American Women in Radio and TV, Board of TV Academy in New York).